CONCORDE
AND THE AMERICANS

Smithsonian History of Aviation Series

Von Hardesty, Series Editor

On December 17, 1903, human flight became a reality when Orville Wright piloted the *Wright Flyer* across a 120-foot course above the sands at Kitty Hawk, North Carolina. That awe-inspiring 12 seconds of powered flight inaugurated a new technology and a new era. The airplane quickly evolved as a means of transportation and a weapon of war. Flying faster, farther, and higher, airplanes soon encircled the globe, dramatically altering human perceptions of time and space. The dream of flight appeared to be without bounds. Having conquered the skies, the heirs to the Wrights eventually orbited Earth and landed on the Moon.

Aerospace history is punctuated with many triumphs, acts of heroism, and technological achievements. But that same history also showcases technological failures and the devastating impact of aviation technology in modern warfare. As adapted to modern life, the airplane—as with many other important technological breakthroughs—mirrors the darker impulses as well as the genius of its creators. For millions, however, commercial aviation provides safe, reliable, and inexpensive travel for business and leisure.

This book series chronicles the development of aerospace technology in all its manifestations and subtlety. International in scope, this scholarly series includes original monographs, biographies, reprints of out-of-print classics, translations, and reference materials. Both civil and military themes are included, along with systematic studies of the cultural impact of the airplane. Together these diverse titles contribute to our overall understanding of aeronautical technology and its evolution.

ADVISORY BOARD: Robert E. Bilstein, *University of Houston at Clear Lake;* Horst Boog, historian, Germany; Emmanuel Chadeau, *Université Charles de Gaulle;* Tom D. Crouch, *National Air and Space Museum;* Carl-Fredrik Geust, historian, Finland; Michael H. Gorn, historian; John T. Greenwood, *Center for Military History;* R. Cargill Hall, *Air Force History Support Office;* James R. Hansen, *Auburn University;* Von Hardesty, *National Air and Space Museum;* Roger D. Launius, *National Air and Space Administration,* chief historian; W. David Lewis, *Auburn University;* Donald S. Lopez, *National Air and Space Museum;* Felix C. Lowe, publisher, South Carolina; John H. Morrow Jr., *University of Georgia;* Richard J. Overy, *King's College, London;* Dominick A. Pisano, *National Air and Space Museum;* Christine White, *Pennsylvania State University;* E. T. Wooldridge, *National Air and Space Museum.*

CONCORDE
AND THE AMERICANS

INTERNATIONAL POLITICS OF THE SUPERSONIC TRANSPORT

KENNETH OWEN

SMITHSONIAN INSTITUTION PRESS
Washington and London

Published in association with the Science Museum, London

Editor: Lorraine Atherton
Designer: Janice Wheeler
Indexer: Dianne L. Hardy

Library of Congress Cataloging-in-Publication Data
Owen, Kenneth.
    Concorde and the Americans: international politics of the supersonic transport / Kenneth
Owen.
      p.   cm. — (Smithsonian history of aviation series)
    Includes bibliographical references and index.
    ISBN 1-56098-736-7 (alk. paper)
     1. Concorde (Jet transports)—History.   2. Concorde (Jet transports)—Political aspects—
United States. I. Title. II. Series.
    TL685.7.O94   1997
    387.7′3349—dc20   96-42415
                                                             CIP

British Library Cataloguing-in-Publication Data available

Manufactured in the United States of America
04 03 02 01 00 99 98 97   5 4 3 2 1

♾ The recycled paper used in this publication meets the minimum requirements of the American
National Standard for Information Sciences—Permanence of Paper for Printed Library Materials
ANSI Z39.48-1984.

To Suzette

CONTENTS

PREFACE

For more than 20 years a fortunate minority of air passengers have enjoyed the luxury of crossing the Atlantic at twice the speed of sound, thanks to an ambitious sixties Anglo-French enterprise to develop a supersonic transport (SST) named Concorde. Britain, France, and the United States each have distinct perceptions of this aircraft, both in its national impacts on society and in its effects on sensitive international relations. For France, the Concorde remains a symbol of national pride, to be championed without question. For Britain, reluctant partner in the project, the national view remains equivocal. In the United States, views are colored by past attitudes toward America's own SST program, which was abandoned in 1971.

In 1976 the Concorde was the first SST to enter regular airline service, and today it remains the only one. Its development marked a unique advance in aviation. It was an unprecedented experiment in international collaboration, and the results of the experiment were striking: after weathering turbulent political storms the Concorde proved at once a technological triumph and an economic disaster.

Concorde and the Americans examines the behind-the-scenes international politics that shaped the history of the first steps, in Europe and America, toward supersonic air transport. Drawing on hitherto unpublished contemporary documents and interviews with key players, it tells the inside story of the remarkable transatlantic interactions that led to today's regular daily passenger flights at twice the speed of sound.

Before the Anglo-French Concorde was launched, Britain first sought a deal to develop a supersonic transport jointly with the United States. The details of this determined but ill-fated attempt by the Macmillan government are here disclosed for the first time. Also exposed is the background to the race between the Concorde and America's own SST, including the role of the Central Intelligence Agency in monitoring Concorde progress and high-level attempts to persuade British ministers to abandon the Anglo-French project. In the end, it was the U.S. machine that was abandoned, on economic and environmental grounds.

The fight to gain approval for regular Concorde services to the United States was headline news during the Ford and Carter administrations in the mid-seventies, as public hearings were held, provisional federal approval was given, and public and congressional opposition mounted. Eventually the British and French airlines took their case to the courts, rising to a final decision by the U.S. Supreme Court. Until now there has been little to illuminate the full story that lay behind the ephemeral headlines in the press and the case detail in the legal journals. In this book I have aimed to trace the moves and motives behind the headlines, cut through the jargon to explain the legal issues, and interpret more fully the seminal approval decision made by William T. Coleman, Jr., President Ford's secretary of transportation. Also, 20 years after the event, it is possible to strip away the facade of a unified Anglo-French front in fighting the battle for New York approval, to expose a sharp, behind-the-scenes conflict between the British and the French on how best to win the day. Eventually the crucial fight for U.S. approval was won, and the aircraft survived. If the fight for approval had been lost—and that could have happened at a stroke had Congress so decided—the Concorde would not have survived.

Today, the heroic technical achievement of the Concorde is widely recognized, not least by the U.S. aeronautical community. From the start the program was a high-risk venture, and its technical success was hard won through the combined skill of British and French engineers. Credit for the early survival of the aircraft, however, must go to the French, who provided the political thrust to overcome the drag of a reluctant partner and keep the program flying.

Other books have recounted the general history and technical development of the Concorde and its two would-be competitors, the aborted United States SST and the Soviet Tupolev Tu-144. They have concentrated on the respective, individual aircraft. Other authors have published polemics attacking all SSTs. *Concorde and the Americans* looks at the transatlantic dimension of the Concorde story, at the complex political interactions between Europe (including Britain) and the United States that lay behind the public controversies. I argue no case, neither for nor against. As for the likely future of supersonic travel, at a time when international collaboration is again being proposed for a new SST that could fly early in the next century, I argue the case for realism.

In summary, the Concorde was born in the early jet age, when national prestige was a prime concern on both sides of the Atlantic, but grew up in a changing world. It exerted a truly remarkable influence on the American SST program, extending as high as the White House. It went on to provoke bitter argument in the United States, not only on its environmental impact but also on the historic constitutional issue of federal versus state authority. This supersonic pioneer, which has been carrying passengers daily across the Atlantic for the past 20 years, may well continue for another 20 years. Looking ahead, it is now the United States, not Europe, that is setting the pace toward a possible successor. But any successor will pose even higher risks. The needs for viable collaboration, sound economics, and environmental acceptance are lessons that have been learned the hard way. If these three needs cannot be met, there will be no supersonic successor to the magnificent flying machine that is the Concorde.

ACKNOWLEDGMENTS

Many people and organizations have helped me to tell this story. First, I am indebted to Prof. John Durant for his positive response to my proposal, which led to a three-year research fellowship at the Science Museum, London. Grants from the Royal Society, the Nuffield Foundation, and the Smithsonian Institution contributed toward the cost of research visits to the United States. My earlier book, *Concorde: New Shape in the Sky,* gave me the original idea for this further study, while Prof. Mel Horwitch's book, *Clipped Wings: The American SST Conflict,* signposted initial U.S. research directions.

My time in Washington, D.C., included a stimulating month in the Aeronautics Department of the Smithsonian's National Air and Space Museum, where I was made welcome by Tom Crouch, Von Hardesty, and Ron Davies. Elsewhere in Washington I was warmly received and helped by old and new friends including Ned Preston, Federal Aviation Administration historian; Len Bruno of the Library of Congress; Lee Saegesser of the NASA history office; Tab Lewis of the U.S. National Archives; Joseph E. Clarkson of the Department of Justice; and Prof. John M. Logsdon of George Washington University. My Washington work took me to a range of locations, from the splendors of the Library of Congress to the rigors of the Washington National Records Center at Suitland, Maryland. Elsewhere in the United States I was welcomed by many people, including the staffs of the Lyndon B. Johnson Library in Austin, the John F. Kennedy Library in Boston, the library of the Port Authority of New York and New Jersey, the Massachusetts Institute of Technology Libraries, and Boeing company archives.

In Britain, I drew on the resources of the Science Museum and Imperial College Libraries, the British Library, the Public Record Office, the Royal Aeronautical Society Library, the British Library of Political and Economic Science, the Civil Aviation Authority library at Gatwick, the USIS Reference Center at the U.S. Embassy in London, the Open University Library, and the George Edwards Library of Surrey University; and I was aided at British Aerospace archives at Bristol by Howard Berry and Mike Fish. In Britain and the United States I benefited from the views of many of those involved in the Concorde and U.S. SST programs. I am particularly indebted to two (unrelated) Clarkes—Alan E. of Bedford, England, and William C. of Bedford, New York—for background information and guidance. I benefited also from the perceptive comments of Sir Peter Masefield, the Rt. Hon. Aubrey Jones, Dr. Edmund Preston, Alexander Gordon-Cumming, Prof. Geoffrey Lilley, and Andrew Nahum of the Science Museum, all of whom found time to read drafts of the text. Finally, I acknowledge the research assistance and patience of my wife, Suzette, throughout, and the U.S. research assistance of my friends Alan C. Brown, Mark E. Kahn, and David H. Keene.

ABBREVIATIONS

AST   Advanced Supersonic Transport
ARB   Air Registration Board
BAC   British Aircraft Corporation
BAe   British Aerospace
BOAC   British Overseas Airways Corporation
CASE   Campaign for Action on Supersonic Engineering
CIA   Central Intelligence Agency
CAB   Civil Aeronautics Board
DOD   Department of Defense
DOT   Department of Transportation
EPNdB   effective perceived noise decibels
EIS   environmental impact statement
EPA   Environmental Protection Agency
FAA   Federal Aviation Agency or Administration
FAR-36   Federal Aviation Regulation Part 36
FAUSST   Franco-Anglo-U.S. Supersonic Transport
HSA   Hawker Siddeley Aviation
HSCT   high-speed civil transport
HSR   High-Speed Research program
IATA   International Air Transport Association
ICAO   International Civil Aviation Organization
IDA   Institute for Defense Analyses

IFALPA   International Federation of Air Line Pilots Associations
IPR   International Public Relations Company
MOA   Ministry of Aviation
MOS   Ministry of Supply
NASA   National Aeronautics and Space Administration
NASP   National Aero-Space Plane
NATO   North Atlantic Treaty Organization
NEF   noise exposure forecast
NPRM   notice of proposed rule-making
OST Office of Science and Technology
OSTP   Office of Science and Technology Policy
OTA   Office of Technology Assessment
PNdB   perceived noise decibels
PAC-SST   President's Advisory Committee on Supersonic Transport
RAE   Royal Aircraft Establishment
SGAC   Secrétariat Général de l'Aviation Civile
SCAR   Supersonic Cruise Aircraft Research
SCR   Supersonic Cruise Research
SCT   Supersonic Commercial Transport
SST   supersonic transport
STAG   Supersonic Transport Advisory Group
STAC   Supersonic Transport Aircraft Committee
TBM   type board meeting
TSS   Transport Supersonique
VLCT   Very Large Commercial Transport

QUEST FOR SPEED | 1

Once upon a time there were three supersonic airliners. One died an early death, one flew first but soon gave up, and one survived controversy to carry passengers across the Atlantic routinely, expensively, and very quickly indeed. The survivor is the Concorde, conceived by the governments of Britain and France (and paid for by their taxpayers), designed and built by British and French firms, flown by British and French airlines, acclaimed by engineers, scorned by economists, hated by environmentalists.

All three were seeking speed. Supersonic flight was believed to be the next logical advance in air transport, but more basically it represented a dream. Aircraft makers had been in the business of translating dreams into reality ever since the Wright brothers. Now the dream was to fly airline passengers at speeds faster than sound—faster than a bullet from a gun. The reality was to prove limited: real engineering achievement coupled with highly unreal economics.

The time was the sixties, a decade that began with the first man in orbit around the earth and ended with the first men on the moon; that began with the inauguration of John F. Kennedy as president of the United States and ended with the resignation of Charles de Gaulle as president of France. In between, memories include the Cuban missile crisis, the Kennedy assassination, the Vietnam War, civil unrest in the United States and France, the repeated rejection by de Gaulle of British attempts to join the European Community, and strikes and sterling crises in Britain. In aviation, toward the end of the decade, three significant aircraft took to the air for the first time: first, the Soviet Tu-144 supersonic transport; next, the subsonic Boeing 747, the so-called jumbo jet; and third, the Concorde.

To create a supersonic airliner was an enormous challenge. Scientists had gradually explored the secrets of aerodynamics during the first half of the twentieth century, translating the theory and experiment of an advancing science into the design and refinement of a succession of aircraft. Air transport had seen progressive increases in speed, but strange effects appeared when aircraft approached the new realm of supersonic flight. Air resistance rose dramatically to impose a serious obstacle—the so-called sound barrier—to conventional flight. The changes were sudden and literally shocking, as the normally orderly airflows broke down and shock waves, analogous to the bow waves of a ship, were generated at the nose and tail of the aircraft.

In 1947 U.S. Air Force Captain Charles E. Yeager, flying the rocket-powered, air-launched Bell XS-1 research aircraft, became the first pilot to exceed the speed of sound in level flight. (Supersonic speeds are expressed in terms of Mach number, which is the ratio of the speed of the aircraft to the local speed of sound. Mach 1 varies from about 760 miles per hour at sea level to about 660 miles per hour at a height of 50,000 to 60,000 feet.) By the end of the fifties a number of fighter aircraft were in service that could fly brief bursts at supersonic speeds, but they could not cruise supersonically for hours at a time.

Hence there were serious aerodynamic problems to be tackled in the design of a supersonic airliner, not only in shaping the aircraft to give the best possible performance but also in handling the complex airflows within the long power-plant intakes. High temperatures also create problems, both within the engine, where materials and components have to withstand very high internal temperatures, and on the aircraft skin. Air friction at supersonic speeds causes the skin of a supersonic airliner to heat and expand—the fuselage of the Concorde extends by about eight inches during a typical transatlantic flight.

Solving those and many other technical problems while keeping the structural weight down so that a reasonable payload could be carried was a high-risk task. The technical task was successfully accomplished on the Concorde, but at the price of economic inefficiency and environmental harm. One of the problems, the shock-wave "boom" heard on the ground as a supersonic aircraft passes overhead, was a fact of nature that could not be overcome; thus it was avoided by limiting airline service to overwater routes. The other factor that played a prominent part in the progress of the American and European supersonic transport (SST) programs, if not that of the Soviet Union, was the unprecedented force of public concern over the aircraft's economic and environmental shortcomings. To set the scene for the story that follows, I begin by introducing briefly the three main characters.

The Anglo-French Concorde

For Britain and France, the Concorde appeared to offer the prospect of gaining a lead over the Americans in what was seen as the next major step in air transport. After separate initial design studies had pointed to similar concepts (except that the British work favored a larger, longer-range machine), the two nations formally decided to embark on a joint project to develop a Mach 2 aircraft in 1962. The aircraft made its first flight in 1969, regular airline service began in 1976, and transatlantic service is still going strong today. The Concorde remains the only supersonic transport aircraft in airline operation, serving its own niche market of super-first-class travel at super-first-class fares.

The two countries' motives in launching the program were different, though both shared the misconception that the supersonic travel market would embrace all classes of airline seats and so would be substantial. For Britain, the Concorde would keep design teams employed and should help in the country's attempts to join the European Community. For France, the project would help to build up the national aircraft industry. Both countries started from the premise that it would be cheaper to share the costs in a joint project than to go it alone in separate programs. The project was expected to cost between £150 million and £170 million (between $420 million and $480 million); as it turned out, the net cost to the public purse was more than ten times that figure, though inflation and devaluation accounted for much of the increase.

The Anglo-French agreement committing both nations to "develop and produce jointly a civil supersonic transport aircraft" was a remarkable document. It had the status of an international treaty. The good news for the Concorde supporters was that it ensured the survival of the program because both sides were locked into it with no provision for unilateral withdrawal. Equally, this was bad news for those who came to realize that the program, by any normal measure, should *not* survive: to build a total of only 16 aircraft is an admission of failure that could not be clearer. Ironically, the lack of any break clause in the agreement had been insisted on by the minister of aviation in Harold Macmillan's Conservative British government to prevent the French from withdrawing; only two years later, it prevented the incoming British Labour government, facing a severe economic crisis, from canceling the project. Another key year was 1974, when again the project was heading for cancellation even before the new Labour government was elected, but Prime Minister Harold Wilson and President Valéry Giscard d'Estaing agreed to complete the program.

The organization of the Concorde program also was remarkable. Flying in the face of accepted tenets of project management, the "equal shares" provision of the

Table 1

Anglo-French Concorde: Key Dates

1962	November	U.K. and French governments sign agreement to develop and produce an SST; British Aircraft Corporation and Sud Aviation to collaborate on aircraft, Bristol Siddeley and SNECMA on engine
1963	June	Pan American, BOAC, and Air France sign Concorde options
1964		Medium-range version abandoned; long-range version enlarged
	October	U.K. Labour government reviews program
1965	May	Preproduction design announced
1967		Preproduction design revised
	May	Options to purchase reach total of 74 from 16 airlines
	December	Prototype 001 rolls out at Toulouse
1968	February	U.K. government announces £125 million production loan
	September	Prototype 002 rolls out at Bristol; production design revised
1969	March	First flight of 001 takes place at Toulouse
	April	First flight of 002 goes from Bristol to Fairford
	June	Both prototypes shown at Paris air show
1970	December	Design changes made
1972	April	Production of 16 aircraft confirmed
	July	BOAC orders 5 Concordes, Air France orders 4
	December	U.K. government increases production loan to £350 million
1973		Design changes made
1974	January	Pan Am and TWA drop Concorde options
	July	U.K. and France agree on only 16 Concordes
1976	January	U.S. Transportation Secretary Coleman holds public hearing on Concorde U.S. service; airline service begins (British Airways London-Bahrain and Air France Paris-Rio via Dakar)
	February	Coleman approves service to Washington and New York
	April	Air France service extended to Caracas via the Azores
	May	Washington service begins, from London and Paris
1977	November	New York service begins, from Paris and London
	December	Bahrain-Singapore extension service opens, but suspended because of overflying ban by Malaysia
1978	September	Air France opens Paris–Mexico City service via Washington
1979	January	Braniff opens subsonic Concorde service between Dallas–Fort Worth and Washington; British Airways resumes Bahrain-Singapore service
	September	U.K. and French governments announce unsold Concordes to be placed with Air France and British Airways
1980	June	Braniff ceases Dallas–Fort Worth service
	November	British Airways ceases service to Bahrain and Singapore
1982	March	Air France ceases service to Caracas and Rio
	October	Air France ceases Washington and Mexico City service
1983	January	Fastest crossing made, New York to London, in 2 hours 56 minutes
1984	March	British Airways opens Washington-Miami Concorde service; British Airways takes over support costs from U.K. government
1987		Air France takes over support costs from French government
1991	March	British Airways ceases Miami service
1994	November	British Airways ceases Washington service

agreement applied to management as well as to costs and work. Decisions—not only strategic decisions but also technical decisions at all levels—were made by joint committees, both governmental and industrial. The resulting process has been described by those involved at the top level as "incredibly tortuous," "absolutely dreadful," and "incredibly cumbersome."[1] It was a dinosaur of an organization to produce a greyhound of an aircraft. Certainly this bureaucracy, coupled with the many technical obstacles to be overcome, created delays. On the other hand, the need to obtain consensus on every point arguably led to a better airplane.

Throughout the program, the two governments (at both ministerial and official levels) continued to exhibit basically different attitudes toward the Concorde, which compounded the delays in the program. The French displayed an unwavering dedication to the program, particularly so during the de Gaulle presidency, while the British appeared to be reluctant partners, concerned about the continually rising costs and seeking to keep all options open. These national differences were reflected also in parliamentary and public attitudes. At a time when the number of Concorde questions asked in the British Parliament was approaching one thousand, the corresponding number in the French National Assembly was two. Typical books in France described "the glory" and "the great adventure" of the Concorde, while British books and newspapers recounted stories of the "Concorde fiasco" and the "Concorde conspiracy."

Among the inefficiencies of the joint program was the decision, made for reasons of national pride, to operate two production lines, one in Britain and the other in France. Production of parts was not duplicated, but they were shipped to Bristol or Toulouse as appropriate. Each factory assembled one prototype, one pre-production version, and eight production aircraft. In addition, one specimen airframe was built for static-load testing at Toulouse and another for fatigue-load testing at the Royal Aircraft Establishment in Farnborough. Air France and British Airways each received seven of the production Concordes, effectively at no cost (though the airlines are now paying for all the in-service support costs). British Caledonian Airways and Pan American each considered Concorde operations, but to no effect. By the end of 1994, the airlines' year-round scheduled services had shrunk to the New York routes—daily from Paris and twice daily from London. The unique "Concorde experience" was also being marketed in a range of exotic charter flights by travel operators.

Despite everything, Britain and France succeeded in building the world's first—and to date the world's only—supersonic airliner able to carry passengers routinely across the Atlantic Ocean faster than sound. It carries 100 passengers and cruises at twice the speed of sound, over 1,300 miles per hour. We know it cost almost $3 billion, we know it is noisy, we know by any normal standards it is economic nonsense, but it works and it can take you from London to New York in under three and a half hours.

The United States SST, 1963–1971

For the United States, the national supersonic transport program was a reaction to the Anglo-French Concorde initiative. Industry and government researchers had studied the technical options for supersonic airliners in the fifties, and development of a supersonic transport was recommended by a national task force on U.S. aviation goals in 1961.[2] But it was the European decision to launch the Concorde program—and the decision of Pan American to take options on the airplane— that stung President Kennedy into announcing the start of a national program in June 1963. It was to be a joint government and industry program to develop the prototype of "a commercially successful supersonic transport superior to that being built in any other country of the world."

Development of the SST was to be managed by the Federal Aviation Agency (FAA), whose head, Najeeb Halaby, was a former test pilot and an SST enthusiast. President Lyndon Johnson also was in favor of the SST, but his right-hand man, Robert McNamara, was not, and McNamara was to play a leading role in the SST decision-making process. Delays and disagreements within the Johnson administration plagued the progress of the program. After a protracted design competition, Boeing of Seattle was selected to build a variable-geometry (swing-wing) machine, to be powered by General Electric engines. It was to be a huge machine, carrying 300 passengers at 2.7 times the speed of sound, about 1,800 miles per hour. But the technical task proved too difficult, and the company changed to a simpler, delta-wing design, further delaying the program.

Airline interest in supersonics, always lukewarm, waned as Boeing began to market the huge 747, the mass-market subsonic aircraft that was to revolutionize air transport as the first jet airliners had a decade before. Public interest, however, waxed strong *against* the SST, and an unprecedented campaign of opposition to the new technology on environmental grounds engulfed what fragile support there was. President Richard Nixon favored the SST but could not save it; congressional votes reflected the public mood, killing the project in 1971. At that time, more than $1 billion and about 8.5 million man-hours had been spent on the SST design. About 1,500 people were working on the project in Seattle, and metal was being cut for the first prototype.[3] Across the country, the project represented a massive industrial effort; the SST team, including subcontractors, was said to total about 14,000 people.[4]

Table 2
United States SST: Key Dates

1961	July	SST steering group formed with members from FAA, NASA, and Defense Department
	August	Congress appropriates $11 million for FAA SST research
	September	FAA SST research program management office established; Project Horizon report recommends SST development
	November	Industry proposals requested for SST research; Supersonic Transport Advisory Group (STAG) formed
1962	October	Congress appropriates $20 million to continue research
	December	STAG recommends SST development
1963	January	SST review committee formed, chaired by Vice President Johnson
	June	President Kennedy announces intention to develop SST
	July	FAA office of SST development formed
	August	Kennedy appoints Eugene Black as special adviser on SST financing, with Stanley Osborne as deputy
	November	Kennedy assassinated; Congress votes $60 million for SST
	December	Black-Osborne report submitted to President Johnson
1964	January	Industry submits initial design proposals
	April	President's advisory committee established, chaired by Robert McNamara
	May	Johnson orders further design work, economic studies, sonic-boom research
	June	Design contracts awarded
	December	Continuation of design effort ordered
1965	July	Eighteen-month design competition announced
1966	July	Phase 3 proposals requested
	September	Proposals submitted; $280 million appropriated for 1966–1967
	December	FAA selects Boeing and General Electric
1967	October	Congress appropriates $142.4 million for 1967–1968
1968	February	Boeing requests more time for design
	October	Boeing selects fixed-wing design
1969	January	Boeing proposes new design to FAA
	February	Interdepartmental ad hoc review committee appointed
	September	President Nixon announces go-ahead
	December	Congress approves $85 million for SST prototype development in 1969–1970
1970	April	William Magruder appointed director of SST development; program transferred from FAA to Transportation Department
	May	House rejects amendment to delete $290 million from SST funds
	December	Senate passes Proxmire amendment to delete SST funds from Transportation appropriations
1971	January	Congress approves funding to 30 March 1971
	March	House votes to delete all SST funds; Senate defeats amendment to restore funds

The Soviet Tu-144, 1961–1984

For the Soviet Union, the year 1961 gave the world two startling demonstrations of Soviet technological strength. Major Yuri Gagarin became the first man to orbit the earth, and an outstanding crop of supersonic military aircraft was unveiled at Tushino airfield in Moscow. It also reportedly was the year when Andrei Tupolev's experimental design bureau began SST design studies.[5] Tupolev, jailed by Stalin and then favored by Khrushchev, was a veteran Russian designer whose many aircraft had included the impressive Tu-104 jet and Tu-114 turboprop airliners, both developed from military types. His son Alexei was to become chief designer of the supersonic Tu-144.

In 1963 a top-level team of British aviation officials and industrialists visited Moscow, were shown a model of a possible Soviet SST, and were surprised and somewhat concerned by its resemblance to the Concorde.[6] Two years later the shape and the designation "Tu-144" were confirmed at the 1965 Paris air show, with a larger model on display. The obvious nickname "Concordski" was seized on by the headline writers of the western world: the shapes were similar, and the quoted speed of the Soviet machine was only slightly higher than that of the Concorde. At the 1967 Paris air show the Tu-144 model showed changes, and on the last day of 1968 a prototype of the real thing took off from the Zhukovski factory runway and into aviation history as the world's first supersonic transport aircraft to fly. The production version was designed to carry 140 passengers at about the same normal cruising speed as the Concorde, though it reportedly reached Mach 2.4.

Table 3
Soviet Tu-144: Key Dates

1965	June	Model shown at Paris air show
1968	December	First prototype flies
1969	June	Prototype exceeds Mach 1 for first time
1970	May	Prototype makes first public appearance, Sheremetyevo airport, Moscow; exceeds Mach 2 for first time
1971	June	Prototype appears at Paris air show
1973	June	A production Tu-144 crashes at Paris air show
1975	December	Freight and mail flights begin, Moscow to Alma-Ata, Kazakhstan
1977	November	Scheduled passenger flights begin, Moscow to Alma-Ata
1978	June	Scheduled passenger service ceases
1979	June	Improved Tu-144D makes proving flight from Moscow to Khabarovsk
1984	August	Aeroflot confirms it has ceased Tu-144 service

The Soviet SST prototype made its first public appearance at Sheremetyevo airport in Moscow, in May 1970, and its first appearance outside the Soviet Union at the 1971 Paris air show. Two years later a production Tu-144 at the Paris show demonstrated that major design changes had been made, much to the gratification of Sir George Edwards, leader of the British Concorde design team, who had pointed out to "young Tupolev" the error of his ways on the prototype six years before.[7] On the final day of the show the Soviet machine crashed during a flying display, killing the six-man crew and eight people on the ground. A Franco-Soviet investigating board concluded that the accident was not caused by any technical fault of the aircraft.[8]

One implication of the Concordski tag was the allegation that the Tu-144 was a copy of the Anglo-French machine. This bald statement is untrue, but there was some evidence of industrial espionage by the Soviet Union. In his book on the Tu-144, Howard Moon reports that one Soviet network was congratulated on obtaining "the entire technical documentation for the Concorde prototype," and other reported espionage efforts were aimed at obtaining Concorde engine information in England and airframe data in France.[9] The head of the Soviet airline Aeroflot office in Paris was arrested and expelled from France for Concorde espionage in 1965.

The operational life of the Soviet SST was short. A major defect in the design was the dependence on reheat, or afterburning, of the Kuznetsov NK-144 engines, leading to high fuel consumption and limited range. A Russian source quoted by Moon says about 18 aircraft were built; they possibly consist of 2 prototypes, 12 production machines, and 2 prototypes plus 2 production versions of the improved, reengined Tu-144D. Announcing in August 1984 that Aeroflot had withdrawn the Tu-144 from service, Nikolai Poluyanchik, head of the airline's international traffic division, blamed high operating costs. "We are not prepared to use an aircraft which is inefficient," he was quoted as saying.[10]

Transatlantic Interactions

The Soviet Union in general went its own way in developing the Tu-144, albeit with a touch of industrial espionage en route, but between Britain and France and the Concorde on the one hand, and the United States and its SST on the other, there were many complex interactions as the projects took shape and advanced. These interactions fell into four distinct phases.

First, there is the story of the aircraft that never was, but might have been. British aviation officials had convinced the Conservative government under Harold

Macmillan that there were sound reasons for trying to regain the aviation lead Britain had briefly held with the de Havilland Comet, the world's first jet-powered airliner. (In 1952 the Comet was the first jet airliner to enter airline service, but after a series of accidents in 1954 the lead in jet transport was taken by the American Boeing 707 and Douglas DC-8.) The way to do this, they argued, was to press ahead to develop the world's first supersonic airliner or, indeed, perhaps two supersonic airliners. Britain had the resources to do this, but a partnership with another country would reduce costs. The preferred partner was the United States, and an enormous effort went into encouraging the American government to join an Anglo-American SST program. In theory, such a collaboration would have offered clear benefits in sharing the costs and the markets. In practice, there were basic obstacles, including differences in technical judgment and in government-industry relations, which were insufficiently appreciated by the Macmillan government at the time. More important, the United States was determined to build its own SST—but at its own pace—in order to retain its world leadership in air transport manufacturing. Thus Britain turned to France as a partner to meet the supersonic challenge.

Second is the perceived race between the Concorde and the American SST, launched by President Kennedy in 1963. Concorde progress and prospects were all-important factors in the planning of the American SST program. It was accepted that, all being well, the Concorde would fly first. But just how big was this lead? The numbers of each SST that could be sold would clearly depend on their respective dates of entry into airline service. President Kennedy was determined that the United States should not be beaten by de Gaulle in the supersonic enterprise, and the Central Intelligence Agency was brought in to keep the U.S. side informed of the pace and problems of the Concorde program. Equally, the Concorde designers were acutely aware of the American SST on their tail as they advanced toward the expected world market. On both sides of the Atlantic, the idea of collaboration surfaced again. Why not mount a two-phase joint program, with the United States joining in the Concorde and Britain and France participating in the expected Mach 3 American design? Logic and economics said it might make sense, proponents on both sides of the Atlantic argued the case, but practical politics once more ruled it out.

Third, the process of obtaining approval for regular Concorde service to the United States proved long, complex, and bitterly controversial. This was the most important phase in the entire history of the Concorde. Approval was crucial, for if it had been denied, the Concorde enterprise would have come to an abrupt end: the aircraft's only remaining scheduled service is on the transatlantic routes. The process began with applications by Air France and British Airways in 1975 and ended with a U.S. Supreme Court decision in 1977. The battle was fought against a background of internal political arguments within the U.S. administration and in Congress and vociferous public opposition to any increase in aircraft noise. The delay in gaining New York approval strained international relations at the highest level—not only between the United States and the two Concorde nations but also between the British and the French.

Fourth, as the Concorde enters its third decade of airline service, a possible successor is being studied by Britain, France, the United States, and other countries. Any such machine would need to be larger, quieter, more economical, and cleaner—but not necessarily faster—than the Concorde and almost certainly would demand a broader international partnership to develop and build it. A substantial program of preliminary research is under way in the United States, companies in Europe have joined together to build on their Concorde experience, and a wider international industrial group is studying the prospects for a joint development effort. Will there be a son of Concorde, or is this the end of the line for the supersonic transport?

Together, these four topics highlight the international political background to the development and operation of the supersonic transport, surely one of the greatest challenges that technology has tackled this century.

ORIGINS | 1

COULD WE, SHOULD WE, GO IT ALONE? 2

Thoughts of supersonic transport aircraft emerged from the research laboratories and entered the cabinet room of Number 10 Downing Street in May 1958, when Derick Heathcoat Amory, chancellor of the exchequer in the Conservative government led by Harold Macmillan, reported the conclusions of an ad hoc inquiry into the future of the British aircraft industry. Among other things, the report concluded that fewer firms were needed (presaging the drastic industry "rationalization" that was to follow) and warned that the development of a future generation of aircraft such as supersonic transports might be possible only with substantial government assistance.[1]

The cabinet learned a little more the following December from Aubrey Jones, minister of supply.[2] The aircraft industry was in a bad way, he indicated, and one way to strengthen it would be to resume the immediate postwar practice of providing government support for the development of selected aircraft, even those for which there was no immediate requirement. The largest such project was likely to be the supersonic civil transport. The prime minister said the Ministerial Committee on Civil Aviation should be reconvened to consider further the Jones suggestion.[3]

The idea that Britain might join with the United States to develop and build a supersonic transport began to solidify the following year. Both countries had SST research under way, and in both countries thoughts were turning to the possible development of supersonic civil airliners. The initiative for collaboration came from the British government.

15

At first the supersonic transport was regarded purely as a possible national venture. Early in 1959, at the first meeting of the ministerial committee (now renamed the Committee on Civil Aviation Policy), Aubrey Jones identified two main problems facing the industry: first, at a time of recession, how to preserve design staffs who would be needed for the longer term, and second, how to exploit ideas and projects, such as the supersonic transport, for which no immediate U.K. requirement existed.[4] The Americans were known to be aiming at a supersonic transport by about 1970, and it would be surprising if the Russians did not cherish a similar ambition. "If we as a country are to be in this race the giving of the project to industry ought not to be delayed. But it would cost money."

Britain believed it had a head start in this race. Initial technical studies into the prospects for transport aircraft that would fly faster than sound had already begun. A group known as the Supersonic Transport Aircraft Committee (STAC), including experts both from industry and from the civil service—notably from the renowned Royal Aircraft Establishment (RAE) at Farnborough—had begun work in 1956. Jones reported the committee's conclusion: supersonic airliners with reasonable economics were a practical proposition.

According to STAC, Britain should develop at least one and possibly two types of aircraft—a long-range (transatlantic) aircraft cruising at twice the speed of sound, and a short-range aircraft cruising at just over the speed of sound. Development of these two types would cost about £100 million and £70 million respectively. No British firm could afford such speculative sums, the minister noted, and so the bulk of the development cost would have to be borne initially by the government. A decision in principle was required on whether to go ahead. No action was taken on the Jones proposal, but its scope was broadened to include the prospects for international collaboration when the views of industry were canvassed by the ministry in May. The firms, however, gave a decidedly lukewarm response to the suggestion that international collaboration on an SST might be a good thing.[5]

Two British SSTs?

Aubrey Jones had received the STAC report in March 1959 and in July brought his prime minister up to date in a note giving his view of SST prospects.[6] He confirmed that STAC had recommended that Britain should start to develop the two proposed supersonic civil aircraft. But the top executives of aircraft firms had argued against the medium-range machine and in favor of the long-range design. Jones summarized the basic dilemma: To embark on such a project would be costly, bearing in mind the small potential U.K. market. On the other hand, "not to embark upon such a project would be tantamount to the exclusion of this country from the field of advanced civil aircraft design." The minister said he had suggested to the French government that the two countries should discuss a possible joint SST project, he was exploring possible cooperation with other countries, and he was placing a design study contract with industry in order to obtain more precise cost estimates.

The American dimension was developed in a note Macmillan received three weeks later from Harold Watkinson, his minister of transport and civil aviation.[7] Watkinson had been talking supersonics with Lieutenant General Elwood Quesada, chosen by U.S. president Dwight Eisenhower to be the first administrator of the Federal Aviation Agency (an organization created by the Federal Aviation Act of 1958). Both men agreed that the airlines ideally should have at least eight to ten years' use of the existing subsonic jets before they were forced to buy supersonic airliners—but they recognized that this would not necessarily happen.

At a recent assembly of the International Civil Aviation Organization (ICAO) in San Diego, Watkinson reported, Britain had called attention to the big problems that would face civil aviation authorities if an SST were to come into operation within the next ten years, and had proposed that ICAO staff examine these matters. His suggestion had been supported by most of the other nations at the meeting but had been opposed by the United States. The U.S. attitude made sense, the minister concluded, only if the Americans had already decided to proceed with a supersonic transport project of their own. This mistaken conclusion by Watkinson was coupled with the mistaken assumption that the American SST would begin life as a military project, which would breed a civil version. The cost of an all-British supersonic project would be enormous, Watkinson continued, and it was doubtful whether Britain could match the United States in straight competition. The government should encourage British firms to set up a joint project with whichever U.S. firm won the SST contract.

In September 1959 Aubrey Jones returned to the topic in a memorandum arguing that the proposed study contract should not be confined to Mach 2 aircraft and should include exploring the possibility of cooperation with American or French industry.[8] Possible cooperation with France should be explored in parallel at the governmental level and by the companies. As for a possible link with the United States, intercompany talks should precede governmental discussions.

On 18 September 1959 the British cabinet agreed to announce the government's intention to place design study contracts for a supersonic transport aircraft.[9] These studies would not be confined to Mach 2 aircraft but—because of the American interest in Mach 3—would encompass higher speeds also. Though

Aubrey Jones's preference was for cooperation with France, cabinet discussion concentrated on prospects for an association with the United States. An approach to the U.S. administration should be made soon, ministers urged.

Writing in 1992, Aubrey Jones gave the background to his 1959 bid to initiate an SST project with the French: he was very much in favor of the European Community, while Macmillan at that time was not.[10] "When I received the STAC report I realized that there was no hope of obtaining the necessary finance from the Treasury, and proceeded to make good what I considered to be a great mistake in foreign policy by going to Paris and proposing to the French government a joint approach in developing a supersonic civil aircraft. This I did in June 1959 on the occasion of the French air show at le Bourget." In an earlier recollection, Jones stated that, when he reported back to London that collaboration with the French was possible, the cabinet "laughed with derision."[11] After the U.K. general election of October 1959, Jones declined the post of minister of works offered by Macmillan and left the government.

Persuading the Companies

Just two days before the cabinet decision of 18 September 1959, a preliminary discussion on the SST studies was held between Ministry of Supply (MOS) officials and representatives of the Hawker Siddeley and Bristol companies.[12] The firms argued against any U.S. involvement at that stage, "since it would cause delays," but believed that an agreement with a European or Canadian firm might be possible later on. Nonetheless the British government continued to insist that the firms explore the prospects for international collaboration. In advance of the actual contracts, the Ministry of Supply wrote to Stuart Davies of Hawker Siddeley Aviation (HSA) and Dr. Archibald Russell of Bristol Aircraft on 6 November, inviting them to prepare an outline plan for the joint study. Among the specific topics the study would have to address was an assessment of prospects for cooperation based on discussions with both American and French companies.

At a meeting in London toward the end of November, ministry officials and senior executives of HSA and Bristol reviewed the work the firms were doing "in anticipation of the proposed feasibility study contract on supersonic transport aircraft."[13] Denis Haviland, an MOS deputy secretary, warned that no government decision was likely without convincing proof that collaboration with America and France had been thoroughly explored. The industrialists suggested that cooperation with the United States would be more rewarding—but intrinsically more difficult—than cooperation with the French. Haviland was to remain a staunch advocate of Anglo-American collaboration.

Thus 1959 was the year when a joint Anglo-American supersonic transport venture began to receive serious attention from the government and the aircraft industry in Britain. The firms, instructed to explore the prospects of collaboration with both the United States and France, questioned the need for collaboration but, when pressed, indicated that their preference lay toward the United States. During 1960 both the United States and France were brought into the SST discussions, while a detailed rationale for collaboration was developed by British officials. British firms examined the prospects for collaboration in more detail.

A French Connection?

In a departmental reshuffle after the U.K. general election of October 1959, the Ministry of Supply and the aviation part of the Ministry of Transport were combined to form the Ministry of Aviation (MOA) under Duncan Sandys as minister. Officials of the new ministry met French Air Ministry officials in February 1960 to discuss the possibilities of SST collaboration.[14] Morien Morgan of the MOA, former deputy director of the RAE and an active SST proponent, disclosed that the U.K. government was interested in contacting the U.S. government to explore the possibility of a cooperative project. General Jean Gerardin said that the French government might contact the United States but first would consult the West German government. Would the British consider a cooperation that included Germany? The U.K. officials replied that SST cooperation would be difficult enough between two countries; it would be well-nigh impossible between four.

The topic was picked up at the ministerial level in April 1960, when Duncan Sandys was in abrasive form at an Anglo-French meeting.[15] Sandys pressed for immediate collaboration between French and British companies. "If we see no possibility of quick collaboration with France," he warned, "we shall turn to the U.S.A." (In November 1961 another U.K. minister of aviation was to warn an American delegation that if Britain saw no possibility of quick collaboration with the United States, she would turn to France.)

Contacts at the governmental level in the United States also were being explored. In Washington, Roy MacGregor, civil air attaché at the British embassy, had exploratory discussions with FAA administrator Quesada. At the end of March he reported back to Sir George Gardner, controller of aircraft at the Ministry of Aviation in London.[16] Quesada was among those who seriously doubted the desirability of the SST, MacGregor reported, but he might respond to the idea of collaborating with Britain. The time was ripe for such an approach to be made, the air attaché suggested.

In July 1960 the "supersonic airliner" came up again for consideration by Harold

Macmillan's cabinet, first in papers by the minister of aviation and the chancellor of the exchequer and then in general discussion. In his cabinet paper, Duncan Sandys reported that following the award of study contracts to Hawker Siddeley and to Bristol Aircraft (by this time part of British Aircraft Corporation, or BAC), each firm had submitted proposals for both a Mach 2.2 aluminum-alloy aircraft and a Mach 2.7 steel or titanium machine.[17] Each type would carry 100–120 passengers nonstop from London to New York. BAC strongly favored the Mach 2.2 aircraft, while Hawker Siddeley recommended that work should continue on both types. Ministry officials favored Mach 2.2. The United States favored a steel aircraft of the highest practicable speed (taken to be about Mach 2.7), based on experience in developing the B-70 supersonic bomber. France was studying medium-range Mach 2.2 designs.

Both British aircraft groups had had inconclusive discussions with U.S. and French firms on possible collaboration, the minister reported. He recommended that one aircraft firm and one engine firm should be authorized to continue design work on a Mach 2.2 aircraft over a period of 12 months. The British firms should then resume discussions with American and French companies, after which the government could decide whether or not to advance to the prototype stage.

At this stage, then, Britain's aviation minister was assuming that if his country was going to embark on the undoubtedly expensive development of a supersonic transport aircraft, it would preferably be in conjunction with another country and preferably directed toward a Mach 2.2 design. The preferred choice of the collaborating nation remained open—but not for long.

The Sandys paper was discussed by the cabinet on 14 July but was not accepted right away. Instead, the minister of aviation was asked to get together with the chancellor of the exchequer and the minister of defense to consider the matter further. Five days later the result of this trio's deliberations was conveyed in a cabinet paper by Heathcoat Amory, the chancellor.[18] The proposal was that the government should place a further contract for a 12-month, £500,000 design study with one of the two main aircraft groups.

Objective: To Secure U.S. Collaboration

The chancellor went on to state categorically the collaboration deal the three ministers had in mind:

> *The object would be to create a negotiating position from which the United Kingdom should attempt to secure United States collaboration in a joint project—since the Americans*

would only be likely to be interested in collaboration with us if they thought that, without it, the United Kingdom would develop a supersonic airliner which would compete in a limited market with any airliner which they might produce themselves.

(Emphasis added; at the time, significantly, this objective was never publicly disclosed in such overt terms.)

Heathcoat Amory's acceptance of this next step along the road to civil supersonics was tempered by the caution instilled in all chancellors by the U.K. Treasury's hallowed reluctance to spend money on anything at all if it can possibly be avoided. His agreement to letting the contract, he stressed, was subject to the proviso (accepted by the minister of aviation) "that we must neither decide nor announce anything now which in any way commits us to proceeding to any stage beyond that of the design study now proposed." He very much doubted whether, if international collaboration proved impossible, Britain should go ahead on its own. Despite the chancellor's lack of enthusiasm, his paper had made the collaboration issue crystal clear. Britain's first-choice collaborator was the United States, with France regarded as a possible third partner.

The limited go-ahead proposed by Sandys and reluctantly endorsed by Heathcoat Amory was confirmed at a cabinet meeting on 21 July. The cabinet broadly agreed with the main points as outlined in the two papers and agreed that one aircraft firm and one engine firm should be authorized to continue design work on a Mach 2.2 aircraft. They agreed also to consider further "the possibility of collaboration with the United States or other countries in the joint development of a supersonic airliner."

Agreement in Principle—Somewhat

A London meeting scheduled for September appeared to offer the ideal opportunity to try to translate this possibility into agreed joint action. This occasion was the first in a planned series of Anglo-American policy review meetings on civil-aviation cooperation, to be attended by officials from the U.K. Ministry of Aviation and a U.S. team led by Elwood Quesada, the FAA administrator. The second item on the five-point agenda was the supersonic transport aircraft. MOA briefing documents for the meeting reviewed the prospects for SST collaboration (noting that West Germany was not interested in SST development), posed several hypothetical questions that Quesada might raise, and suggested possible answers.[19] For example, why did Britain want collaboration? In essence, to share costs and market and to avoid unnecessary competition. What could the United Kingdom offer the United States? Know-how (especially on slender wings), cost-sharing, time-saving, and cheaper research and development effort.

Those questions, as it turned out, were not raised at the September meeting. Discussion of the supersonic transport at that meeting was thorough but inconclusive in terms of any firm commitment to Anglo-American collaboration in SST development.[20] Quesada's FAA team was supported by John Stack of the National Aeronautics and Space Administration (NASA). The British team was led by Sir William Strath, permanent secretary at the Ministry of Aviation; senior officials included Denis Haviland, Sir George Gardner, Morien Morgan, and L. F. Nicholson. Peter Thorneycroft, who had succeeded Sandys as minister of aviation, did not participate formally in the meeting but was joined by Strath and Quesada for an informal discussion over lunch.

The FAA chief described supersonic transport aircraft as the next major step for the civil air transport industry. (At that time he was not alone in this assumption, but in fact, the next major step turned out to be the Boeing 747 high-capacity subsonic aircraft.) The general discussion included a debate on the technical factors that had led Britain to favor an aluminum-alloy Mach 2.2 aircraft and the United States, drawing on the military B-70 experience, to favor Mach 3 or thereabouts. Sir William Strath said that Britain was keen to avoid duplication of the very high costs of developing an SST for a very limited market, and was suggesting a full collaboration between the two countries in development and production. If the U.S. government intended to hold a design competition, a full discussion of arrangements for collaboration might have to wait until that competition had been concluded.

Indeed it would, Quesada indicated. The FAA head said he agreed in principle that collaboration would be of mutual benefit. But he had given no thought to methods of achieving such collaboration, and competitive factors might make a mutually acceptable joint project difficult. An American airframe powered by a British engine might be feasible, he suggested. That was not at all what the British team had in mind. If that type of deal did emerge, Sir William said, he hoped there would be a full exchange of information. It was impossible to take the discussion farther. The official U.K. note of the meeting records: "It was agreed that both countries should give further consideration to the possible means of collaboration." In terms of the sort of commitment that the United Kingdom was seeking, that sentence was hardly a stirring call to action.

Implications of the September meeting were analyzed in a follow-up discussion in Sir George Gardner's office at the Ministry of Aviation. In particular, officials tackled the tricky question of how to keep open the possibility of U.S. collaboration while maintaining the momentum of the U.K. work. Following the joint meeting the minister had decreed that the link with the United States must be maintained, the United Kingdom should proceed with the design study contract but should not give the impression of "going it alone," and the United Kingdom should propose further technical discussions at the government level in the new year. The flavor of the ministry's enthusiasm for supersonics, though constrained by administrative caution and the need to be nice to the Americans yet firm with British industry, comes across in this extract from the official note of the meeting:

> Mr. Morgan said that we must keep the momentum of the project up. We could not afford to wait for the Americans to make up their minds. Sir George Gardner agreed and said that we must declare our policy, pick our firm and say exactly what was to be done. He stressed however that nobody could now predict our attitude in a year's time and we should therefore still maintain our collaboration with Mr. Quesada. Mr. Meeres [N. V. Meeres, an MOA under secretary] said that any announcement on the design study contract would need to be qualified by the statement that no decision had yet been taken to build prototypes. Sir George Gardner thought this was too negative and would not generate the enthusiasm we wanted nor would the management put the best men on the job if they thought there was no future in it. He recognised that there was at present a stop at the end of a year but maintained we must paint as rosy a picture as possible. He thought "we are proceeding to the next stage" was the right tone.[21]

Summing up, Sir George Gardner said, "whilst we must go ahead with our design studies and be prepared to stand alone on the project if necessary, we must keep the door of collaboration open."

The Morgan Rationale

The British government's policy during 1960 was based on a detailed appraisal by senior Ministry of Aviation officials—Gardner, Morgan, and Nicholson—of the likely prospects for supersonic transport aircraft in general and for possible Anglo-American projects in particular. Papers by Nicholson and by Morgan in October 1960 give a revealing insight into the technical view at that time.[22] (Morgan's is reproduced in appendix 1.) Morgan's argument, in essence, ran as follows. Supersonic long-range air transport was coming, and the United Kingdom could not afford to be edged out of this field by the United States and the Soviet Union. Britain held a lead of two or three years over the United States in SST research and had the resources to develop a Mach 2 light-alloy design. It appeared that the United States, unwisely, would go for a Mach 3 steel machine. Anglo-American and Anglo-French cooperation could be explored but was not essential. Britain could go it alone on a light-alloy machine even if the Americans went for steel, provided no time was wasted. If, after further study, the Americans settled on Mach 2 and light alloy, that would be the time for a commercial deal between U.S. and U.K. firms to share the market, split design responsibility, and split production. There was everything to be gained by moving ahead with a British Mach 2 project.

The essential message from the British aviation officials, then, was that Anglo-American SST collaboration would be difficult to agree on and implement because of the two disparate technical approaches to the design, quite apart from organizational, political, and industrial problems. Anglo-French collaboration might be possible. If no international collaboration proved achievable, then Britain could go it alone with a fair chance of a reasonable share of the expected market.

U.S. Prototypes, Built in Britain?

Meanwhile, top management of British and American aircraft companies had begun to explore possible SST collaboration. At the Farnborough air show in September 1959 Hall L. Hibbard, senior vice president of Lockheed Aircraft Corporation, Burbank, California, called in at the Hawker Siddeley chalet with a novel proposition to put to John Kay and Stuart Davies.[23] Lockheed had already spent $3.5 million in preliminary design work on a Mach 2 supersonic transport to carry about 90 passengers, Hibbard reported; the company was ready to go ahead with detailed engineering but was seeking additional finance. Lockheed did not expect the U.S. government to put up any SST funds for some time but believed that the British government might welcome U.S. cooperation. In return for U.K. investment, Lockheed proposed that Hawker Siddeley could share in detailed design and engineering of the SST—and indeed could build the envisaged two prototypes in Britain and go on to share the production. Lockheed estimated the market at about 300 SSTs. The British executives said they were certainly interested in Hibbard's proposal.

At that time, in September 1959, the prospects for a joint venture had appeared reasonable, but the following March Hibbard wrote to Kay to report a change of plan.[24] The previous September, he recalled, there had seemed to be no hope whatsoever of any U.S. government interest in developing an SST. Lockheed had been keen to get started, hence the suggestion of collaboration with the British company. But things had changed: there had been a quickening of interest in the U.S. supersonic transport, and it appeared that it might be started soon. Thus Lockheed intended to await U.S. developments rather than pursue foreign possibilities.

"Therefore, it seems that any ideas which we might have had for collaborative agreements must be shelved, certainly for the time being."

Just prior to this shelving of ideas with Lockheed, Hawker Siddeley had discussed collaboration with Boeing also.[25] Stuart Davies of Hawker reported that Boeing was keen to establish exactly what type of agreement might be feasible: a joint company, sharing the development of a common design, or a technology-pooling arrangement, for example. But the Seattle firm envisaged SST competition with at least one other U.S. firm and appeared "profoundly distrustful of trying to conduct this battle with hands tied by some prior agreement with a British company and indirectly with the U.K. government." Boeing felt that the time was not yet ripe for the company to be tied to any specific proposal, Davies concluded, but it might utilize the services of a British company for early feasibility studies. In the end, this idea also was to remain on the shelf.

As part of the government-inspired process of rationalizing the British aircraft industry, the aviation elements of Vickers, Bristol, and English Electric came together in 1960 to form British Aircraft Corporation (BAC). In May 1960, the merged group gave its considered view on international SST collaboration in a letter from Reginald Verdon Smith, BAC director and chairman of Bristol Aircraft, to the Ministry of Aviation.[26] BAC had been in touch with Boeing, Douglas, and General Dynamics in the United States, the letter reported, and with Sud Aviation in France. Each of the three American firms had shown some general interest. More positively, Sud Aviation was "most willing" to cooperate as soon as British and French governmental approval was obtained and suitable areas for technical collaboration had been identified. After listing the advantages and disadvantages of foreign cooperation, Verdon Smith suggested an initial cooperative arrangement in Europe, after which it might become easier to select a possible American partner.

Hawker Siddeley Aviation, also, had been examining the issue of collaboration in some detail, following the discussions with Lockheed and Boeing. In an appendix to an SST study report, the company's advanced projects group not only examined the prospects for collaboration with other countries, as required by the ministry, but also first took one step back to examine critically the three assumed reasons for such collaboration.[27] First, the international market might not be big enough to support economically two or more competitive designs. Second, the costs of design, development, and manufacture could be shared. Third, the technical strength and resources of the U.S. airframe industry were believed to be very much greater than those of the United Kingdom.

The group queried those assumptions. The world market was greater than had been suggested; any substantial saving to the British taxpayer through a joint project was doubtful; and to design, develop, and produce a supersonic transport was well within the capacity of the United Kingdom. As for the mechanisms of collaboration, the report went on to consider possible approaches, but the overall flavor of the Hawker response was that collaboration with the United States was likely to give Britain only a minor role and would seriously damage the U.K. industry's ability and prestige.

SERIOUSLY SEEKING A PARTNER | 3
The Quest Continues

Meanwhile, in the United States, the prospects for an American supersonic transport were beginning to be explored on Capitol Hill. Hearings were held in May 1960 by a special subcommittee of the House Committee on Science and Astronautics, at which witnesses tended to talk in terms of foreign competition rather than foreign collaboration.[1] No mention of international collaboration appeared in the resulting committee report.[2]

In October, a joint report signed by FAA administrator Quesada, NASA administrator T. Keith Glennan, and Secretary of Defense Thomas S. Gates recommended "the immediate initiation of an orderly national program for the development of a commercial supersonic transport aircraft."[3] At this stage, it appeared that the trio retained fairly open minds on the merits of international cooperation—up to a point. They accepted that cooperation could be of mutual benefit but disliked the idea of intergovernmental agreements, which might impose unacceptable constraints on "the best engineering and economic courses of action." The gist of this message was repeated in a fuller report produced by the FAA in December to spell out in more detail the key issues surrounding the case for an American SST.[4]

"Join with Us"

At the September 1960 Ministry of Aviation debriefing following the Anglo-American talks in London, Sir George Gardner had insisted that the door of collaboration be kept open. The following month his minister, Peter Thorneycroft, proffered an appropriate doorstop in a letter to Elwood Quesada.[5] After bringing the American up to date on U.K. developments, Thorneycroft went on to propose something more than just another round of talks:

> Join with us in our studies, or if you prefer it, ask us to join with you, in a study of the Mach 2.2 aircraft. There is no commitment to make it but no one can judge it until they have really studied it and at the moment it looks to us by far the best bet from an economic point of view. If we agree that the study shows this to be the best approach, then in the event of either of us deciding to go ahead we will find ways to enable the other to have an opportunity if he so desired to share in the development and production of it. If either of us prefer the Mach 3 or higher we will give the other a chance to join in going ahead with that.

Quesada's reply brought no joy to the British minister.[6] In a "Don't call us, we'll call you" response, the FAA head promised, "Your proposal for cooperation will certainly be given our fullest consideration. A specific reply will not be easy but please be assured I will communicate with you on this matter as soon as I am able." Mr. Quesada was not able. On the same day that he signed his letter to the British minister, the U.S. presidential election was won by John F. Kennedy, and the following January a new administrator was appointed to head the FAA. Thus Thorneycroft ended the year 1960 with high hopes for SST collaboration with the United States, but facing a great unknown: how would the incoming Democratic administration react to his proposal for collaborative studies?

At the beginning of 1961 Dr. Archibald Russell, technical director of Bristol Aircraft (part of British Aircraft Corporation) moved to pursue the question of international collaboration more actively. He contacted Denis Haviland of the Ministry of Aviation for an update of the British government's policy and progress on collaboration, and he wrote to Pierre Satre, technical director of Sud Aviation in Paris, suggesting the time was now ripe for the two men to get together to try to work out a basis for Anglo-French collaboration on a supersonic transport project.[7]

Satre replied that his engineers were busy working on a draft SST scheme, which had to meet a March deadline, and so could not be spared for joint studies with the British.[8] However, if Sud were to be selected by the French government for further SST development, the two men could perhaps meet in April to discuss collaboration. The French designer could not resist the opportunity of a gentle twist of the British lion's tail. It appeared that Britain was looking to the United States for an agreement, he noted, and if that implied a design speed of Mach 3 then clearly Anglo-French cooperation would be "less interesting."

Russell doubtless appreciated this tongue-in-cheek comment, but as technical director at Bristol, he was taking seriously the question of the choice of Mach number. He had taken part in the STAC studies and concurred with the Mach 2 recommendations but was keen to make sure that his judgment was based on the fullest available information. At a meeting at the ministry on 18 January and in a letter to the ministry five days later, he was concerned to try to determine whether the Americans knew anything that he and his team did not.[9] "The conflict between the technical assessments of supersonic transports in this country and the U.S.A. has been disturbing us all for a long time," he wrote. Both sides should "come clean" on a number of specific technical questions. It would be a "great relief" to learn the basis for the U.S. view.

New President, New Administrator

Britain's aviation man in Washington, Roy MacGregor, was over in London again for the 18 January meeting, giving his views on the U.S. scene.[10] Experience with the B-70 bomber, other technical arguments, and an American desire to outdo other nations all pointed to Mach 3, he suggested. The possibilities of collaboration therefore seemed remote if the United Kingdom persisted with a Mach 2 project.

In Washington, D.C., the next day the FAA announced that the president-elect had chosen Najeeb E. Halaby, a Los Angeles lawyer, to be the agency's new administrator and Kennedy's principal aviation adviser. Halaby had been a private pilot since 1933 and during the forties had been a test pilot, first for Lockheed and later for the U.S. Navy. Between 1948 and 1954 he was deputy assistant secretary of defense for international security. Now he was to put his own strong, distinctive stamp on the FAA.

Soon after moving into his office at the FAA, Halaby accepted an invitation from Sir Harold Caccia, the British ambassador, to lunch at the embassy. Sir Harold raised the question of coordinating the British and American SST efforts, suggesting that there was not enough room in the market for two SSTs. Halaby stonewalled; *intra*-American cooperation was difficult enough, he claimed, let alone an Anglo-American joint venture.[11] The embassy lunch had clearly been intended to prepare the ground for an approach from the British minister of aviation, and in March Thorneycroft duly renewed his efforts at collaboration with a letter to Halaby.[12] "I am anxious that no time should be lost," he wrote, "in pursuing the possibilities of collaboration between our two countries on a supersonic transport project." Halaby's reply was noncommittal on the question of possible joint projects—and, indeed, on any possible U.S. government-funded SST studies.[13]

French Possibilities

By June 1961 British MOA officials were briefing their minister that "the situation appears to be hardening against collaboration with the U.S.A., whereas on the other hand the French possibilities seem increasingly worthy of consideration."[14] The basis for British governmental thinking on SST collaboration by then had become focused on the ideal of an Anglo-French-American joint venture, tempered by a realization that perhaps the most likely outcome would be an association with France rather than the United States.

This was the view of industry, also. The results of British Aircraft Corporation's further exploration of international SST collaboration were spelled out in July in a report to the Ministry of Aviation.[15] Approaches to American firms had produced only negative responses, the British firm reported, and the U.S. authorities saw little benefit from British involvement in SST development or production. Collaboration with France appeared more promising. There were two options. First, if Britain and France decided to proceed with their respective long-range and medium-range machines, BAC and Sud had agreed, subject to official approval, to collaborate in all possible areas, including the adoption of a common, British engine. The second option was to join with France in developing a single, medium-range aircraft, which implied leaving the development of a transatlantic aircraft to the United States. This industry assessment was reflected in an internal MOA review of SST prospects made later the same month as the design study period drew toward its close.[16]

"I am deeply concerned as to the future of the aircraft industry," declared Minister of Aviation Thorneycroft in a paper presented to his cabinet colleagues in October 1961.[17] And the future of the industry could depend largely on the future of supersonic air transport, he indicated, as well as on international cooperation— not only with countries in Europe "but naturally also, where possible, with the United States." The seventies would almost certainly see the introduction of supersonic air travel, Thorneycroft predicted. The Americans' Mach 3, all-steel aircraft was "an extremely ambitious project, even for them." With a Mach 2, light-alloy machine, Britain had an opportunity to gain "the leadership we so narrowly missed with the Comet." The Mach 2 aircraft could be first in the field, and it promised to be the more economical machine. Thorneycroft disclosed that he had already met Robert Buron, the French minister of transport, to explore possible Anglo-French collaboration on such a project.

The Thorneycroft-Buron meeting was of interest to the United States, also. In a dispatch from the American embassy in Paris, the State Department in Washington was apprised of the meeting and its outcome in some detail.[18] Behind this

American interest in the Thorneycroft-Buron meeting lay the prospect that if the Anglo-French joint venture did not materialize and the French decided to go it alone, they could be interested in using a U.S. Pratt & Whitney engine for their SST. The dispatch went on to discuss this. Finally, the dispatch claimed that Sud Aviation was giving serious thought to an "intermediate" short-range SST based on the subsonic Caravelle, which would cruise at about Mach 1.2. Though the outcome of the Thorneycroft-Buron meeting had been inconclusive, the dispatch concluded, both countries were seriously considering a joint project.

Within a week of Thorneycroft's cabinet paper the chancellor of the exchequer, now Selwyn Lloyd, responded with one of his own, demonstrating that he was just as alert as his predecessor in defending the public purse against the proposals of would-be big-spender ministers.[19] Civil aircraft development in general and the "highly speculative" supersonic airliner in particular would demand large sums of public money over the next decade, he warned. Britain's general economic position was such that "we should think very carefully indeed before embarking on what I fear might prove to be a major project of a wholly uneconomic character." The chancellor's fear was to prove singularly well-founded.

At about the same time, Georges Hereil, Sud Aviation president—ignoring the cross-channel links that were already being forged—presented a more ambitious collaborative SST vista in a lecture at the Technological University in Delft.[20] The countries of the western world, he suggested in an epilogue to his lecture, should collaborate to build not one but two supersonic transports: a European-led "transcontinental" Mach 2.2 machine and an American-led "transoceanic" Mach 3.5 model. There was no question of a commercial objective, Hereil later admitted: "It was just to lead the way, as the aeronautics industry has to do always."[21] Not this time, however: the western world declined to take any such action. In 1962 Hereil was to resign from Sud before the Concorde project was launched; his stated reason was the two governments' refusal to allow him to chair the joint industrial committee for at least five years, instead of two.

Thorneycroft and Halaby

Despite his officials' warnings that the prospects for SST collaboration with the United States were fading fast, Peter Thorneycroft continued to argue the general case for an Anglo-American project. His next platform was a meeting in Washington in November, second in the series begun the previous year by Quesada.

In preparation for the Washington meeting, an internal FAA brief conveyed the Anglo-French intelligence from the Paris dispatch and concluded, "Since there appears to be no basis for a U.S. accommodation with the British on a Mach 2 air-craft, nor they with the U.S. on a Mach 3 aircraft, it is recommended that we inform the British that a government-to-government agreement for the joint develop-ment of a supersonic transport can serve no useful purpose."[22] This was the broad line followed by Halaby and his FAA team at the November meeting, though Halaby softened the "no useful purpose" phrase. The U.S. note of the meeting records, "Mr. Halaby stated that it is difficult to foresee at this time government-to-government collaboration on the manufacture of supersonic aircraft."[23] Thorney-croft repeated his call for a joint Anglo-American project. "If the U.S. and U.K. are not able to reach an agreement," the note records, "Mr. Thorneycroft advised that he will probably recommend that the U.K. and the French proceed on a joint proj-ect as the United Kingdom desires to proceed in a commercially sensible way."

The Soviet Threat

Throughout 1962, as the British and French struggled toward an agreement, one or two unusual variations were played on the by then familiar theme of interna-tional SST collaboration. The idea of possible U.S. involvement persisted and re-mained a live issue on both sides of the Atlantic. Though Halaby had in effect dis-missed Thorneycroft's repeated "Join us" plea, there were isolated American voices calling for careful consideration of an international effort before the United States embarked on its own program. One such voice was that of Dr. Theodore P. Wright, an internationally respected U.S. aeronautical scientist.

The American SST studies were being coordinated by a high-level committee of FAA, NASA, and Department of Defense (DOD) representatives known as the Supersonic Transport Advisory Group (STAG). Within the FAA, a small manage-ment office had been created for the supersonic transport program, headed by Colonel Lucien S. Rochte. Wright, a member of the advisory group, wrote to Rochte and to Halaby to argue the case for SST collaboration between NATO na-tions in an Atlantic Union approach in the face of the perceived threat from the Soviet Union.[24] Wright's argument, couched in terms of the "east-west conflict," reflected the cold-war attitudes of the time but related also to the probable limited market for supersonic airliners. French and British SSTs could usurp the world market by the time a U.S. machine appeared, hence a three-nation consortium ap-proach should be considered. The first approach should be on the political level, Wright argued, with the United States inviting Britain and France to an exchange of views on possible SST collaboration. "The mere fact of calling the conference would be important from the standpoint of advancing the cause of NATO or At-lantic community solidarity." Colonel Rochte's reply was politely noncommittal.[25]

In the summer of 1962 the issue was raised again within the FAA in a memorandum written by Arnold Kotz, a policy planning officer.[26] The thrust of his argument was that SST economic and market uncertainties were such that a three-nation consortium might prove the most economical solution in meeting U.S. objectives. France and Britain could contribute $150 million each to the consortium for research and development, plus $600 million from the United States. National commercial jealousies would inhibit an efficient joint venture, Kotz admitted, and there would be many technical, management, and economic problems.

> However, if the obstacles can be overcome, the west will preserve its prestige vis-a-vis the Soviet bloc; uneconomic competition for a very small market among the western allies will be reduced or precluded; the claim on U.S. public funds will be substantially reduced; the strain on the U.S. private aircraft industry will be lightened *while they would still achieve the largest share of the market* since U.S. airlines would presumably order the largest number of aircraft; all western participating countries would share in the advanced technology, and there would be a definite political gain in having key western nations work closely together on a program of this magnitude.

And, Kotz pointed out, there were precedents in military aircraft and missiles for such international collaboration, involving government-to-government agreements and industrial participation. These included U.S. Department of Defense programs for the European production of the F-104G fighter and Hawk and Sidewinder missiles.

Frank E. Loy, acting director of the policy development office, passed on Kotz's "penetrating and incisive" memo, urging that it be given very serious consideration.[27] "I don't want to beat a dead horse," he wrote, "but I don't believe this is a dead horse." Raymond B. Maloy, international aviation services director, responded with a step-by-step argument that began with Anglo-French disagreements and led to a somewhat different conclusion.[28] There were obstacles to a tripartite SST program: the timing was out of phase and the practical difficulties of jointly designing or producing anything as complex as an SST were tremendous. The United States should concentrate on a long-range SST, Maloy concluded, leaving Britain and France to build a medium-range machine.

"The Race Has Started"

Traditional ties and a common language had meant that transatlantic SST collaboration with the United States had been explored first by the British, rather than by the French. Indeed, French suspicion of the special relationship between

Britain and the United States was an inhibiting factor in the early Anglo-French collaborative discussions. But in March 1962 Georges Hereil and Jean Gelos of Sud Aviation flew to Seattle for talks with Wellwood Beall and colleagues in the Boeing company. At that time Sud had been chosen by the French government (as BAC had been chosen in Britain) to pursue the national SST effort; no American "chosen instrument" had been selected for a U.S. program, but Sud believed that Boeing was the company most likely to succeed. Hereil began with a progress report on the proposed 100-passenger, Mach 2.2 Anglo-French design and went on to suggest U.S. involvement. Giving a resume of the discussions to William M. Allen, Boeing president, Beall reported that the Frenchmen had suggested two options for the United States.[29] First, join with France and Britain on the Mach 2.2 aircraft and forget about Mach 3.5. Second, act as sales agent for the European aircraft, with France and Britain providing both sales and technical assistance on the Mach 3.5 machine later.

"This means to me," Beall warned, "that the race for the supersonic transport has started and we are going to be faced with competition in the United States from foreign manufacturers." Beall went on to send a copy of his note to Najeeb Halaby at the FAA. In a covering letter he warned again, "I believe the foreign threat, particularly that of the French, to our air transport image and our national prestige is so great that an effort much more vigorous than our present national supersonic transport program must be organized."[30]

Rearguard Action

Though a formal Anglo-French agreement was approaching the final stages of negotiation, a valiant rearguard action to secure American involvement was being waged at the senior-official level by Denis Haviland at the Ministry of Aviation in London. At the end of May, at the invitation of the ministry, Wellwood Beall and three Boeing colleagues called on Haviland (after a preliminary meeting with Morien Morgan) in London. Haviland's message was that the British government would welcome the participation of Boeing in the Anglo-French project; that approaches to the U.S. government had failed, but joint discussions by Boeing and BAC would be welcome; and that the Anglo-French design was by no means frozen, and there would be scope for Boeing to influence it if they wished. No, he indicated, his government had no specific proposal to make to Boeing. Beall, after mentioning his earlier discussions with Sud, indicated that Boeing had no specific proposal either.

On the evening of the same day, the Americans dined with Sir George Edwards,

Geoffrey Knight, and Jim Harper of BAC. Sir George outlined the Anglo-French progress and indicated he would welcome Boeing participation—though he did not think there was much time left to improve the design. One of Beall's colleagues, Vernon Crudge, in a note of the London meetings, concluded bluntly, "It may be that the British and French will be left to do this thing on the philosophy that it is a stupidity of their own and will lead them nowhere, and we shall ultimately overtake them with something more versatile, more economical and better suited to solve the problem."[31] But Boeing could consider a limited tie-up with safeguards. At that time Denis Haviland was expected to visit the company soon in Seattle for further talks; he never made the trip, and the prospect of U.S. industrial involvement in a tripartite deal with Britain and France evaporated.

Common Market Context

Meanwhile, in the summer of 1962, the British and French governments were moving toward a formal accord. On 29 May the British cabinet considered a short progress report by Peter Thorneycroft.[32] Buron and Thorneycroft had "gone a long way towards agreeing a possible plan" to develop jointly a Mach 2.2 aircraft prior to Buron's recent resignation. The French cabinet had already authorized substantial funds for the project. The issue should now be passed to "a small group of ministers most concerned" for further consideration, Thorneycroft suggested, and the newly formed Cabinet Committee on Civil Scientific Research and Development seemed a suitable forum. The cabinet concurred.

Chairman of the committee was Harold Macmillan's minister without portfolio, Lord Mills. He had not previously been among those "most concerned" with the proposed SST, but he was highly regarded by Macmillan as an effective general troubleshooter. It took the committee three meetings to complete their SST business. At the first meeting the group discussed papers by Thorneycroft and by Henry Brooke, chief secretary to the Treasury.[33] Thorneycroft reported that the Americans were determined to go it alone, and he went on to spell out the political implications of a joint Anglo-French venture.[34] The project could be of great political significance in the context of Britain's negotiations to enter the Common Market, he emphasized.

Henry Brooke's view was unequivocal: the man from the Treasury did not think that the supersonic airliner was a commercially viable project. The group decided that more information was needed. This was provided on 13 July by Sir George Edwards of BAC and Sir Arnold Hall of Bristol Siddeley Engines. The industrialists' view of American competition included a touch of wishful thinking on the choice of speed: U.S. industry still harbored doubts on the wisdom of its "initial" preference for Mach 3, they averred.[35]

Only days later, Harold Macmillan shocked Britain in a sudden, wholesale shake-up of his ministers that became known as "the night of the long knives." In the new cabinet, Peter Thorneycroft was moved from aviation to defense, and Julian Amery, Macmillan's son-in-law, became the new minister of aviation. Just as significant was the change in chairmanship of the Committee on Civil Scientific Research and Development: out went the faithful Percy Mills and in came R. A. Butler, first secretary of state and deputy prime minister.

In preparation for the next meeting of the committee, MOA and Treasury officials prepared a number of reports on specific aspects of the proposed Anglo-French program. On 27 September the committee assembled for what was to be its final discussion of the SST. Amery and Thorneycroft urged an immediate go-ahead, while other members were more cautious. The balance of opinion in the committee, according to the minutes of the meeting, "appeared to be that the project was unlikely to be justifiable as an economic proposition in ordinary commercial terms, and indeed that there were considerable risks, both technical and financial, in undertaking it."[36]

Butler drafted, circulated, revised, and presented the committee's report to the cabinet on 6 November. The report reviewed the complex issues involved, but it left the final decision fairly and squarely in the lap of the cabinet: it contained no firm recommendation for or against.[37] At its 6 November meeting the cabinet began with foreign affairs ("The Foreign Secretary said that the dismantling and withdrawal of Soviet missiles from Cuba appeared to be proceeding smoothly") and continued with the proposed supersonic airliner.[38] Butler presented the gist of his committee's report, ending with the equivocal conclusion:

> To sum up, this proposal may well constitute a natural and inevitable step in techno-logical advance, offering the benefits of such advance and a moment of opportunity to enhance British and French prestige, but we may find in later years that United States industry ousts it with something better, and we are left with too small a market for our pains. And some of us believe that the right lines of technological advance for this country to exploit cannot be selected without regard to commercial prospects. On the other hand to decide not to venture in this field while America and perhaps Russia and France go ahead could well mean contracting out of the large passenger aircraft business.

Julian Amery argued for the project. John Boyd-Carpenter, chief secretary to the Treasury, "hesitated to commend the proposal because of its poor showing in commercial and financial terms." If an SST were to be thrust upon British Overseas

Airways Corporation (BOAC) before its fleet of subsonic jets had reached the end of their useful lives, he said, further massive aid from public funds might be required.

The SST topic itself had been thrust upon the cabinet at that particular meeting because the minister of aviation (now Julian Amery) was about to meet his French opposite number (now Roger Dusseaulx) and needed to know the government's attitude. Otherwise, Butler indicated, his committee would have liked to assess the relative priorities between the SST and other candidate projects. A decision should not turn on the timing of the meeting with Dusseaulx, it was suggested; on the other hand (and every point in the argument appeared to have its "other hand"), it would be wrong to let a major opportunity slip by.

Summing up, the prime minister said that it was peculiarly difficult to judge the proposal. For commercial reasons the airlines would tend to oppose the aircraft. The project would not make money, because of its own high cost and possibly also because of U.S. competition. It would demonstrate an Anglo-French interdependence, while it would be to Britain's disadvantage to allow France to go it alone. If the project did go ahead, it was important to ensure that the companies would contribute financially "and that the aircraft was known by a name which would reflect the joint participation of the United Kingdom and France in the project." (In other words, it should not be known as the Super-Caravelle, the name of the French SST design.)

This was hardly an enthusiastic endorsement. Nonetheless the cabinet authorized the minister of aviation to inform the French government that the proposal for the joint development of an Anglo-French SST was in principle acceptable, "subject to satisfactory assurances on the participation of French airlines and to final examination of market prospects." Amery would have good news for Dusseaulx. The cabinet moved on to item 3 on the agenda, a familiar 1960s British industrial topic ("The Minister of Labour informed the cabinet that the unions concerned had now given notice of an official strike to be called at the Ford Motor Company works at Dagenham").

Thus the die was cast, and events moved rapidly toward a formal engagement between the two countries. Julian Amery saw Dusseaulx on 8 November, and on 14 November President de Gaulle approved the joint project. On 20 November Amery reported back to his cabinet colleagues.[39] Assurances of French airline participation had been obtained, he said, and he had persuaded the French authorities that the aircraft should *not* be called the Super-Caravelle. Other names had been discussed, of which "Concorde"—with and without the final "e"—seemed to be the best. After further discussion, the prime minister summed up. The agreement with the French should be signed, and the aircraft should be called "Concord."

The deal was sealed on 29 November, when Amery and French ambassador Geoffroy de Courcel met in London to sign the historic Anglo-French Agreement "regarding the development and production of a civil supersonic transport aircraft."[40] That was the end of any thought of cooperation with the Americans—or so it appeared at the time.

As for Britain's Common Market hopes, they proved premature. President de Gaulle bluntly vetoed British entry less than two months later.

IMPACTS $\Big|$ 2

THE RACE BEGINS | 4

Najeeb Halaby lost no time in warning President Kennedy of the implications of the Anglo-French initiative. The day after President de Gaulle approved the joint program, in a memo significantly headed "Race to the supersonic transport," Halaby listed the dire effects that could follow if the United States failed to take action.[1] If the Anglo-French consortium succeeded unchallenged in capturing the world market for supersonic transports in 1968–1975, he advised, the United States would be forced (in Halaby's own words) to:

—Relinquish world civil transport leadership;
—Spend as much as $3 billion for U.K.-French imports, with consequent balance of payments deficit (one U.S. carrier is already discussing an order);
—Forego exports of as much as $4 billion if we could capture all of the foreign market;
—Fail to provide about 50,000 jobs per year over a ten-year span in the major airframe and jet engine centers of the West Coast, Middle West, and New England;
—Be dependent on foreign sources for supersonic military airlift if this becomes a defense requirement;
—Conceivably, persuade the President of the United States to fly in a foreign aircraft!

The danger that the United States would be forced to "relinquish world civil transport leadership," placed at the top of Halaby's list, summed up the prime argument that was to be advanced repeatedly in the years to come in support of an American

41

supersonic transport program. This issue was coupled to the assumption, widely accepted in world aviation circles, that supersonic travel would be the next major advance in civil air transport. The world-leadership argument was pressed forward again by Halaby in May 1963 in an FAA report to an SST advisory group, set up by Kennedy and chaired by Vice President Lyndon Johnson.[2] The report recommended that an SST development program be started as soon as possible, aiming at a potential market of 210–250 aircraft. The SST was the next inevitable advance in commercial aviation, and to opt out would cast doubt on the merit of the American political and economic systems.

Halaby's emphasis on national prestige as an end in itself was not shared by the White House Bureau of the Budget, where Kermit Gordon, bureau director, and Walter Heller, chairman of the Council of Economic Advisers, stressed that the federal government should take part in the development of an SST only if there was a reasonable prospect of commercial success.[3]

Halaby developed his proposed plans for an SST development program in a memorandum to the president on 3 June 1963.[4] Again the first topic addressed was "national considerations," and again the first point within this topic was the Anglo-French program's challenge to U.S. world leadership in civil aviation. U.S. industry could and should develop a safe and economically feasible SST that was superior to "de Gaulle's and Macmillan's Concorde." Halaby knew that Pan American was about to announce an order for six Concordes; he urged the president to announce a go-ahead for a U.S. program in a speech planned for 5 June at the U.S. Air Force Academy at Colorado Springs. Pan American's Concorde order was announced on 4 June, much to Kennedy's annoyance, and the following day the president told his USAF Academy audience, and the world, that the United States was embarking on an important new program in civil aviation.[5] After referring to supersonic flight as the challenging new frontier in commercial aviation, and to the feasibility studies conducted under the chairmanship of the vice president, he declared:

> Having reviewed their recommendations, it is my judgment that this government should immediately commence a new program in partnership with private industry to develop at the earliest practical date the prototype of a commercially successful supersonic transport superior to that being built in any other country of the world.

A preliminary design competition would be opened, with a more detailed design phase to follow. If these studies did not produce an aircraft that could transport people and goods "safely, swiftly and at prices the traveler can afford and the airlines find profitable," the project would go no farther.

But if we can build the best operational plane of this type—and I believe we can—then the Congress and the country should be prepared to invest funds and effort necessary to maintain this nation's lead in long-range aircraft, a lead we have held since the end of the second world war, a lead we should make every responsible effort to maintain.

International Rivalries

Closely linked to the national-prestige issue, as the U.S. SST program began to get under way, were the various manifestations of international rivalries and perceived international threats. At the highest level, President Kennedy's view of the Concorde was colored by his view of the French president, Charles de Gaulle. In an internal memo on 31 January 1963, Najeeb Halaby wrote, "In a conversation with the President on Tuesday, January 29, it became clear that he is much more nearly in favor of going ahead with the procurement of an SST prototype. One of the factors is the desire to out-do de Gaulle."[6]

Explaining this relationship some years later in his autobiography, Halaby wrote of the French president's rejection of Britain's entry to the European Economic Community (the Common Market) in January 1963, coupled with his strong endorsement of the Anglo-French collaboration on the Concorde.

> When de Gaulle embraced the joint Concorde project, it seemed to trigger competitiveness in John Fitzgerald Kennedy. In fact I think JFK associated the Concorde most with de Gaulle; on more than one occasion he said: "We'll beat that bastard de Gaulle." Kennedy resented the Frenchman's simultaneous support of the British-French SST and his rejection of the British from the Common Market.[7]

Halaby had been well aware of the impending Anglo-French collaboration before it was officially announced, and there were others who in 1962 were concerned about the foreign threat to the United States. In March, following Georges Hereil's visit to Seattle, William Allen of Boeing told Roswell Gilpatric, deputy secretary of defense, of his concern about the serious threat of subsidized foreign competition.[8] Allen drafted a letter to President Kennedy stressing that "our present evaluation of their [Britain and France's] proposed airplane and its potential usefulness to our airline customers, both domestic and foreign, causes us deep concern."[9]

A discussion of foreign competition formed part of the deliberations of the Supersonic Transport Advisory Group, which in December 1962 had submitted its report as an input to the study process that led to the president's announcement the following June. Foreign competition, they declared, demanded "an accelerated research and development program, prototype fabrication and testing without jeopardizing safety of operation standards and satisfactory economics."[10] The primary competitive forces were those of Britain and France, fully subsidized by the two governments; Soviet competition, also, should not be underestimated. Foreign competition intended to offer a supersonic transport for commercial operation in 1970, and although this timing appeared optimistic, "the importance of proceeding expeditiously cannot be overemphasized" if the United States expected to maintain its leadership.

The president's June 1963 announcement was backed up later that month by an FAA report, which described the envisaged U.S. program.[11] On foreign competition, after outlining main features of the Anglo-French program, the report warned: "It would be unwise for the United States to assume that these objectives will not be substantially attained since both the British and French Governments have fully mobilized their aeronautical resources and have earmarked approximately $450 million for the development program." Turning to the expected return on investment, the report emphasized that, whether or not the United States were to develop an SST, the U.S. subsonic fleets would face direct competition with the Concorde—"with deleterious effects upon revenues of U.S. carriers." The Concorde might not prove economical; if a U.S. SST were not available, U.S. airlines, compelled for competitive reasons to buy Concordes, "would face the serious penalty of operating against subsidized foreign airlines."

After visiting the international air show at Le Bourget Airport in Paris in June 1963, Halaby warned that the European nations were cooperating ever more closely "to pool their technical and economic resources to topple the United States from the position of pre-eminence it has held in transport aviation for the past 30 years."[12] In October that year he told a Senate committee, "We would not seriously entertain the thought that we should rely solely on British-French efforts to produce ships or buses for the free world, and no more can we avoid our responsibility to meet our obligation to maintain U.S. leadership in the field of commercial aviation."[13] The message that the United States must beware the foreign threat was an essential thread in the fabric of the continuing SST controversies throughout the decade of the sixties and beyond. It was easy for proponents to use, and overuse, this argument, but the basis of their case was to be subjected to deeper scrutiny as the initiative for the SST program was taken away from the FAA.

Mr. Black and Mr. Osborne

One early problem Kennedy and Halaby encountered in moving the SST program forward was the industry's objection to a proposed arrangement under which development costs would be shared between government and industry on a 75 percent–25 percent basis. To help resolve this problem, in August 1963 the president invited Eugene R. Black, former president of the World Bank, to review financial aspects of the program planning, with Stanley de J. Osborne, chairman of Olin Mathieson, as his deputy. Following the assassination of President Kennedy in Dallas on 22 November 1963, it was to President Lyndon Johnson that Mr. Black and Mr. Osborne reported back in December. Their report covered much more than the financial issues, including the possibility that the United States would join the Concorde program and the relative timing between the two programs.[14] "The Franco-British 'Concorde' program, now well underway," they declared, "sets the pace, poses our problems and defines the competitive and technical necessities of the United States supersonic transport."

The two financiers rejected the idea that the United States should join in the Concorde program; to do so would not now be in the national interest. As for the relative timing, one of the basic philosophies of the current U.S. program—that of tying the U.S. effort to the Concorde, so compressing the time of development and construction—was dangerous, both technically and economically. A superior aircraft, available two to three years after the first Concorde deliveries, would still be able to capture the bulk of the world market. (The Black-Osborne arguments on these two issues are reproduced in appendix 2.)

The Black-Osborne report proved a controversial document—among other things, it recommended that a new, independent authority should take over management of the SST program from the FAA. That did not happen, but the report correctly predicted the two key problem areas in the entire program: the tolerability of the sonic boom and the economic viability of the aircraft in airline operations. These were to be subjects of intense study as determinant factors throughout the life of the American program—in contrast to a much less rigorous approach by the Anglo-French team. Even more important than the report itself was its significance in stimulating a top-level change in influence in the American program: Najeeb Halaby had been John Kennedy's principal aviation adviser; following the Black-Osborne report Robert McNamara, secretary of defense, was to emerge as Lyndon Johnson's leading adviser on the supersonic transport.

Collaboration Revisited

After the signing of the Anglo-French agreement in November 1962, it appeared that the idea of any U.S. participation in a combined program was dead. At least, Halaby and George Edwards of BAC thought so, as Halaby recorded in his account of a discussion the two men had the following month:

Sir George felt that two years ago or even 18 months ago it might have been possible for the British and the Americans to get together, but he thinks it is impossible now, except on the environmental factors. . . . We both agreed that there were great difficulties in two countries and several companies building an airplane, and to add a third country and additional companies three thousand miles away would be to "court a camel," that is, a horse designed by a committee.[15]

But the idea persisted, even within Sir George's company. At the Paris air show in June 1963, BAC and Sud gave a Concorde presentation to a U.S. delegation. After the formal meeting (an FAA colleague reported to Halaby),[16] Alan Greenwood and Charles Gardner, respectively sales and public relations managers of BAC, had sought an informal discussion. Both men had pressed strongly for an Anglo-French-American SST consortium, to share development of both a Mach 2.2 aircraft and, later, a Mach 3 machine.

Robert McNamara's increasing influence in the SST program was exerted not as secretary of defense but as chairman of the President's Advisory Committee on Supersonic Transport (PAC-SST), a top-level group set up by Johnson in April 1964. In this role he received strong staff support from his aide Joseph A. Califano, Jr., who acted as the first executive secretary to the committee, and in May 1964 Califano reported a conversation at the French embassy.[17] The occasion was a lunch hosted by the French ambassador in order to discuss possible American cooperation with the Concorde program. Paul Simonet of Sud Aviation had suggested that U.S. firms might build parts for the Concorde and assemble the aircraft under license, in return for a reciprocal deal on the U.S. SST. "I left with the distinct impression that the Franco-British effort is in real trouble," Califano concluded, "and that the French and British are looking for help."

Not so, declared Gordon M. Bain, the FAA's SST program director.[18] "I cannot agree with Mr. Califano's conclusion that the French-British program is in real trouble, and that they want help from us. It is my belief that they would like to eliminate any competitive factor but, from all the reports we can obtain concerning Concorde's progress, they are not slackening off and, indeed, seem to be accentuating their program." He continued: "I would not like to think that the United States would fall for the 'broken wing approach' in order to draw us away from the nest leaving our own transport unhatched."

The following year, after attending the 1965 Paris air show, Bain reported to Halaby on Concorde intelligence gleaned at a BAC-Sud briefing at the show.[19] The British and the French were again seeking some way to "work in harmony" with the American program, he noted, and might well approach the United States with some cooperative plan. "There is no way in which we can meld these competing programs," he commented, "nor should the United States retard its development program to give them a 'head start.'"

By late 1965, the Federal Aviation Agency had a new administrator and a new SST director. General William F. "Bozo" McKee was chosen by President Johnson to succeed Halaby, and Gordon Bain was succeeded by another senior Air Force officer, Brigadier General Jewell C. Maxwell. In March 1967 Arnold E. Briddon, the FAA agency historian, responded to three questions from Maxwell, one of which was "Why no collaboration?" Before tracing the history of British approaches in detail, Briddon summarized the key obstacles.[20] U.S. firms were reluctant to collaborate with foreign companies, the Pentagon was reluctant to release classified SST data to foreign companies, the respective timing of the two programs made their fusion difficult, each side valued the national-prestige argument, and the two SST designs were basically different. Given the will, as the FAA historian noted, all of these inhibiting factors—save the last—could have been swept aside. But it would have taken more than will to reconcile the differences in the choice of speed, even at the beginning. As time passed and the designs hardened, these differences became even more difficult to reconcile.

A Change of Government

In September 1964 Halaby and a small FAA team visited the United Kingdom to discuss Concorde progress with high-level ministry and company officials. One sentence in Halaby's extensive report read, "The next financial climax will occur after the British election when the United Kingdom will have 'an agonizing reappraisal' of the rising costs of development of the Concord."[21]

Halaby was correct. In October, the rising costs of the Concorde were indeed among the many economic problems facing Britain's newly (and narrowly) elected Labour government led by Harold Wilson. Drastic economic measures were announced to improve the country's deteriorating balance of payments, and loans totaling about $3,000 million from foreign central banks and the Bank for International Settlements were negotiated. In an economic statement the government warned that expenditure on items of low economic priority such as "prestige projects" was to be cut out, and added, "The Government have already communicated to the French Government their wish to re-examine urgently the Concord project."[22] (Not until much later did the British government accept the French spelling of the aircraft's name.)

Behind the euphemistic "wish to re-examine" lay a clear intention to cancel— as the U.S. administration was assured in Washington by the British foreign secretary, Patrick Gordon Walker.[23] (The U.S. Treasury secretary, Douglas Dillon, said his government would be relieved to hear this.)[24] But the Anglo-French agreement contained no cancellation clause, and the fear of being sued for heavy damages by the French in the Hague Court of International Justice was to lead to Britain's reluctant continuation of the program.

In the delicate negotiations that prefaced that decision, the suggestion of transatlantic collaboration surfaced once more. Marc Jacquet, the French minister of transport, floated the idea of an Anglo-French approach to the United States— on an "off the record" basis—in a conversation with Roy Jenkins, Harold Wilson's new minister of aviation. At a meeting of the cabinet's Economic Development Committee on 16 November 1964, Jenkins presented a discussion paper offering five options: break the treaty unilaterally, propose an alternative £3 million research program, try to renegotiate the agreement to cover only the development of two prototype aircraft, suggest bringing Germany and Italy into the Concorde program, and propose a joint approach to the United States for a tripartite project, as suggested by Jacquet.[25]

In a Foreign Office telegram of background instructions to Sir Pierson Dixon, the British ambassador in Paris, accompanying a formal aide-mémoire intended for the French foreign minister, the ambassador was told that ministers were attracted by Jacquet's idea of an approach to the United States but was warned of a possible ulterior motive: "There is, of course, a danger that in dropping hints about a joint Anglo-French approach to the Americans the French are baiting a trap for us. If we propose such a move formally they may take it (quite wrongly) as confirmation of their suspicions that we and the Americans have been up to something."[26] Nevertheless, the risk must be accepted, the message continued; the advantages of reaching an understanding with the United States on a more sensible approach to the supersonic era were obvious.

Accordingly, in the aide-mémoire delivered to Maurice Couve de Murville, Britain suggested that if the French government agreed on a joint approach to the United States, possible proposals could include U.S. participation in the construction of two Concorde prototypes and further development and production, a U.S. agreement to slow up the development of a Mach 3 SST, and a British and French share in development of the American SST.

Whatever Minister Jacquet may have indicated off the record, the official, on-the-record response from Paris was skeptical. The French government did not reject the idea of a joint approach to the Americans but insisted that Britain and France should make it clear that the Concorde program would continue whether or not any joint approach bore fruit.[27] Despite considerable doubts on Concorde economics, Britain concurred, and in January 1965 Prime Minister Wilson and

President Georges Pompidou confirmed the continuation of the program. It was left to the hapless Jenkins and Jacquet to pursue the attempt to forge an agreement with the United States. Possible Concorde participation by West Germany and Italy also was explored, but to no avail.

With hindsight, Jenkins (now Lord Jenkins of Hillhead) regards the collaboration option as having been only a "semi-serious" proposal at that time.[28] He explains: "Wilson (who always half-wanted to save the plane) and Callaghan (who as Chancellor did not) were both then more Atlantic than Channel orientated. If the Americans would play, the costs would be spread and the chances of saving the plane much better. For these reasons I, although more sceptical, was quite willing to play along, particularly as I like Halaby very much."

Halaby was closely following the Anglo-French discussions on the Concorde after the Labour government's election and, toward the end of November 1964, had received a report from Raymond B. Maloy, his assistant administrator for international aviation affairs.[29] Now as in the past, Maloy wrote, the French would prefer to go it alone—if they had an engine and the necessary capital. A suitable non-British engine could be obtained only from the United States, while capital might come from Germany or other European countries. The French industry could be more severely hurt than the British by cancellation. Recommendation: the U.S. government should as a matter of priority explore the degree to which it would be prepared to offer assistance to the French if the British withdrew. Reporting official U.K.-French exchanges in a telegram from the American embassy in Paris to the State Department the following month, Charles E. Bohlen, the American ambassador, noted, "Source remarked that British bending over backward avoid any impression serving as U.S. cat's paw in affair."[30]

Prime Minister Harold Wilson paid his first official visit to President Johnson in Washington in December. Defense, foreign policy, and economic policy were the main items on the agenda, but as Najeeb Halaby pointed out in a prior memo to the president, the British might well suggest an Anglo-American or tripartite review of the need for and timing of an SST.[31] Halaby strongly advised the president not to become involved in Concorde discussions. "There is now no basis for our agreement to collaborate on the construction of any supersonic transport."

As it turned out, neither side raised the SST issue at the Wilson-Johnson talks that December. But, Halaby informed the White House in January, it was to be raised the following month at a tripartite ministerial meeting in London.[32] Roy Jenkins had proposed that he, Halaby, and Marc Jacquet should "discuss the possibility of *an agreement on rate of progress* on the U.S. SST and the Concorde" (Halaby's emphasis). Although Jenkins had stated that he felt agreements to delay volume production until more experience was available would benefit both aircraft,

Halaby correctly opined that "it appears the real objective is to preserve the two-year time advantage they believe the Concorde now has."

Thus the topic of supersonic transport programs was picked up again in London in February 1965 by Jenkins, Halaby, Jacquet, and their officials. As expected, the suggestion of closer collaboration was again raised by Jenkins and again stonewalled by Halaby. But first the British minister confirmed that the British government had completed its review of the Concorde project; both Britain and France had determined to go ahead with the project "with determination and speed."[33] Speaking for both Britain and France, Jenkins admitted that it was probably now too late for the United States to participate in the Concorde program, while it would probably prove too costly for Britain and France to participate in the U.S. program. A third possibility remained: a "time-phasing" arrangement under which they agreed on the two program schedules could avoid much wastage of resources.

Halaby agreed that it would be very wrong for the three countries to race into the supersonic transport era, and repeated that arrangements between manufacturers were open at any time, subject only to the requirements of U.S. legislation. But he insisted that he could not agree with the time-phasing idea if it involved a limitation on competition or on his government's discretion in the program.

While the Concorde review and other aviation matters had been occupying Roy Jenkins in the autumn of 1964, he had found time to set up an independent inquiry into the aircraft industry—an inquiry, he wrote later, "which I hoped would result in shining a beam of rational light on to what was becoming the smoke-obscured battleground of the too-political aircraft industry."[34] He appointed Lord Plowden, industrialist and former head of the U.K. Atomic Energy Authority, to chair a handpicked committee to tackle the task. The resulting Plowden Report was published in December 1965.[35] It favored the principle of international collaboration in aircraft projects, in the interests of sharing in wider markets and in development costs—but with Europe rather than with the United States. The essence of the Plowden argument, couched in general terms, clearly applied to the specific case of the SST.

> The U.S., unlike Britain, has no overriding need for a partnership in aircraft development and production. Partnerships occur between those for whom they satisfy needs which are held in common. . . . The committee fully recognise the value to Britain of her present aeronautical links with the U.S. and see no reason why these should not be extended. . . . But we do not see a real prospect of a comprehensive programme of collaboration on aircraft development with the United States.

Hence the key Plowden recommendation: "Wholehearted collaboration on a comprehensive range of civil and military aircraft projects with European countries, with the aim of evolving a European industry to produce aircraft fully competitive with those from the United States." Thirty-plus years after Plowden this still remains in the category of wishful thinking, with the notable exception of the Airbus Industrie family of large airliners, a number of generally problematical joint military projects, and an embryonic collaboration on regional airliners.

Pause for Thought

The tentative suggestion by Roy Jenkins of "time-phasing"—that the Americans and Europeans might agree on schedules for the two machines in the interests of avoiding an unseemly and expensive race—was to be picked up and reexamined periodically in the latter half of the sixties. But in November 1964, in a follow-up letter to their 1963 report, Black and Osborne came up with a more drastic suggestion: a development moratorium.[36] Both sides should pause in their SST programs in order to refine their studies and obtain better information on costs and environmental effects. In the United States, studies had shown widely differing cost estimates, while Concorde cost estimates had risen substantially. Nobody believed that a supersonic race was healthy. On the other hand, there were the problems of national pride and of the special interests of the national aircraft and engine industries. Hence a revised version of the Black-Osborne proposals:

(a) That the United States, Great Britain and France reach an inter-governmental agreement to stretch out the SST development and construction period for an agreed period and consequently not now to fund the heavy costs of pre-production and prototype construction which now faces the "Concorde" nations, as well as the United States.

(b) A technological undertaking with Britain and France devoted to the problems of the sonic boom, airport and community noise levels and all the other new phenomena which will be met with supersonic flight at altitudes never before used by commercial aircraft. . . .

(c) A further period wherein our government will underwrite a series of improvement studies in the aircraft and engine industries designed to lower still further the direct operating costs, further improve flight characteristics, and more nearly reach a period when there will be more protracted and definite flight experience with the variable geometry wing and the double delta configurations.

Black and Osborne emphasized that they were not recommending that the SST programs should be abandoned. But the heavy additional costs faced by the Concorde program and the lack of knowledge in important areas within the whole SST field pointed to a temporary slowdown. "It also seems to us that our own current budgetary requirements and Britain's economic situation may well coincide with the need to slow down what has tended to become an uneconomic pressure to the SST program." To have a billion-dollar failure in Europe or the United States would serve nobody; a sensible delay appeared to be in order. "After such an hiatus, we can both proceed to the construction of prototypes and production aircraft if we will, and compete for the markets of the world on the basis of the excellence of our respective aircraft."

Something similar had already crossed Halaby's mind, during his visit to the United Kingdom in September 1964, just before the British general election. In his report of the trip he recounted a discussion with Sir George Edwards.[37] Supposing all three governments concluded that neither the Concorde nor the U.S. SST could be profitable, what in theory were the options? One was that if, in 1964, it appeared obvious that current technology could not produce a safe and profitable SST within the next five years, then the three governments should agree "to keep the program at the prototype research and development level, and that under no conditions would any one of the three parties offer a transport for operation prior to 1975." Such a cooling-off period might be to all three countries' advantage. But Mr. Halaby and Sir George both knew it would never happen—General de Gaulle would veto any such moratorium, and the industry and the unions were unlikely to forgo the competitive opportunities.

MR. MCNAMARA AND HIS SYSTEMS MEN | 5

For Robert McNamara, U.S. defense secretary, the top priority in the mid-sixties was clearly the conduct of the controversially escalating Vietnam war. But the SST question was one of many other important issues that crossed his desk, and from April 1964 onward he exerted increasing influence over SST matters as chairman of the President's Advisory Committee on Supersonic Transport. Thirty years on, he is candid about his bias against the SST and his thoughts on how to kill it:

> Right at the beginning I thought the project was not justified, because you couldn't fly a large enough payload over a long enough nonstop distance at a low enough cost to make it pay. I'm not an aeronautical engineer or a technical expert or an airline specialist or an aircraft manufacturer but I knew that; I could make the calculation on the back of an envelope.
>
> So I approached the SST with that bias. President Johnson was in favor of it. As chairman of the committee I was very skeptical from the beginning. The question, in a sense, was how to kill it. I conceived an approach that said: maybe you're right, maybe there is a commercial market, maybe what we should do is to take it with government funds up to the point where the manufacturers and the airlines can determine the economic viability of the aircraft. We'll draw up a program on that basis.[1]

McNamara made no secret of his skepticism at the time, though he would hardly have declared so bluntly his mission to kill in the face of his president's enthusiasm.

His team of systems-thinking analysts fed the committee a regular diet of skeptical reports in which the economic viability of the SST was continually questioned. The Concorde became an important element in the economic assessments of the SST that were considered by the committee. Initially the committee consisted of the secretaries of defense, commerce, and the Treasury and the NASA and FAA administrators; later it was expanded to include Black, Osborne—and John McCone, director of the Central Intelligence Agency. Among the defense secretary's analysts, Dr. Stephen Enke (initially a Rand Corporation consultant and later on the staff of the DOD systems analysis office headed by Dr. Alain Enthoven) was to play a key role in subjecting both the Concorde and the U.S. SST to rigorous economic scrutiny.

"How best can the U.S. counter the Concorde?" asked Enke in a wide-ranging SST report in April 1965.[2] Not by engaging in a race, he suggested; crash development programs would be costly, and airlines were in no hurry to operate SSTs. Psychologically, the United States appeared to be responding to foreign programs; far better first to determine what was in America's own best interests and then influence foreign competition. The DOD consultant went on to consider three possible countermoves the United States could make: First, a "gentlemen's agreement" with France and Britain on deferred dates for first flights of airline prototypes (as suggested by Roy Jenkins) and possibly on dates of first deliveries to airlines. Second, the U.S. government could prevent U.S. airlines from purchasing the Concorde—or any airline from operating it into and out of the United States. Certification of the Concorde—as in the case of the early British Comets, Enke noted—might "long be delayed by the U.S." The use of U.S. airports by Concordes might even be delayed pending further sonic boom tests—"with these being completed 'satisfactorily' shortly before airline operation of the U.S. SST commences." And U.S. import duties might be imposed if the Concorde sales price reflected British and French subsidies. Third, but an extreme measure involving major international reactions, Enke admitted, the United States might aim to detach Britain from its agreement with France.

A Treasury Plot

Enke was not the only one considering how the United States might inhibit, damage, or even stop the Concorde program. In another SST working paper, Daniel J. Edwards, a U.S. Treasury analyst, presented a startling plan for deliberate misinformation, which was endorsed by Dr. J. Stockfisch, deputy assistant secretary of the Treasury.[3] The Concorde was probably more a psychological threat than an economic one, Edwards wrote, and it was time to consider counterpsychological warfare on the Concorde developers:

> Public relations people might devote some of our resources to "saying" that the United States is giving serious consideration to meeting the Concorde on entry date. This tactic could be done either without specifying the date, in which case it may actually turn out to be the truth, or, alternatively, we could state that the United States will try to make the 1970 entry date because of some unspecified technological breakthrough. Resources devoted in this manner could buy us a great deal of really precious research and development time. *An announcement of a 1970 target date might be the straw that broke the Concorde "back." Under this pressure the Concorde people might crash their program so drastically that they would produce a very uneconomical aircraft.* The Concorde people might even come running to the United States to negotiate earliest entry dates for each. If we could negotiate for earliest entry of Concorde in mid-1973 and earliest entry of the American SST for the beginning of 1975 we would gain worthwhile advantages over the Concorde, although this alternative would be a second-best. The American SST has great growth potential, the Concorde almost none. We need to consider buying R&D time in many different ways. [Emphasis added.]

This would-be conspiracy apparently was not pursued, but at the next meeting of the president's advisory committee, in May 1965, the question of relative timing between the two programs was an important factor in the committee's discussion of the speed at which the U.S. project should proceed.[4] Dr. Alexander Flax, assistant secretary of the Air Force for research and development, accepted the claimed Concorde estimates of early 1968 for first flight and mid-1971 for airline availability and reported that both Boeing and Lockheed believed that a delay of up to two years for the American machine would be acceptable. Treasury Secretary Henry "Joe" Fowler clearly remembered his people's briefing; how about negotiating an arrangement to agree on schedules and so, in effect, buy R&D time? The British and French would be delighted for the United States to agree to a schedule that would assure them a lead time in the market of two to three years, McNamara replied. Najeeb Halaby agreed.

One important way to reduce the importance of the Concorde's first-flight date, McNamara argued, was for the United States to be able to demonstrate the superiority of the American SST in flight before the Concorde entered airline service. Halaby stressed the urgent need for a U.S. decision and his differing perceptions of the British and French attitudes. Following the cancellation of the TSR-2 bomber, on which Britain was counting for many hundreds of Olympus engine hours, the attitude of the British government would change when the U.S. president announced his commitment to an economic, 200–250-passenger SST. Whether the attitude of the French government also would change was another matter. "Do you think they [the British] might throw in the sponge?" asked Eugene Black. "I think there is a possibility of it," replied Halaby.

Papers prepared for the committee's next meeting, held 16 days later, included another novel suggestion from the Treasury in answer to the question "What should our posture with the British and French be?"[5] The British and the French should be encouraged to "boom Paris and London" to see how Europeans reacted, the Treasury suggested. Also, both Concorde nations had been reported to be concerned with the development of the aircraft; if the United States were to offer them 25 percent of subcontracts on the first 200 American SSTs and 10 percent of all others "they might jump at the opportunity."

Another paper, unsigned but clearly reflecting its Department of Defense origin (and probable Enke authorship), addressed a number of overall strategic issues affecting the SST program.[6] It began by calling for an SST "mission" to be specified, as was the custom in military projects, before deciding whether or not to build an SST. In a wide-ranging comment on the effect of the Concorde on American strategy, the paper noted that to date, the Anglo-French project had done a good deal to structure the U.S. SST program. Much of the immediacy of the U.S. program stemmed from the assumption that the Concorde would be developed and introduced on time. The paper continued:

> It is not clear how the U.S. ought to respond to the Concorde; what is appropriate depends on what we are trying to do and this is not yet clearly defined. There are numerous possible responses which include use of diplomatic and economic resources to delay the Concorde, to make it look less promising to the consortium, and to detach Britain from the effort. *The current response resembles "war" more than "economics."* There has been little explicit analysis of how much the U.S. would be willing to "pay" for a delay or cessation of competition. Similarly, no one has analyzed what the consortium would "pay" for a delay in U.S. competition. An agreement might take the form of a guaranteed low Concorde price and early delivery to U.S. airlines combined with British and French support for lower IATA [International Air Transport Association] subsonic fares and purchase of some U.S. subsonics in return for a stretch-out or abandonment of the current U.S. SST effort. Such agreements ought to be considered in some detail to see if there are not some which would serve the goals of the U.S. even better than the present SST program. [Emphasis added.]

On 1 July 1965, Halaby's departure from the FAA coincided with a quickening tempo in the American SST program, though falling short of any commitment to build a prototype. Speaking at the swearing-in of General McKee as the new FAA administrator, President Johnson announced an intensified 18-month preliminary design phase, as recommended by his advisory committee, starting in August. But Halaby was not leaving without again urging a faster pace of development; in a memo to Johnson written the same day, he argued that the selection of companies to build prototypes should begin "much sooner than the first part of 1967."[7] The United States could not afford further delay, he insisted; that would play into the hands "psychologically and commercially" of the French, British, and Russian governments and industries. Halaby urged the president to give General McKee the authority to "carry out an expedited program to achieve the objectives you have so wisely set"—and to abolish the president's advisory committee by the end of the year. Nice try, Jeeb, as McNamara might have said. The committee was to stay in business, and in control, until September 1968.

Dr. Enke's Mission

Stephen Enke remained concerned that the U.S. SST program was being driven by the perceived progress and prospects of the Concorde, and in October 1965 he widened the intelligence net by enlisting the help of John S. Meadows, civil air attaché in the American embassy in London, to answer a long list of questions on the Anglo-French project.[8] Enke went on to suggest that Meadows and his opposite number in Paris might piece together "a reasonable facsimile of the truth" on these matters. "Perhaps there is another 'David Henderson' in Paris who would be useful," he suggested. This revealing reference was to P. D. Henderson, chief economist at the British Ministry of Aviation, noted Concorde critic, and, for Enke, a useful fellow skeptic on supersonics in general.

Toward the end of 1965 Henderson visited Enke and Pentagon colleagues in Washington with the evaluation of Concorde and the American SST at the top of his list of topics to be discussed.[9] This visit was seen as an opportunity to influence the Concorde program, and so, at McNamara's level, the question of how much information Henderson should be given was linked to the answers to two questions of U.S. policy. First, was it in the U.S. interest to slow the Concorde development and perhaps shorten its production run? Second, if so, how could this be done? McNamara was advised that a Concorde stretch-out would enable the United States to pursue its own program in "a more orderly and economical manner," and a reduced British commitment could prevent "an embarrassing competitive defeat later, together with the anti-American emotions that would then be aroused." Henderson might be provided with selected "ammunition" from the

U.S. studies, or if the French were "calling the shots," they might be provided—in the "least official manner possible"—with study results "that should prove disquieting."[10]

In 1965–1966 Stephen Enke made two fact-finding visits to Europe in order to make his own appraisal of Concorde status and prospects. In May 1965 he had suggested to the McNamara committee that both the United States and the Concorde partnership had much to gain from slowing the SST race.[11] Several kinds of mutually advantageous arrangements were conceivable. "Or," he repeated bluntly, "the U.S. might detach the U.K. from the consortium by offers of subcontracting work on the U.S. SST." The following month he flew to Britain for talks with BAC at Bristol and the Ministry of Aviation in London, gaining the impression that the British officials were very worried about the expected U.S. competition.[12] "Although never openly suggested," he reported, "a possible deal was in the air." Detailed economic studies to determine the probable sales of the Concorde in competition with the U.S. SST were needed, the Pentagon economist declared. Only then could the negotiating possibilities be assessed. "At present," he warned, "the two countries may unknowingly and unnecessarily be on a collision course."

A few months later, Enke was amplifying that message and seeking wider backing within the executive branch. There was an urgent need to limit wasteful SST competition through formal agreements with Britain and France, he told the Bureau of the Budget and the State Department Policy Planning Council.[13] The DOD analyst examined possible strategies in detail but admitted that there was hardly any support within the McNamara committee for a Concorde deal. The FAA had become emotionally attached to the SST program; broader national interests should be considered.

In January 1966 Enke, by then a deputy assistant secretary of defense, flew over to Europe for further talks in Paris and London. "Some French and British officials want a 'deal' on the Concorde," he reported back to McNamara on his return.[14] In a fuller report, the thrust of his message was:

1. A significant number of influential government officials in France and especially in Britain appeared anxious to reach some agreement with the United States to rationalize competition in commercial supersonics.
2. The keenest interest was in "time phasing."
3. The principal French official on Concorde (Robert Vergnaud) still appeared interested in a division of the market, with the Anglo-French team concentrating on a medium-range machine and the United States on long-range SSTs.

4. Any negotiations by the United States would have to be conducted jointly with France and Britain. Britain was a reluctant partner in the Concorde enterprise, and "a weak flank that can be exploited indirectly," but any attempt to detach the United Kingdom from the Concorde venture was now unrealistic.

5. A pretext existed for continuing the dialogue at the ministerial level, but it was questionable whether the FAA could best represent the total interests of the United States.[15]

In his detailed account of his talks in Paris and London, Enke was blunt in reporting his impressions. At a meeting with Ministry of Aviation officials in London, the general mood was one of "subdued despair." None of the officials expected that many Concordes would be sold or that the price would cover more than prime costs of production. There seemed to be a "dumb acceptance" that, unless the French took the lead in somehow alleviating the impending collision with the U.S. SST, the Concorde was one of the prices the United Kingdom must pay to avoid a French veto of Britain's entry into Europe. At a separate meeting, G. R. Bell of the Treasury "conveyed a general impression of fatalistic hopelessness that combined an awareness of financial losses ahead with a belief that little could be done about it." In Paris, at a dinner hosted by Stanley M. Cleveland, minister for economic affairs at the American embassy, General R. Le Camus of the French Ministry of Defense accused the Americans of trying to destroy the French and European aircraft industries. Enke retorted that it was true only that the Anglo-French and U.S. SST programs seemed to be on a collision course and increasing speed; was it really necessary that someone be hurt? At a meeting with Robert Vergnaud, cochairman of the Concorde Committee of Officials, the French official was worried about Concorde economics and pointed out that France and Britain were still waiting for a response to the time-phasing suggestion put forward by Roy Jenkins at the February 1965 meeting.

Though the time-phasing issue continued to be discussed, the discussions proved inconclusive. Eugene Black raised the topic in London with James Callaghan, the British chancellor of the exchequer; and both Black and Osborne continued to provide useful informal channels for the exchange of SST ideas between Washington and London. Robert McNamara's view remained unchanged: the United States should make no move to propose a transatlantic agreement to rationalize SST competition. It would probably be impossible to reach any such agreement that would benefit the United States, and in any case the competition between the Concorde and the American SST was healthy and should not be discouraged.[16]

Setting the Pace

Throughout 1966 the president's advisory committee wrestled with a basic dilemma: to what extent should the timing of the American SST program reflect the development pace of the Concorde? And if the Concorde timing was relevant—despite the no-race arguments, it clearly was highly relevant in market terms—how credible were the announced Concorde target dates? Conflicting intelligence and conflicting opinions somehow had to be accommodated, against a background of a widening gap between the FAA proponents of a "fastest, soonest" program and the Department of Defense caution that all options should be checked and double-checked before proceeding to the next phase. It was ironic that Defense, a department with no direct interest in operating a supersonic transport, emerged as the most influential agency in shaping the U.S. effort. The basic reason for this was President Johnson's high opinion of Robert McNamara. Writing in 1978, Najeeb Halaby referred to the "paralysis by analysis" of the SST program that occurred in the later days of the Johnson administration "as inspiration yielded to calculation."[17] He added, "The greatest calculator of them all was Bob McNamara, and with a very bright, aggressively analytical Joe Califano at his side, he had maximum authority and minimum responsibility for diagnosis and dissection of the SST program."

A brief, early difference of opinion on the question of timing had arisen in May 1964 in the advisory committee's first report to the president.[18] Recommending further study, the committee argued that the U.S. program would not suffer commercially if a superior aircraft lagged the Concorde by as much as two to three years. But Najeeb Halaby placed his dissent on record: he could not agree that a delay of three years could be tolerated without jeopardizing the market for the U.S. SST, and the United States could not safely assume that France and the United Kingdom would fail in their challenge to U.S. leadership.

For obvious reasons, the U.S. aircraft manufacturers were keeping a close eye on the progress of the Concorde, and in 1965, Boeing and Lockheed had assessed the impacts of differences in the lead expected to be enjoyed by the Anglo-French machine. Even assuming a three-year advantage for the Concorde, Lockheed believed there would still be a market for 200 American SSTs.[19] In the Boeing view, the Concorde was quite simply the controlling factor in the timing of the American SST.[20] The company concluded that the U.S. machine could not afford to lag the Concorde by more than two years. At that time, in mid-1965, the Concorde was scheduled to be certificated for commercial service in 1971, and the FAA was stating that the U.S. SST could be certificated in 1973–1975.[21]

In March 1966, McNamara advised General McKee of the view of a group of PAC-SST members, including the chairman.[22] The U.S. SST program should be scheduled at an optimal rate to provide a safe aircraft as soon as possible that would be profitable to its developers, manufacturers, and operators. The pace of the U.S. program should *not* depend on an uneconomic desire to race the Concorde into commercial service.

At a meeting of the full committee two months later, McNamara posed a key question: "Are we today doing anything different than we would be doing if there were no Concorde and, if so, what is it?"[23] U.S. airlines had indicated that a two-year gap after the Concorde would be acceptable, but a three-year gap would not. The answer to the question appeared to be no, the U.S. program at that time was not responding to the Concorde, but an accelerated program might have to be considered at some future date. The credibility of the claimed Concorde dates was again queried. More information was needed, McNamara declared.

Stanley Osborne returned to these issues in a note to McNamara the following month.[24] If airlines were forced to buy the Concorde for competitive reasons because of a wide gap between the two aircraft, this might become a serious matter for the U.S. program. On present plans the United States was trying to maintain a gap of not more than three years. An alternative plan would be to accept as a calculated risk (based on U.S. military supersonic experience) that the Concorde could not operate successfully in airline service at Mach 2 by its announced dates, and publicize to airlines and the British the problems of accumulating supersonic flight hours. The U.S. program could then proceed to prototype development and test flying, before accelerating to make up the supposed gap with the Concorde. This could well become a "less risky, cheaper, and technologically superior approach" for a high-risk enterprise such as the SST.

The defense secretary also had received a letter from John McCone (who had remained a member of the committee after leaving the Central Intelligence Agency to join Joshua Hendry Corporation of Los Angeles) reporting on an informal visit to General André Puget, head of Sud Aviation in Paris.[25] The general had given a full briefing on the Concorde program, and McCone had warned him of the problems encountered in the U.S. military programs. Puget said more information on the U.S. problems might greatly assist the Concorde program; equally, information on Concorde flight-test problems in 1968–1971 might greatly assist the U.S. program. Yet again the question of an agreed relaxation of program schedules was raised by the Frenchman. If the two governments did consider such cooperation, General Puget stressed, General de Gaulle would of course have to be approached very carefully.

Calculating the Concorde Impact

McNamara's May 1966 request for more information was in part answered in papers prepared for the committee's meeting on 9 July, though conflicting FAA and Defense views obscured a ready conclusion. The effect on sales of a slippage in the U.S. program could not be assessed until detailed economic studies were completed, the FAA argued.[26] But it was clear that airlines, which were hedging their bets by taking delivery positions for both aircraft, would move to protect their interests if the timing of either program were to change. If the U.S. program slipped appreciably, they would order significantly more Concordes. On the other hand, a three-year interval could enable the U.S. program to learn from oversights and errors in the Concorde program and so improve the U.S. design. "This was the case with the early Comet aircraft which benefited later U.S. subsonic jet designs," the paper noted.

Enke was unimpressed with the FAA paper. It was "not an adequate response" to the committee's request, he declared bluntly; the FAA's original calculations had been replaced by General McKee by "a few pages of trivia"—apparently because the calculations "were unfavorable to the argument that the U.S. must adopt a risky and possibly unprofitable schedule because of Concorde competition."[27] Defense Department calculations had shown that the Concorde would have a very short-lived market and that it made little difference to sales of the American SST in the long run whether the U.S. program did or did not slip a year.[28] Indeed, Enke argued, a one-year slippage could benefit the U.S. program if it resulted in even a slight improvement in performance.

Enke disagreed also with the FAA view on whether the present U.S. schedule was the one that would be followed were there no Concorde.[29] The schedule included a one-year overlap between prototype test-flying and production. This overlap represented a degree of risk, the FAA admitted, and could be considered a response to the Concorde competition. Should the Concorde prove to pose a serious market threat, the overlap could be increased. This risky overlap was one example of the desire to stay within two years of the Concorde, Enke argued.[30] Almost no analysis had been made of the supposed Concorde threat; important aspects of the interacting programs had been overlooked; and collectively the British, French, and United States governments were not in control. Each side was being driven by the other side, and no one was prepared to break out of the dilemma. (Enke's paper is reproduced in appendix 3.)

Airline views were explored at the July meeting in testimony by Juan T. Trippe, chairman of Pan American World Airways, and by Charles A. Lindbergh, pioneer of solo transatlantic aviation and a director of Pan American.[31] "The whole Concorde picture as we see it is a sort of an insurance program,"Trippe told the committee. "If they did get going and we were left behind we would find that we would be in a pretty bad shape from the point of view of public patronage and public acceptance without something on the oceans that would stay in the ring with them." If the U.S. SST program did not go forward, Trippe forecast, at least 600 Concordes would be built and operated.

Trans World Airlines' views were conveyed to the committee in December by Charles C. Tillinghast, Jr., the airline's president.[32] "We would love to skip the Concorde," he declared—not because it was not a serious contender but because having an extra aircraft type in the fleet created problems. TWA would like to avoid having to buy the Concorde, but a longer interval between the two machines would make this impossible. He concluded, "The British and French are in. They may have been silly to have done it. They are in. They are going ahead. I think anyone who has a tendency to write off the Concorde as a lot of flop is being very unrealistic. Its economics are considerably less than sensational but it will fly, it will fly well. . . . If there isn't anything better we will all be buying them. I could wish they never had the idea but it does not do me any good."

Balance of Payments

In emphasizing the threat of the Concorde, American SST proponents relied heavily on the balance-of-payments argument. Members of Congress, aircraft industrialists, and airline chiefs repeatedly stressed what they saw as the obvious danger of replacing exports of U.S. SSTs by imports of Concordes. At the president's advisory committee meeting noted above, for example, Charles Tillinghast of TWA declared, "The swing on balance of payments between equipping the airlines of the United States with Concordes on the one hand and equipping the airlines of the world primarily with a U.S. SST supersonic is just a tremendous figure, and people differ as to its exact magnitude but it is the magnitude of five, ten or 15 billion dollars." But this argument was not accepted by everyone; it had not been accepted in the past and would not be accepted in the future.

An early assessment, covering the potential effects of the U.S. SST program not only on balance of payments but also on domestic employment and on defense readiness, had been made by the Department of Commerce in 1963.[33] It considered the extent to which an SST would displace subsonic long-range jet airliners, and interestingly, it included estimates for a Mach 2.2 U.S. machine as well as for the expected Mach 3 design. The results were equivocal. For the Mach 3 design, the impact on the U.S. balance of trade in aircraft would range from a deficit of

$1.64 billion to a surplus of $2.07 billion. For the Mach 2.2 design, the range was from the same deficit to a surplus of only $1.08 billion. In each case the impact would be spread over 15 to 20 years (approximately 1970 to 1987). The potential impact on balance of payments, the department told Vice President Johnson, provided no compelling reason for undertaking an SST program (neither did the impact on employment, or on defense readiness).[34]

Within the White House, Kermit Gordon and Walter Heller came to a similar conclusion by a slightly different route.[35] A successful SST program *would* benefit the country's balance of payments, they told Vice President Johnson, but the Treasury believed that the balance of payments would be much stronger in five years' time. Thus, from the point of view of balance of payments, public funds would be better expended on projects with a more immediate payoff.

Three years and many more estimates later, President Johnson's advisory committee was still wrestling with the issue. In preparation for drafting their fourth report to the president, they assembled for a Saturday-morning meeting at the Pentagon just three days after hearing Tillinghast's comments.[36] They had before them a special study prepared for the FAA by the Institute for Defense Analyses (IDA), which, as interpreted by Treasury Secretary Fowler, went even farther than the 1963 Commerce study in dismissing the balance-of-payments case for the SST. "The creation of any commercial supersonic plane, SST, Concorde or both," he said, "is going to accelerate significantly the worsening of the U.S. balance of payments that accompanies an increasing flow of trans-oceanic travel."

Robert McNamara repeated his previously expressed view: "I am not influenced in the slightest degree by either a favorable effect, adverse effect, or a neutral effect." There were other ways of solving the balance-of-payments problem, he indicated. Joe Fowler clarified a key assumption in his reading of the IDA report: the neutral balance-of-payments conclusion was based on the assumed restriction of commercial supersonic flight to overwater routes because of sonic booms; if there were no such restriction, and so greater numbers of SSTs, the balance-of-payments case could be more positive. The conflicting views of the members were reflected in the resulting carefully worded report to the president.[37] In essence, and subject to the contrary views of certain members, the message was that the likely balance-of-payments benefit of a U.S. SST program was far less than previously thought; indeed, the program might even increase the deficit, as the overseas spending of an increased number of travelers overshadowed the domestic SST sales.

THE INTELLIGENCERS' TALE | 6

As plans for the U.S. supersonic transport steadily advanced, by way of technical studies, cost studies, and market studies by a host of interested agencies and advisory groups, the need for accurate information on the progress and plans of the Anglo–French Concorde team became clear. The American program was not being formulated in a vacuum; as noted, it was a national response to an existing, foreign venture. For the response to be effective, it had to be based on the fullest possible information on the competition. In assembling the total picture, pieces of the jigsaw came from a variety of sources, ranging from ad hoc reports by individuals to the considered judgments handed down by the Central Intelligence Agency (CIA). "I will be in London and Paris next week reconnoitering the British–French effort," Halaby told Vice President Johnson at the end of January 1963.[1]

To attempt to develop an evaluation of the British-French SST seemed "eminently appropriate," Walter Heller, chairman of the Council of Economic Advisers, told the vice president in March 1963.[2] "We understand the great difficulties in obtaining detailed 'hard' intelligence on this program and of making authoritative economic analysis of its prospects, but we endorse any efforts to improve and expand our information on this venture." In his comment on the Black–Osborne report one year later, Donald F. Hornig, the president's science adviser, told Kermit Gordon, budget bureau director, "An effort should perhaps be made to assign the highest priority to acquisition of more complete intelligence than is now available concerning the technical details of the Concorde program."[3] Within the FAA, Bain gave Halaby an "intelligence estimate of Concorde" based on a careful screening of "the information reports received within the past six months from the Central Intelligence Agency, the Department of Defense Intelligence, the Department of State, and, to a very limited extent, press reports."[4] Bain's report listed ten problem areas, including the fact that "each airplane will be partly metric (French portion) and partly in inches (British portion)." Other reports following visits to the French and British companies working on the Concorde were made both by FAA officials and by others.

Among the inputs during 1964, John McCone promised Califano a CIA report "on the progress of the Concorde and the estimated operational date; also the British engineer's opinion of a few of the problems and questions raised in the committee's memorandum to the President."[5] (The committee's first interim report to the president had been submitted in May; the identity of the "British engineer" remains a mystery.) Items of published information were scrutinized, also, as in a detailed assessment of two documents presented by Lieutenant Colonel Robert E. Pursley, a DOD analyst.[6] These documents were a BAC-Sud report on "the revised long-range aircraft" published in April 1964 and Sir George Edwards's Concorde lecture to the Institute of Transport in London in February that year. Pursley subjected the economics portion of the BAC-Sud paper to a long and critical analysis but spent little time on Sir George's lecture, which he described as a statement of faith. "It is not appropriate to evaluate Sir George's thesis critically," the DOD analyst declared. "His purpose was to report favorably on progress to date and to exhort the faithful to greater effort in the future." Sir George was an SST believer, and the role of the believer was important for any venture—but, Pursley commented sternly, belief should be viewed as a supplement to judgment and analysis and not as a substitute for them.

From the views of secret CIA informants to public calls to the faithful, all was grist for the mill of the American SST analysts. In the summer of 1964 particular importance was attached to a report on the "mission performance potential" of the Concorde compiled by staff at the NASA Langley Research Center in Virginia. Based on information supplied to the president's advisory committee and other data obtained by NASA, augmented by wind-tunnel tests, the Langley analysis was probably the best Concorde information available outside the Anglo-French design team—indeed, "maybe better than theirs," according to the director of aeronautics research and engineering at the Pentagon.[7] The main question appeared to be the reliability of the fuel-transfer system needed to adjust the Concorde's center of gravity; another question was whether the engine could be developed on schedule.

Events following the election of the Labour government in Britain in October 1964 were outlined in the previous chapter. The CIA view of the situation was reported to McNamara by Califano early in November.[8] The election of the Wilson government in the United Kingdom had had serious repercussions on the Concorde program, the CIA reported. The ability of the French to continue alone was now doubtful. Whatever the outcome, the CIA concluded, "the introduction of so much strain and uncertainty into the Concorde program because of the political factors makes it doubtful whether the degree of cooperation that has thus far prevailed between the British and French can be maintained."

Airline assessments of the Concorde, including one by TWA in March 1965, also were fed into the deliberations of the U.S. federal agencies and the president's advisory committee. At a meeting of the committee in May 1965, members discussed how information on the Concorde should be obtained. "We have talked many times about gathering information on the Concorde," McNamara told the meeting.[9] "We have not evolved any systematic way of doing it." The meeting went on to evolve a systematic way of doing it: the FAA administrator would submit regular status reports on both the American and foreign SST programs, drawing on information from the CIA, the Defense Intelligence Agency, and NASA as appropriate.

Regular reports continued to chronicle Concorde and Tu-144 progress over the next few years. In October 1965 a Concorde intelligence summary reported that management of the program was "operating smoothly," which doubtless would have surprised the British and French program managers at the time.[10] In March 1967 the CIA produced a special nine-page report on the European SSTs, a sanitized version of which was declassified in July 1993.[11] This version discloses little that was not public knowledge at the time; the only feature of interest is the high proportion of the report—almost half—that 26 years later was still judged unsanitary.

Techniques for acquiring useful intelligence covered a broad spectrum, from the sophisticated mysteries of the CIA to rather more down-to-earth efforts. Records left by Bernard J. Vierling, Maxwell's deputy in the FAA SST office, include a choice example of the latter genre. A list of Concorde questions prepared prior to a visit to the BAC plant at Bristol begins: "1. Request to look at a representative part such as a bulkhead on premise of looking at type and thickness of structure. Count number of same bulkheads that are available. This may show us how many airplanes are committed."[12]

Common Market, Uncommon Interest

The quest for Concorde intelligence continued at different levels. Production rates, design changes, and schedules were among the raw data fed into the various U.S. studies of Concorde competitiveness at what might be termed the working level. At the political level, there was great interest in the assumed link between the

Anglo-French SST program and Britain's continuing efforts to enter the Common Market in the face of steadfast opposition from General de Gaulle. Certainly it was a highly relevant issue, as noted by Lord Callaghan, the former British prime minister. At its most basic, the perception of most outside observers was that Britain's participation in the Concorde project was an earnest of its commitment to Europe. In December 1966 the McNamara committee sought to pin this down in more detail.

Was there some tie-in between Britain's continued support for the Concorde and her eventual acceptance in the Common Market? After a comprehensive search that yielded nothing, the State Department concluded that this was most unlikely.[13] Contrasting views were offered by the Central Intelligence Agency and the FAA's man in Brussels. It is worth recording the CIA assessment in full:

> 1. Economic and technical considerations have weighed heavily in decisions on the future course of the joint Anglo-French Concorde project, but from the beginning the project has had political significance as well. At the time of its initiation, Britain was seeking practical cooperative ties with its European neighbors and De Gaulle was eager to demonstrate that British entry in the EEC was not essential to such cooperation. The project continues to have political significance and has relevance to prospects for British entry in the Common Market.
> 2. Even if Prime Minister Wilson were not now making approaches toward the EEC, the political and technical arguments for going on with the Concorde would probably prevail. If, however, Wilson were under any temptation to pull out of the project London's desire to enter the EEC would be an additional factor arguing for its continuation.
> 3. If Britain withdrew from the project while EEC negotiations were in progress, De Gaulle would almost certainly cite it as proof that the United Kingdom was not sufficiently European-minded. On the other hand, should De Gaulle veto the British bid for EEC membership, Wilson would be under strong pressure to withdraw from the project.[14]

Raymond Maloy, FAA assistant administrator for the Europe, Africa, and Middle East region, took a broader view. The Concorde was "only one pawn in big game and probably not a key one at this point in time," he reported from Brussels.[15]

Concorde Production

Concorde intelligence continued to be scrutinized in the ongoing discussions of relative program timing. By the end of 1965 Maxwell had reported that revision number 2 of the *Concorde Intelligence Handbook* had been distributed,[16] and "a secret file of other foreign SST documents" was contained in a certain safe in the SST office. The main focus of the policy discussions—exhaustively analyzing whether, how, and at what pace U.S. public money should go into the SST program—remained the president's advisory committee.

In June 1966, the FAA's seventh summary status report to the committee included a CIA assessment of a variety of technical problems reportedly being encountered on the Concorde.[17] None was insurmountable, most would succumb to a normal engineering approach, but their solution could easily delay the program by 18 months to two years. Nontechnical factors might have more bearing on the success of the program, and here the report confirmed major differences between the two partners. In particular, the French attached a very high priority to the Concorde program, were worried by the competition of the U.S. SST, and wanted a first-generation vehicle operational as soon as possible. By contrast the British felt that a developed, 167-passenger machine could compete favorably with the U.S. SST. A later version of this CIA report formed the basis of the eighth summary status report to the committee.[18] Seizing on the CIA estimate of a delay of 18 months to two years, Enke told McNamara, "This factor should help the U.S. to resist pressures to adopt a 'crash' program to meet the earlier introduction of the Concorde."[19]

In turn, the committee included a digest of up-to-date information on the Concorde (and on the Soviet Tu-144) in its fourth report to the president in December 1966. Once more the differences between the French and British attitudes to their joint project were noted:

> *Concorde production program* General de Gaulle continues to view the Concorde as an important step in demonstrating the technical competence required of a major power. He sees the project as a means to enhance French prestige, particularly vis-a-vis the U.S. and has taken a personal interest in it. The French Government's determination that the project be completed, despite growing British disenchantment, also stems from Gaullist assertions that France's "independent" foreign policy has not harmed its friendship with its allies. Although France has been anxious to conclude a production agreement for some time, no such agreement with Britain has been concluded. (Although the treaty speaks generally of development "and production" of the Concorde, it appears that this is essentially a statement of intention and is not a binding commitment to produce the Concorde.) The U.K. Treasury has independently conducted an economic analysis of the Concorde, and the British are highly concerned over increasing cost and market prospects for the aircraft. Commercial production of Concorde is not a foregone conclusion.

Concorde intelligence continued to be supplied regularly via the FAA to the president's advisory committee and irregularly by various interested individuals. In

March 1968 the FAA head of international aviation affairs reported to General Maxwell, "In being responsive to your request for recent data pertinent to the status of foreign SST programs, we have taken certain actions which we feel will reemphasize our interest in this area to the Intelligence Community."[20] One way and another the interested U.S. agencies were kept well informed on the technical progress of the Concorde; in April that year BAC engineers in Bristol were surprised that visiting NASA officials were aware of a particular problem on the aircraft's droop-nose mechanism, and asked how they had learned of it. "The question was passed off with a vague reply about press reports," a State Department airgram reported.[21]

Information to the Enemy?

On the reverse side of the coin of Concorde intelligence—gaining information on the European project that might assist the U.S. program—was the question of how much information on U.S. work should be supplied to the British and the French. Some argued for a "We'll tell you if you tell us" approach, while others urged a total security blackout in order not to help the enemy. Linked issues that soon arose included whether to approve exports of U.S. equipment for use on the Concorde and whether to grant permission for the use of U.S. wind-tunnel or other facilities by British and French engineers.

The central question had been addressed as early as February 1962 by the SST steering group chaired by Najeeb Halaby as FAA administrator.[22] No official position was taken, but the consensus at that meeting was to withhold or delay relevant research information. "To provide the results of Government-sponsored research to foreign manufacturers," the minutes of the meeting recorded, "would enhance their position in developing a supersonic transport to the detriment of the economic position of the U.S. manufacturers and the nation." This basic issue was to be pursued more comprehensively and formally in later years, but in 1964 an unusual aspect of the question was posed in connection with a major series of sonic-boom tests conducted by the FAA at Oklahoma City.

A leading opponent of supersonic flight during the sixties was Bo Lundberg, director general of the Aeronautical Research Institute of Sweden, and in June 1964, after observing the Oklahoma City tests, the Swedish scientist urged "representatives of governments of countries likely to be overflown by SSTs" to come to Oklahoma City and observe for themselves. This idea was enthusiastically picked up by Charles G. Warnick, the FAA's director of information services, who proposed to Halaby that the Washington-based foreign air attachés should be invited to observe the tests.[23] It might be useful to have a record of such a visit when the time came to certificate the Concorde, Warnick suggested; besides, it would be good for the civic pride of Oklahoma City. Alas for civic pride, this visitation was not to be. "Attaches are members of the intelligence profession," Halaby was warned by Raymond Maloy, at that time FAA assistant administrator for international aviation affairs, "and we have not yet approved a general exchange of SST data with the United Kingdom and France."[24] Also, as a matter of policy, outside observers were not being given the full story. (Presumably the full story included details of the negative public reaction to the tests.) Thus the proposed visit was judged to be premature.

From disagreement on a minor point within the FAA, the issue turned into a major clash between the Department of Commerce and the Department of Defense on the central principle when it came up for scrutiny by Commerce's Advisory Committee on Export Policy Structure.[25] In this forum in 1965 a new dimension of the problem was addressed: the supply of U.S. technology via the Concorde to communist countries to which such exports were normally banned. The questions were:

A. Shall the United States Government authorize U.S. private firms to export U.S.-origin materials, equipment, supplies and technical data for use in the design, engineering and construction of the British-French supersonic aircraft Concorde, some of which may be exported to any country in the world?
B. Shall the United States Government authorize the export of U.S.-origin materials, equipment, supplies and technical data for the maintenance, repair, replacement and servicing of the British-French supersonic aircraft Concorde regardless of such aircraft's location, ownership or control?

Yes, in both cases it should, declared the Department of Commerce—but the British and French governments should be told that the United States hoped they would avoid selling the Concorde to Communist China, North Korea, North Vietnam, and Cuba. The issue had arisen because of contract commitments being demanded by British and French firms from potential U.S. suppliers. The B. F. Goodrich company, for example, anticipated a loss of about $9.5 million in U.S. exports if it was unable to make those commitments.

The Commerce recommendation was too broad, the Department of Defense retorted; it might even embrace the export of complete engines to power the Concorde.[26] Each application for export should be reviewed on its merits, with the paramount factor being the U.S. national interest. Military security was important; the landing gear involved in the Goodrich proposal, for example, was a sophisticated item based on military aircraft technology—what if this technology was to find its way behind the Iron Curtain?

Twenty-one months later, in February 1967, the issue was still exercising the FAA, which had received requests for release of U.S. technology not only for the Concorde but also "through the British" for the Soviet Tu-144.[27] Two arguments pointed for release, and two against. Release would maximize the exploitation of U.S. technology, and airlines (and U.S. suppliers) would welcome the maximum amount of equipment that was common to the Concorde and the U.S. SST. On the other hand, many of the requested items had potential military uses (as did the foreign SSTs themselves); and if Britain, France, and the Soviet Union had to develop their own alternative technology their lead over the U.S. SST would be narrowed. In the FAA view, the best policy would be to exercise leniency in the export of U.S. *hardware* but to be much stricter in the export of *technology.*

An unusual variation on the theme of information release came before the president's advisory committee in 1966, when McNamara was very conscious of the problems encountered by American military aircraft operating at Mach 2 and above. Details of these problems might be given to the Concorde consortium and to the airlines, it was suggested. This would "make the Concorde management aware of the difficulties to be faced and perhaps to induce them to proceed at a slower pace and, further, to discourage the U.S. airlines from over-optimistic evaluation of the Concorde."[28] Bad idea, the FAA advised: instead of deterring the consortium, such action might well encourage them to greater efforts.

NASA, the FAA, and the Departments of State, Commerce, and Defense were all involved in 1966–1967 in deciding how to handle an inquiry by Pierre Satre, engineering director of Sud Aviation, on the possibility of conducting certain Concorde wind-tunnel tests in the United States. Satre also sought reports on the American B-70 aircraft that compared wind-tunnel test results with in-flight performance data, offering to provide comparable Concorde data in exchange. Vierling, Maxwell's deputy, was in no doubt on the wind-tunnel issue: "I can see no reason why the U.S. Government should subsidize the Concorde program which is in direct competition with our own supersonic transport."[29]

Following an interagency meeting, Arnold W. Frutkin, NASA assistant administrator for international affairs, noted that U.S. wind-tunnel tests would provide useful information on Concorde performance.[30] He suggested a low-key approach to the French that could lead to Concorde model testing at NASA's Ames and Langley research centers and the exchange of B-70 and Concorde data. Vierling was not convinced, however, warning that the Concorde delivery date represented an important competitive factor; the United States should think carefully before assisting the Anglo-French project to meet its schedule.[31]

From the other side of the Atlantic, David Bruce, American ambassador to Britain, recommended cooperation for wider reasons. The issues involved were broader than those of the commercial race between the Concorde and the U.S. SST, he suggested; a European autarky in aerospace was in no one's interest, and U.S. cooperation should be limited only by considerations of national security. Considerations of diplomacy also exercised the ambassador: "If discussions with French on wind tunnel testing proceed further, believe it would be desirable at some point to inform British informally what is going on so that they don't get impression we are dealing behind their backs with French."[32] In the end, Maxwell noted, Satre "was overruled by his government superiors" in his bid to run tunnel tests in the United States.[33]

Though the use of NASA wind tunnels was not pursued, another NASA resource, an advanced flight simulator at Ames Research Center in northern California, proved invaluable in the Concorde airworthiness program. Eventually, a number of U.S. companies contributed to Concorde production, notably Rohr Corporation (stainless steel honeycomb panels for the engine bays) and Stresskin Products (powerplant nozzle design) in California. A list of 41 U.S. participating companies accompanied the U.S. press release announcing the rollout of the first Concorde prototype at Toulouse on 11 December 1967.[34] By 1973, on the occasion of the first Concorde visit to the United States, the number had risen to more than 75.[35]

Friendly Persuasion

A further dimension of the "information to the enemy" issue is what might be called "pressure on the enemy." Conflicting accounts have been given of alleged American pressure on British politicians to cancel the Concorde. Quite apart from the official meetings, examples of direct approaches have been described by British politicians of both main parties. Speaking in 1976, Julian Amery, the Conservative minister of aviation who signed the Anglo-French agreement, recalled the first approach:

> Before we took the decision in cabinet, the former president of the World Bank, Mr. Eugene Black, asked to see me in London. . . . We had a bit of a talk about international monetary problems and then he went straight into an effort, a very gifted effort, to try and persuade me not to go ahead with the supersonic transport. That was in 1962. This in fact encouraged me to think if the Americans were so much against it, we'd be wise to try. We'd probably get a lead on them.[36]

The argument that Britain should join France in launching a supersonic transport program because an eminent American thought it was a bad idea would hardly have been presented in those terms at the time. But attempts at persuasion continued, according to Amery:

> Even after the Concorde agreement had been signed, we were subjected to a ceaseless barrage of advice from Washington to stop the project. Senior American ministers and officials visiting London to see the chancellor of the exchequer or foreign secretary or the minister of defence or the prime minister would, at the end of their conversations on other and larger issues, raise the question of Concorde. Without producing particular arguments, they would make the concerted point that there were very strong feelings in Washington that Britain ought to cancel it.[37]

The assumption that the influential Americans' "ceaseless barrage of advice" to U.K. ministers to cancel the Concorde was aimed at leaving the field open to the U.S. SST is questionable. It is equally possible, as pointed out by British politicians Jock Bruce-Gardyne and Nigel Lawson, that the aim of some, at least, of the advisers was to increase the chances that the U.S. machine itself would be canceled.[38] Research for this book reinforces that interpretation. With the Concorde out of the way, there would be no race, and so less reason for the United States to commit itself to an expensive adventure of doubtful merit.

In at least one case, according to a former British Labour minister, this was made quite explicit. Denis Healey, U.K. minister of defense from 1964 to 1970, recalls:

> In Washington, McNamara was equally hostile to the supersonic transport aircraft that Boeing and the Congress were pressing on him. At one point he offered me an SST disarmament pact—Washington would not support the Boeing SST if we cancelled Concorde. I told him that such a pact would be meaningless; Britain could not get out of its agreement with France, and if Congress wanted an SST the United States would build one, whatever McNamara promised.[39]

Speaking in 1994, Robert McNamara says he cannot recollect this conversation with Denis Healey.[40] But he does recollect a similar exchange with Roy Jenkins, then minister of aviation. "I said 'This is not commercially viable for us, it's not commercially viable for you, let's do a deal.' My recollection is that Roy said he agreed with me, but later the French would not agree to cancellation. But Roy was wanting to cancel, based on our conversation." Roy was indeed wanting to cancel, though based primarily on conversation within the Wilson cabinet. As for the exchange with McNamara, Roy Jenkins (now Lord Jenkins of Hillhead) in turn recollects no such discussion.[41]

American and British records confirm that McNamara did meet Healey in December 1964 and that the two men did discuss Concorde topics as well as defense matters. Though no "disarmament pact" was mentioned in the official records of that meeting, London took care to inform the French of the exchange. "It is important that the French should not hear of this conversation from some other source," Sir Pierson Dixon, British ambassador in Paris, was warned, "and suspect that the Anglo-Saxons have been ganging-up on them."[42]

As noted, informal contacts by Eugene Black and Stanley Osborne were a useful and continuing mechanism for obtaining high-level British and French views on matters supersonic for the benefit of McNamara's committee. In March 1966, at an informal meeting of some PAC-SST members, Black reported on a talk he had had in London in February with James Callaghan, chancellor of the exchequer (and future prime minister). The possibility of reaching some sort of agreement on SSTs between the United States and Britain and France had been raised—not on cancellation but once again, according to Maxwell, on some form of either time phasing or market sharing.[43]

James Callaghan, now Lord Callaghan of Cardiff, recalls a rather different message.[44] Black reported U.S. concern about the cost of the American SST and the results of the Oklahoma sonic-boom tests, but he was confident that the machine, though coming into service two years later than the Anglo-French effort, would render the Concorde dead as a commercial venture. Lord Callaghan adds:

> He emphasised that his approach was made personally—"speaking as a friend of mine." His advice was that we should cut our losses and get out and, if we could not do that, we should approach the United States for a tripartite production. His approach was typical of a number of approaches made to me by Joe Fowler, the secretary to the U.S. Treasury, and by Robert McNamara. On each occasion my reply was the same: namely, I was very worried about the cost, which was increasing dramatically; that following advice from the attorney general, Elwyn Jones, it was difficult if not impossible to escape from our treaty obligations; that we had tried out the prospect of cancellation on the French but had failed; and that because of our desire to enter the Common Market and the sensitivity caused by our past approaches, it was not politically possible for us to suggest U.S. participation to the French.

7 | THE NIXON YEARS

After the defeat of Hubert Humphrey, the Democratic candidate in the 1968 U.S. presidential election, the future of the American SST program became one of the urgent questions facing the incoming Republican administration headed by Richard Nixon. Hence a high-level review of the program formed part of the briefing material prepared that December for the new administration.[1] Since 1967 the Federal Aviation Agency, renamed the Federal Aviation Administration, had formed part of the newly created Department of Transportation (DOT). In its brief for the incoming administration in 1968, the FAA admitted candidly that the SST had evolved into a response to the challenge of the Concorde. Airlines held options to buy a total of 78 Concordes, including 38 in the United States. In comparison, there were 122 options for the U.S. SST, 58 of them for foreign airlines.

Though U.S. airlines had reservations about Concorde economics, the FAA paper continued, the Anglo-French machine now held a potential lead of five to seven years. "With such a time advantage it is entirely possible that not only could the initial SST market be exploited, but an improved Concorde might be built and introduced into the market concurrently with the U.S. SST." The paper went on to raise again the balance-of-payments argument, estimating "a $17 billion adverse balance of payments swing by 1990" if a successful Concorde had the field to itself.

The much-discussed, much-rejected issue of international cooperation emerged once more. In cooperation's favor were the large costs and the need for government financing. Against it were the private ownership of commercial aircraft makers and operators in the United States, as against their public ownership or control in Europe, together with "the advanced state of U.S. aircraft technology compared with Europe." Three current issues—delays in the first flight of the Concorde, British and French financial problems, and the slippage of the U.S. program—might create new interest in cooperation.

> There is little enthusiasm among U.S. manufacturers to participate in the Concorde program and even less if they must invest in it. This is due to the low airline opinion of the economic merit of the Concorde, the already complicated problems of Anglo-French partnership, and the excess production capacity already committed to the Concorde. Further, both Britain and France would require a substantial technological upgrading to equip them to manufacture large, high performance SSTs constructed of titanium. U.S. manufacturers would resist sharing such knowhow with their foreign competitors. On the other hand it is possible that some other agreement might be sought. For example, if the Concorde is in serious technical trouble, slow down or cancellation of both programs might be agreed upon.

Elsewhere in the Department of Transportation, Donald G. Agger, assistant secretary for international affairs and special programs, urged that a cooperative effort with the British and French should be reconsidered.[2] David D. Thomas, acting FAA administrator, suggested that Agger himself needed a briefing on the SST, since it was evident that he was not completely familiar with the subject.[3] John E. Robson, DOT under secretary, pointed out that there had been differences of view within the department, the government, and Congress; he recommended that the new president be advised to create an SST task force to help him reach a speedy decision.[4] Agger, in another guise, was to become very familiar with the Concorde project some years later.

On 7 February 1969, President Nixon introduced John A. Volpe as secretary of transportation at a White House news conference, and in turn Volpe announced that an ad hoc interdepartmental committee would be formed to review the SST program and to recommend whether it should continue. Chairman of the committee would be James M. Beggs, under secretary of transportation and a former NASA associate administrator, and the group's review would be conducted in coordination with the Bureau of the Budget.

Just two days earlier, Charles O. Cary, assistant administrator for international affairs at the FAA, had spelled out for David Thomas the international implications of the forthcoming decision on the U.S. SST.[5] The consequences might be serious and might affect other aspects of the United States' international position, he stressed, whichever way the decision went. The Cary document was important in illuminating a number of the international issues that were to emerge; its full text is reproduced in appendix 4.

Delays and Dissent

Strongly conflicting advice within the administration and funding problems were among the factors that delayed a presidential decision on the American SST during 1969. Looming large among the conflicting views of the advisers were differing assessments of the Concorde threat. Soliciting airline views on behalf of the Beggs committee, the FAA asked specifically for views on the probable market for the Concorde and how that market might be affected (a) if the U.S. program continued as planned and (b) if a decision were made to delay it.[6] Writing to John H. Shaffer, a Thompson Ramo Wooldridge executive who was to be the new FAA administrator, Beggs entered a familiar blind alley: "The English are very anxious to talk to us regarding possible collaboration between their Concorde effort and our SST effort. The competitive nature of this entire supersonic transport area would, of course, change if the English decided to join us in some kind of a joint effort."[7] On the same subject, Beggs told Volpe, "I believe that the present inquiry is just another in a series of attempts by the English to get a better deal from us than they have with the French."[8] (Presumably the Welsh, the Scots, and the Northern Irish were also in on the deal.) One of the airline replies came from Najeeb Halaby, now president of Pan American, urging continuation of the program as planned in the face of the European and Soviet competition.[9]

The White House Office of Science and Technology (OST) was among the agencies with a view on the SST question. First, in a letter to Beggs, OST director Lee A. DuBridge judged the competition of "French and Russian SSTs" to be far less serious than had been thought two years previously.[10] Second, in a report by the OST's own ad hoc SST review committee, the balance-of-payments arguments in favor of the U.S. SST were dismissed and "substantial doubt" was cast on the commercial viability of the Concorde and the Tu-144.[11] For those and other reasons, the OST committee recommended a withdrawal of government support from the SST program.

Panel reports of the Beggs committee produced no consensus for or against the program. Once more there were conflicting views on the balance-of-payments issue. On the foreign relations impact of the U.S. decision, the relevant panel report warned that U.S. actions apparently designed to scuttle the Concorde would undoubtedly lead to an adverse political reaction in Britain and France.[12] U.S. noise standards might bar the Concorde from major American airports, "which would undoubtedly doom the Concorde program," and so Britain and France should be kept informed of U.S. noise developments.

The State Department concurred, adding that there was no overriding foreign policy reason for going ahead with, delaying, or canceling the SST program.[13] But a delay would ease the time pressure on the Concorde builders, possibly enabling them to reduce the noise of the aircraft. This would be important for the United States, "since at present it looks as if the United States, France and the U.K. will become involved in quite serious differences over the operation of the Concorde in U.S. airspace." Also, a delay would enable the two sides to discuss their program schedules.

On 23 September 1969, President Nixon announced his decision on the SST.[14] It had been a difficult decision, he said, in terms of a spirited debate within the administration and within Congress on the proper priority for funds. "I have made the decision that we should go ahead. I have made it first because I want the United States to continue to lead the world in air transport."

At the time of the Nixon announcement, flight-testing of prototypes of both the Concorde and the Soviet Tu-144 was under way. Now that the two competing SSTs were in the air, there was an added urgency in the continuing U.S. assessments of their likely impact on the market for the U.S. SST. Taking into account the delays encountered on all three SST programs, the FAA came up with some interesting numbers.[15] Sales of more than 200 Concordes or Tu-144s could be expected if these aircraft had a lead of four or five years over the American machine. The president's announcement had placed the in-service date for the U.S. SST at 1978, and if the Concorde met its certification date of late 1972, the Anglo-French machine would indeed have a lead of at least five years over the American product.

Between 1973 and 1978, about 240 Concordes could be produced and delivered. Production of the American SST would begin in 1978, rising to a total of 500 by the end of 1990. During their monopoly period the Concordes would fly high-density routes at high load factors, enabling their airlines to recover their investments in three to four years. Assessing the impact of the Tu-144 was difficult, but since the Soviet aircraft was similar in size and schedule to the Concorde, sales were likely to come from the estimated Concorde market. The Soviet airline Aeroflot, as principal user of the Tu-144, could require about 130 aircraft, on the assumption that there would be no sonic-boom restriction on domestic flights.

The End Is Nigh

In the latter half of 1970 the American SST program was in deep trouble, buffeted by the intense lobbying of environmentalists, economists, and politicians. Newly appointed SST director—at the Department of Transportation, not the FAA—was William M. Magruder, an aeronautical engineer and former test pilot who had been second-in-command of the Lockheed SST project in the mid-sixties. Magruder fought to save the project by presenting the case for the SST before a variety of audiences—and enlisted the help of Sir George Edwards to provide supporting information on the Concorde. In a "Dear Bill" letter dated 17 September, Sir George acknowledged a telephone message and hoped that the attached letter was the sort of thing Magruder wanted.[16] The attached "Dear Mr. Magruder" letter began innocently: "I thought you would be interested to know how the Concorde is doing," and went on to give an impressive report of Concorde progress— valuable ammunition for the beleaguered SST defenders across the ocean.

Addressing New York security analysts on 2 October, Magruder quoted the State Department, Treasury, and Council of Economic Advisers—as well as Sir George—to reinforce his case for the SST, based substantially on the promising prospects for the Concorde.[17] "This broad support of the program by the president's closest advisers," he said, "reflects the new acceptance of the Concorde as a legitimate competitor to be taken seriously." Speaking before the Aircraft Industries Association later that month, he admitted that the U.S. SST would be about four years behind the Concorde—in airline service in 1978 rather than 1974—but it would be "a better, more appealing article."[18]

Boeing's efforts to promote the importance of the SST had included a 1970 leaflet that again drew attention to the balance-of-payments claims for the U.S. project.[19] The deficit could reach $22 billion over the period of the SST program, the company warned. With a U.S. SST program, 270 SSTs would be exported and 60 Concordes would be imported. If there were no U.S. program, 130 first-generation Concordes and 250 expected advanced Concordes would be imported—hence the swing from $10 billion net exports to $12 billion imports. This assumption of a forthcoming advanced version of the Concorde was a key misconception in the United States at that time.

In May 1970 the Appropriations Committee of the House of Representatives had voted to continue funding for the SST. A period of intensive lobbying by both proponents and opponents prefaced a crucial vote in the U.S. Senate on 3 December. By 52 votes to 41 the Senate rejected further SST funding, a decision President Nixon described as "a devastating mistake." After complicated congressional maneuvering, including a filibuster by Senator William Proxmire, a compromise was reached under which SST funding was extended until 31 March 1971.

As the lobbying pressures intensified, Boeing took the unprecedented step of working with BAC and Aérospatiale (by then Sud had become part of Société Nationale Industrielle Aérospatiale) in the face of the common anti-SST enemies. In October 1970 the three companies agreed to exchange environmental information, and in January representatives of the three companies met to discuss environmental and other issues.[20] The Seattle team sought environmental data from Con-

The Anglo-French agreement to develop and build an SST was signed in London on 29 November 1962 by Geoffroy de Courcel (left) for France and Julian Amery for Britain. (Hulton Getty Collection Limited, formerly Hulton Deutsch, copyright)

LEFT: William Coleman was U.S. secretary of transportation in the Ford administration. His 1976 decision to approve Concorde operations marked a crucial point in the history of the Anglo-French SST. (U.S. Department of Transportation)

RIGHT: In 1977, smiles concealed concern over the Concorde's U.S. approval, as President Carter was visited by Prime Minister Raymond Barre of France. The British prime minister, James Callaghan, also presented the Concorde case to the President. (Jimmy Carter Library)

Léonce Lancelot-Bassou (left) and Sandy Gordon-Cumming, aviation counselors at the French and British embassies in Washington, worked—and here celebrated—together in the fight for U.S. approval for Concorde services. (U.K. Department of Industry)

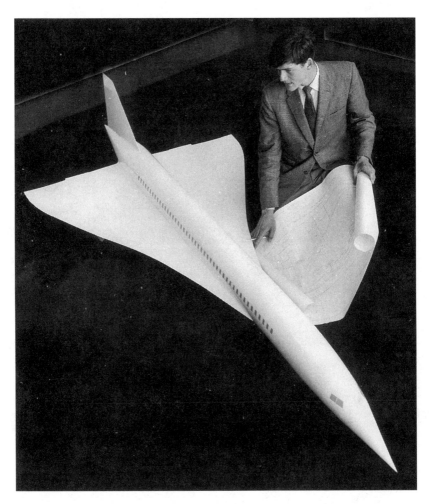

First impression: This model of the proposed Anglo-French SST was shown by British Aircraft Corporation and Sud Aviation in 1962. (British Aircraft Corporation)

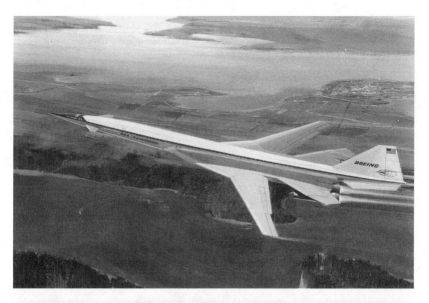

Top: America's first SST design, as envisaged in this sketch, was the proposed Boeing 2707 Dash 200, an ambitious swing-wing design. Technical problems with the wing mechanism forced a drastic revision. (Boeing Company Archives)

Bottom: Full-scale mockup of Boeing's second attempt, the 2707 Dash 300 SST. Development funding was withdrawn by Congress in March 1971, leaving the SST field to the Anglo-French Concorde and the Soviet Tu-144. (Boeing Company Archives)

TOP: The Soviet Tu-144 was the first SST to fly but proved uneconomic in service. This machine crashed at the Paris air show in 1973; note the foreplanes, which give pitch control at low speeds but are retracted for supersonic flight. [© Novosti (London)]

BELOW: Dulles Airport, Washington, provided appropriate security when British Airways and Air France inaugurated Concorde services to the United States on 24 May 1976. (Adrian Meredith Photography, copyright)

Runway-level view: The massive powerplant nacelles, stalky landing gear, and delicately shaped wing contribute to the Concorde's most unusual head-on appearance. (British Airways, copyright)

TOP: Nonscheduled service: In December 1985, on the eve of a decade of airline service, four British Airways Concordes flew a celebratory photographic mission in formation. (Adrian Meredith Photography, copyright)

BELOW: Europe's SST studies in the nineties were focused on this conceptual Mach-2, 250-passenger design. British, French, and German firms were working jointly in the European Supersonic Research Programme. (British Aerospace Airbus)

corde flight testing and suggested a number of further actions that would help their case in the United States. Tupolev participation in the next joint meeting should be considered, the forthcoming appearance of the Tu-144 at that year's Paris air show should be publicized, and influential Americans such as Senator Barry Goldwater and astronaut Neil Armstrong should be invited to fly in the Concorde and comment favorably on it. The January meeting was followed the next month by a joint BAC-Boeing press conference in London, nominally addressing "Concorde and the environment" but in fact embracing environmental aspects of supersonic transports in general.[21] William Strang of BAC and H. W. "Bob" Withington of Boeing joined forces to argue that, relatively speaking, supersonic transport aircraft would be environmentally friendly—except perhaps on noise.

In fighting his battle against the SST opponents, William Magruder assembled a comprehensive array of facts and arguments to combat every critical point. The February 1971 version of the DOT's "SST question and answer index" included the department's latest assessment of the Concorde competition.[22] Assuming a U.S. SST, it was estimated that 240 Concordes would be sold by the time the American machine entered service. Assuming no U.S. SST and no later "Concorde 2," 600 of the initial Concordes would be sold by 1990. The Concorde would be sufficiently profitable in operation to enable airlines to write off the investment in their early aircraft before the U.S. SST entered service.

But the threat of competition from the British and the French was by now of little consequence in the battle to save the American supersonic transport. Far bigger issues were already set to decide the outcome. On 18 March the House voted 215 to 204 to delete all SST funds, and on 24 March the Senate followed suit by defeating by 51 votes to 46 an amendment to restore the funds. America's SST was dead, leaving the world SST market to the Anglo-French Concorde, and perhaps the Soviet Tu-144. An FAA history of the period concludes:

> Those intent on changing the patterns of government spending, its close cooperation with large corporations, and its determination of national priorities had selected the SST as their chief target. But most of all the advanced airliner became the symbol of America's past response to its environment. The ecology movement, needing a clear-cut victory to establish itself as a credible political force, turned the SST into a suitably grotesque dragon, which it slew in heroic combat.[23]

Certainly the environmental concerns were a major influence, but as noted in chapter 14, there were other issues that contributed to the demise of America's supersonic transport.

The Concorde continued its flight test program. Ahead lay a turbulent journey toward limited airline service, during which the Anglo-French craft would impinge once more—directly and painfully—on the collective American consciousness. In the lull before the coming storm, on 20 September 1973, a Concorde landed at Dallas–Fort Worth International Airport in Texas on the type's first visit to the United States. That same morning in Washington, D.C., President Nixon presented the U.S. Harmon Trophy for outstanding contributions to aeronautical science to Concorde chief test pilots Brian Trubshaw of BAC and André Turcat of Aérospatiale.

Collaboration on a Concorde 2?

Sir George Edwards, last of the old-style chief designers of the British aircraft industry and doughty head of British Aircraft Corporation throughout the Concorde program, was a consistent advocate of transatlantic cooperation. Before a variety of American audiences throughout the late sixties he had argued the case for collaboration, and in particular for a two-stage deal encompassing both U.S. production of the Concorde and European production of the Boeing SST. After the demise of the U.S. SST program, he returned to the subject in December 1971 in relation to an advanced Concorde in a speech to the American Chamber of Commerce in London.[24] His earlier suggestions for a wider collaboration had been received politely, he remarked, but not very seriously. Now, after the U.S. cancellation, the situation had changed: "It seems to me much more sensible for you to build an advanced version of the Concorde in collaboration with us than to go off on your own, many years behind us in an advanced technology which could well cost you the earth, and in which you still could very well come unstuck."

Sir George's European optimism extended to his professed expectations of Concorde sales. Even in the unlikely event of a Mach 3 transport's becoming operational by, say, 1985, he remained sure that developments of the Concorde would be required over the next 30 years. That meant there could well be 1,500 Concordes in service by the end of the century. This, then, was the stated view of the BAC chairman at the end of 1971, just two days before the first flight of the first preproduction version of the Concorde. Within five years it was clear that the number of Concordes in service by the end of the century would not reach 15, let alone 1500.

Concorde Versus the United States: Preliminary Skirmishes

In the final years of the American SST program, an important new issue had begun to surface. This involved not the perceived impact of the Concorde on the U.S.

project but, in the reverse sense, the potential impact of American attitudes to the approach of supersonic services by the Anglo-French machine. The main battle for U.S. approval of Concorde services is described in part 3, but a number of preliminary skirmishes took place during the Nixon administration. They concerned noise regulations, a possible U.S. ban on the Concorde, and, after the U.S. SST cancellation, secret letters from President Nixon to the French president and the British prime minister.

In the spring of 1970 the potential impact on the Concorde of American regulations on SST noise and the sonic boom provoked formal protests from France and Britain. Ministers of the two countries objected strongly that the United States was taking precipitate action in proposing to ban civil supersonic flight over the United States and to regulate SST noise around airports. French transport minister Raymond Mondon was particularly incensed, Secretary Volpe was told, and had protested "in the strongest possible language" against the proposed ban.[25] The British also had objected and had filed a "less threatening but very positive" protest.

In April the British view was further explored by Secretary Volpe and FAA administrator Shaffer with Anthony Wedgwood Benn, U.K. minister of technology, in an Anglo-American meeting in Washington. Benn repeated his government's concern over the sonic-boom regulation and the proposed noise regulation. According to the official summary of the meeting, "He stated he thought it somewhat absurd if we should build SSTs ahead of the rest of the world and then, at the same time, ban them ahead of the rest of the world."[26] French concern was reinforced at the industrial level in July, when Henri Ziegler, president of Aérospatiale, called on Secretary Volpe at the Department of Transportation.[27] The Frenchman repeatedly stressed that premature actions to restrict supersonic flight could seriously jeopardize the future of both the Concorde and the U.S. SST. The secretary was suitably diplomatic in his response.

"Ban the Concorde"

Files titled "Ban the Concorde" are to be found in the archives of the Federal Aviation Administration, now held at the Washington National Records Center at Suitland, Maryland. The files were not declaring an imperative, but were the focus for a range of opinions, for and against, which give an illuminating snapshot of official U.S. thinking in the summer of 1970. SST director William Magruder had asked government departments and agencies three questions. First, could the United States ban the Concorde from U.S. operations? Second, what retaliation might be expected? Third, would such a ban be wise?

In summary, the consensus was that the FAA could ban the Concorde (or the Tu-144) for reasons of unacceptable noise, related environmental effects, or safety; or the U.S. Congress could enact a law prohibiting the Concorde from U.S. airspace.[28] But any such action would be extreme, would provoke retaliatory measures, and would prove costly to the United States in the long run. If the United States were to set SST certification noise rules that the Concorde could not meet, this would prevent U.S. airlines from operating the machine anywhere in the world, while non-U.S. airlines could in principle fly their Concordes (certificated elsewhere) into the United States. A total ban on the Concorde from U.S. airports could turn the United States into a subsonic island in an otherwise supersonic air transport world. Foreign countries might impose reciprocal bans on U.S. aircraft in their airspace and discourage their airlines from buying American aircraft.

"The United States should not ban the Concorde if we expect to operate in a free Bermuda environment," declared the Civil Aeronautics Board (CAB).[29] "If technology and economics justify a supersonic, and we agree they do, it would be foolhardy to attempt to ban the Concorde." The reference was to the bilateral agreements governing air transport between the main nations of the world, such as the Bermuda Agreement between the United States and Britain. A U.S. ban on the Concorde would violate those agreements, the CAB argued, and major foreign powers would violently object. The board went on to make a prescient comment: it was important to recognize the power held by the various local authorities that controlled airport operations. Bodies such as the Port of New York Authority had great influence over the type of aircraft using their airports, and their support for U.S. national policies should be enlisted. "A ban imposed at this lower level could have equally disastrous consequences abroad." So it was to prove in 1976 and 1977.

The Commerce Department listed eight retaliatory measures that in theory could be taken against the United States in the event of a Concorde ban.[30] Purchases of American-built aircraft could be cut; operations of U.S. airlines could be restricted on environmental grounds; U.S. airlines could be forced to use alternative, less favorably located airports; and U.S. airlines' passenger service operations could be restricted at airport terminals. Also their cargo operations could be similarly affected, including delays in customs clearance; flight quotas could be imposed at busy airports; pressure could be exerted to renegotiate bilateral air transport agreements and compensation could be demanded; and a comparable ban on the U.S. SST could be imposed.

The State Department argued against a ban: "We do not think that we are in a situation where we must seek to stop the Concorde at all costs."[31] But if there were to be a ban, it should be based on legitimate grounds, not on poor economics or competitive impact. The department did not believe that retaliation would be a major problem. The Treasury Department warned that the structuring of general restrictions might be tantamount to an outright ban on the Concorde and would indeed incite retaliation—not only against the U.S. SST but conceivably against U.S. subsonic sales also.[32]

The Nixon Letters

A secret exchange of letters between President Richard Nixon, Prime Minister Edward Heath, and President Georges Pompidou in January 1973 was to erupt into a major public controversy three years later when their contents were disclosed. The Nixon letters followed cabinet-level discussion on the single most important Concorde issue in the history of the project, then looming on the horizon: approval for scheduled Concorde services to the United States. Setting the scene was the immediate question of what to do about the Concorde in relation to noise rules being proposed by the FAA.

"There are a number of problems facing the Administration with the expected entry into service of the Anglo-French Concorde in 1975," noted Peter M. Flanigan, a special assistant to the president, in November 1972.[33] On the one hand, the British and French governments would exert strong pressures to gain approval. On the other hand, rising U.S. congressional and public pressures to ban the Concorde on environmental grounds were expected. Flanigan listed eight problems. The FAA wished to issue a notice of proposed rule-making that would progressively reduce the average noise level in U.S. airline fleets; this rule would discourage U.S. Concorde purchases. The FAA also had drafted a proposed rule to require SSTs to meet the FAA Part 36 subsonic noise standard; since the Concorde could not meet this standard, Britain and France would undoubtedly request an exemption— which in turn would be opposed by environmentalists. The Concorde would have difficulty meeting FAA requirements for type certification and for operating in U.S. airspace. The Environmental Protection Agency (EPA) had drafted a rule governing engine emissions that the Concorde might not be able to meet. Congress might propose legislation to ban SSTs that exceeded subsonic noise levels; environmentalists would urge the president to sign such a bill, which Britain and France would consider an unfriendly act. The CAB insisted that Concorde fares be economic, i.e. possibly so high that few people would use the aircraft. Regardless of any federal action, U.S. airport operators could ban the Concorde because of local reaction. Finally, both Congress and the public were concerned about the environmental effects of SSTs.

Flanigan listed three options:

1. Seek to support the Concorde, by notifying Britain and France of the problems and indicating that the Administration will do what it can to admit the aircraft.
2. Proceed vigorously with U.S. environmental standards and insist that the Concorde must comply.
3. Adopt a hands-off attitude, allowing the problems to work themselves out without intervention by the White House.

Flanigan's memo formed the agenda for a December 1972 meeting of the "Senior Review Group"—the secretaries of state, treasury, commerce, and transportation, and the assistants to the president for national security affairs and for domestic affairs. Prior to the meeting John Volpe, transportation secretary, submitted his department's conclusions in a paper, which in effect recommended a version of option 3: the FAA should issue both notices of proposed rule making, without any specific exemption for the Concorde.[34] Volpe argued that since the action involved publishing proposed rules, not the adoption of final ones, Britain and France would have the opportunity to seek an exemption during the rule-making process. The government did not have to decide now on whether to grant any such exemption.

Oh, yes, it did, the senior review group decided. The DOT would redraft the advanced notice of the proposed fleet noise rule so as to exempt the Concorde, directly or indirectly, from its terms. In other words, the Volpe recommendation had been overruled; this decision, the minutes of the meeting claimed, was unanimously approved—as were the decisions on the other seven points under consideration.[35] The all-important issue of preemption—whether a federal decision automatically overrules decisions by states, local authorities, and airport proprietors—was touched on at the meeting. The DOT claimed that it had the legal authority to preempt state and local noise regulations, but would not seek to do so.

Anglo-French sensitivity on the noise-regulation issue was reflected the same month in letters to President Nixon from Prime Minister Heath and President Pompidou, and by high-level meetings of officials of the three countries in Washington. Heath and Pompidou both expressed their concern over the likely impact of the proposed rules on the Concorde, while an eight-man team of British and French officials discussed the rules and argued for a Concorde exemption with representatives of the FAA, DOT, State Department, EPA, and OST. On 19 January 1973, Nixon was able to reassure Heath (with a similar letter to Pompidou) along the lines agreed to by the senior review group:

Dear Mr. Prime Minister:

I welcome your recent letter concerning the problems which the Concorde may face in conforming to proposed Federal regulations on excessive aircraft noise. This is, as we both recognize, an issue of major importance with both domestic and international ramifications.

I can assure you that my Administration will make every effort to see that the Concorde is treated fairly in all aspects of the United States governmental regulations, so that it can compete for sales in this country on its merits. As a consequence of this policy, the Federal Aviation Administration will issue its proposed fleet noise rule in a form which will make it inapplicable to the Concorde. I have also directed officials of my Administration to continue to work with representatives of the British and French governments in order to determine whether a United States supersonic aircraft noise standard can be developed that will meet our domestic requirements without damaging the prospects of the Concorde.

You have noted, Mr. Prime Minister, that many aspects of the regulation of civil aviation are in this country outside the jurisdiction of the executive branch of our Federal Government. You must know that the Federal Government's power to influence these aspects, particularly with regard to state and local jurisdictions, is limited. On the other hand, my Administration is committed to principles of non-interference with free and private commerce and non-discriminatory formulation and application of Federal regulations. We will act in keeping with these principles to assure equitable treatment for the Concorde, bearing in mind that it, as well as all supersonic aircraft, raises unprecedented problems of environmental and social costs.

With warm personal regards.

Sincerely,[36]

Nixon's assurance that the FAA would issue its proposed rule "in a form which will make it inapplicable to the Concorde" was not quite correct. In the instructions given to the FAA the distinction was not between subsonic and supersonic aircraft, which clearly would have exempted the Concorde, but between aircraft engaged in "interstate" (domestic) operations and "foreign" (international) operations. In late January 1973 John W. Barnum, DOT general counsel, reported that the British were concerned by this discrepancy, since the proposed rule would prevent U.S. airlines from flying the Concorde on such interstate routes as California to Hawaii or Alaska, and New York to Miami.[37] The DOT answer was that the stated concern of the British and the French had been that U.S. airlines should be able to fly Concordes on the North Atlantic routes, which the rule would permit. Barnum advised his department that "the White House is willing to take the heat from the British and French concerning this domestic applicability to Concorde operations."[38]

As it turned out, the proposed fleet noise rule was never put into effect. The Nixon promise was "a commitment without much substance," suggested Representative John W. Wydler in December 1975. "You put your finger on it," agreed William T. Coleman, Jr., secretary of transportation, who went on to wax Shakespearean in describing the commitment as "a tale told by an idiot, full of sound and fury, signifying nothing."[39] Coleman was to signify much in the contemporary production that lay ahead.

FIGHT FOR APPROVAL | 3

ENVIRONMENTAL IMPACT | 8

Air transport's supersonic era began on 21 January 1976 with the entry of the Concorde into regular airline service. Air France flew between Paris and Rio de Janeiro via Dakar, while British Airways flew from London to Bahrain, first leg of the planned route to Australia. But for the future, the transatlantic routes were crucial. To fly or not to fly into the lucrative United States market would alone determine whether the supersonic dream would take shape, take root, and survive.

The approach of supersonic airline services to the United States was to prove a turbulent passage through unfriendly skies, at least as perceived by the British and French. Normally, for subsonic aircraft, the process is straightforward: existing international agreements include the mutual acceptance of national airworthiness and licensing standards, and reciprocal agreement on routes. These international agreements are subject to relevant national regulations, applied fairly and without discrimination. Hence U.S. approval was required for British Airways and Air France to begin scheduled services by Concorde to that country, and in a completely separate process, a U.S. certificate of airworthiness was required before any American airline could operate the aircraft.

These customary aviation procedures were soon engulfed in a wider storm, however, as political and environmental arguments, set in the fragile framework of international relations, clouded the normally straightforward resolution of technical issues. The Concorde approval process involved not only aviation authorities but also presidents and the public. The key issue would prove to be the environmental impact of the aircraft and, above all, the noise of its engines.

British Aircraft Corporation's American subsidiary had taken a first look at the problems of combating the potential opposition to the Concorde in the United States in an internal report in September 1972.[1] Anti-SST feeling in the country was still strong, the report warned. The company should maintain a low profile for the next 18 months—"Time is the great healer"—and then gradually increase the publicity effort in order to create favorable opinions of the aircraft "within all segments of the United States that could affect its sales prospects." As it turned out, America's SST wounds were far from healed with the passage of time, and the modest, orderly publicity campaign proposed was soon overtaken by an all-out Anglo-French effort, intended not to enhance sales prospects but simply to ensure survival.

In the summer of 1974—the summer when President Richard Nixon was forced to resign after the Watergate scandal, to be succeeded by Gerald Ford—the British and French governments advised the FAA that the two national airlines wished to begin scheduled Concorde services to the United States in 1976, prefaced by a series of noncommercial, route-proving flights. The Concorde's extensive program of route-proving flights was eventually rearranged to avoid the United States, but the process of obtaining approval for the scheduled services was to become a prolonged and bitter conflict. The formal process began politely enough with brief letters from Air France and British Airways to the FAA in February 1975.[2] The airlines were requesting "amendments to their operations specifications" to enable them to begin scheduled services to the United States in early 1976. Specifically, they each sought approval for two flights a day to New York (John F. Kennedy International Airport) and one a day to Washington, D.C. (Dulles Airport). Operations specifications define an airline's aircraft types, airports served, routes, and flight procedures, and normally any change was likely to be approved automatically. But the Concorde was abnormal. It was the world's first supersonic transport aircraft, and its engines would be noisier and would emit more pollutants than those of its subsonic predecessors. Fortunately for the American authorities, if not for British Airways and Air France, the United States had a suitable piece of legislation on hand—the Environmental Policy Act of 1969. Under this act, any "major federal action significantly affecting the quality of the human environment" requires the environmental consequences of the action to be analyzed in a comprehensive environmental impact statement (EIS). Accordingly, a draft EIS covering the proposed Concorde services was completed and published by the FAA.[3] The Concorde was the first aircraft—and to date remains the only one—to be subjected to this scrutiny.

The EIS process was not the only federal action to affect the Concorde; the draft statement noted that proposed SST noise regulations were expected from the Environmental Protection Agency (EPA). As for sonic booms, the FAA had banned all civil supersonic flight over the United States; this rule had not been waived in the past and would not be waived in the future.

Against this background, the draft statement ranged widely in its analysis, discussing not only environmental factors but also technical, economic, and general issues. It pointed to the marked changes in air transport that had taken place in the 14 years since Concorde development began. The machine faced environmental constraints, worldwide concern over fuel shortages, rising fuel costs, and rapidly rising costs of labor and materials, all while airlines were heavily in debt, with poor earnings and a market now dominated by mass, low-cost travel—none of which existed in 1961. Unless initial Concorde services generated sustained high passenger load factors, it was unlikely that more than the 16 Concordes already committed to production would fly in international commercial service.

Noise test data obtained on Concorde visits to Dallas–Fort Worth, Washington, and Boston had confirmed the manufacturers' figures; in common with noise levels of early U.S. subsonic jet transports such as the Boeing 707 and the Douglas DC-8, the Concorde levels were above those specified in Federal Aviation Regulation Part 36 (FAR-36). The Concorde's low-frequency noise, causing vibration in buildings, was greater than that of other aircraft. The draft statement considered whether to reject, grant, or impose further limitations on the applications by British Airways and Air France. Granting the applications was the preferred option. The volume of Concorde operations, and so the environmental impact, would be limited and would not prejudice any subsequent general SST rule making.

That conclusion was not the end of the process, however, merely the beginning. Public comment on the draft EIS was invited—and was received in large measure. Written comments were submitted by a host of interested parties, including one from the U.K. government and an identical one, in French, from the French government. In April the FAA held a series of public hearings in Washington, New York, and Sterling Park, Virginia. Strong opposition to the Concorde was evident, including protests from the organized groups that had contributed to (and had claimed credit for) the cancellation of the American SST program four years before. Now they relished the prospect of a foreign dragon to be slain.

Three If by Air

"I am Ken Binning, director-general, Concorde, in the U.K. Department of Industry, responsible jointly with my French colleague, l'Ingénieur en Chef Gérard

Guibé, for the supervision at government level of the Concorde program." The British official was opening for the Anglo-French team at the FAA public hearing on the draft EIS, held in the agency's headquarters in Washington on 14 April 1975. The team represented not only the two governments but also the two national airworthiness authorities, the four aircraft and engine manufacturers, and the two airlines.

Binning and his colleagues went on to make eight main points. The effect on the stratosphere of the proposed operations was small. The Concorde would raise by less than 2 percent the overall pollution level at Kennedy Airport. The noise level of the aircraft was similar to that of the Boeing 707, DC-8, and VC-10 subsonic jets. The low-frequency noise of the engines would harm neither persons nor property. The aircraft could comply safely with the noise control regulation of the Port Authority of New York and New Jersey. A noise abatement procedure to achieve this had already been demonstrated. The airlines had no intention of operating the aircraft during the hours of sleep. In summary, the environmental impact of the proposed operations was not significant.

Others at the hearing begged to differ. At the second EIS hearing, held later that week in New York, Binning and his colleagues repeated their eight points—in the face of opposition that included a group of banner-carrying senior citizens led by Bella S. Abzug, a New York member of the U.S. House of Representatives. The redoubtable Representative Abzug said she regarded the Concorde debate as "a rare opportunity for us to put a halt to blind, senseless technology which is applied at the expense of the general public." Another speaker struck a historic chord. Recalling that in 1775 the lantern signal for the approach of the British was "One if by land, two if by sea," he continued, "We have to add another signal—three if by air. Today, we have many Paul Reveres here to warn us of this latest British invasion, this time accompanied by the French. We hope the result will be the same."[4]

In the summer of 1975, members of the U.S. Congress were presented with a succinct summary of the Concorde issue in a report by a Library of Congress analyst, which presented the arguments on both sides.[5] In its discussion of international relations, the report extracted the essence of the controversy in blunt terms, first as seen by the Concorde promoters:

> *Pro:* Britain and France are important fellow members of the Western community of nations. Those two nations have invested over ten years of effort and vast sums of money in the development of the Concorde. To ban it now from American airports might result in the collapse of the entire Concorde program, which is in difficulty already as a result of the worldwide economic recession and energy crisis. It would be regarded by Britain and France as a stab in the back, because of the his-

tory of the development of FAA's anti-noise regulations. As a way of permitting the 707s and DC-8s to continue to operate after the introduction of FAR-36, the United States (FAA) agreed that FAR-36 would only apply to aircraft applying for certification after 1969. The French and British, who applied for Concorde certification long before that date, regard this as a binding international commitment. Proceeding on the faith that a U.S. commitment was a solid one, they have invested over two billion dollars in their Concorde program. If the United States should revoke its commitment, the act could shake the confidence of any foreign power in future promises or commitments made by the United States. It might also provoke Britain and France into some form of retaliation against the United States, such as banning our aircraft from their air space, or cancelling purchase agreements for U.S. manufactured transports.

On the other hand, there were equally cogent arguments against the aircraft:

Con: Why should the American people have to suffer as a result of the bad judgment of the British and French? The Concorde is an enormous white elephant, which should have been scrapped years ago. It is uneconomical, a waste of fuel, and a polluter of the environment. If our action results in cancellation of the program, the British and French taxpayers would thank us for removing this burden from their backs. Retaliation is highly unlikely, since Britain and France need us more than we need them. Anyway, this whole argument is irrelevant. The Concorde should be judged on its merits, and should be banned because of its excessive noisiness, regardless of the nationality of its manufacturers. Why should we allow a foreign aircraft to violate standards to which American aircraft are required to conform?

This distillation of the main ingredients of the U.S. Concorde controversy illuminated the heart of the matter, but many variations were to be played on the two opposing themes in the long battle that lay ahead.

Comments for and against the EIS conclusions continued to pour into the FAA following the public hearings. British Airways' U.S. counsel quoted legal chapter and verse to sustain the contention that the airline had the right to operate any properly certificated, U.K.-registered aircraft, including the Concorde, to and from the United States and that no EIS process was required.[6] The British government, also, made the point that its participation in the EIS process did not prejudice its rights under international agreements.[7] In an appendix, David Davies, chief test pilot of the U.K. Civil Aviation Authority, confirmed that the proposed Concorde takeoff procedure for runway 31L at Kennedy Airport was safe. This involved a turn after takeoff at a height of 100 feet—relatively low by subsonic aircraft standards but feasible for the Concorde because of its more precise control.

Collective replies to the "extraordinary volume of comments" on the draft statement were included in the FAA's final environmental impact statement, which was issued on 13 November 1975. More than 100 comments on general issues, noise impact, air quality, stratospheric pollution, economic impact, and the FAA's possible actions were discussed. Some critics were concerned about the possible increase in the number of Concorde flights; the FAA response was that any increase in flight frequency would require a new environmental assessment. Several commentators had suggested that the EIS should be widened to include political, diplomatic, and economic considerations; effects on investment and social structure; and problems of international law. The FAA response was that the EIS legally was concerned only with environmental issues, as one of a number of factors that would be considered by the decision maker.

Final Approach

The decision maker in the case of the Concorde was William T. Coleman, Jr., a distinguished lawyer who had become secretary of transportation in the Ford administration the previous March. When the final EIS was published, Secretary Coleman explained in detail how he intended to reach a decision on the highly controversial application.[8] The Concorde decision raised unique questions of public policy, he noted. In essence, the task was to achieve the proper balance between technological advances, international relationships, and environmental quality. Because those issues were novel and difficult, and were of great public and congressional interest, the secretary had decided to hold a public hearing and to invite comment on the main concerns.

A joint written submission to Secretary Coleman was made by the British and French governments at the beginning of the new year, 1976.[9] Realizing that this was the crucial preliminary to the forthcoming Coleman hearing, the two governments put forward the case for the Concorde as convincingly as they could. The environmental impact of the machine had been grossly exaggerated by its opponents, they argued. The Concorde had been subjected to the most thorough environmental scrutiny given any aircraft, and the results of that study showed that the impact of the proposed operations would be small. The limited environmental impact of Concorde service to the United States would be far outweighed by the benefits and by the important international considerations of technological progress and economic harmony.

Answering specific questions posed by Secretary Coleman, the two governments declared that a negative decision would be discriminatory, because the Concorde met all relevant U.S. and international regulations and the environmental impact of the proposed flights would be marginal. The United States had a commitment to the principles of fair treatment and reciprocity. To ban Concorde operations by British Airways and Air France would be widely viewed as a double standard and could lead to reciprocal limitations on U.S. manufacturers and airlines.

The Coleman Hearing

From nine-thirty in the morning to seven o'clock in the evening of Monday, 5 January 1976, less 45 minutes for lunch, the Department of Transportation auditorium on Constitution Avenue was the scene of a unique confrontation between Concorde proponents and opponents.[10] Secretary Coleman, listening patiently to statements by some 70 interested parties, only occasionally interrupting to clarify points or put specific questions, saw to it that it was a civilized confrontation. All those who spoke, and many more, had already submitted written comments, some at great length, and some would submit further papers after the hearing, but here they could present, in person, the essence of their cases. It was a remarkable event, atmospherically part trial, part medieval disputation. For a trial, the rules of evidence were rather lax. For a medieval disputation, emotion and politics supplemented pure reason.

The Anglo-French team was led by Gerald Kaufman, minister of state in the U.K. Department of Industry, supported by Claude Abraham of the French Civil Aviation Department, Michael Wilde of BAC, Roger Chevalier of Aérospatiale, Claude Lalanne of Air France, and Ross Stainton of British Airways. Their case rested on the argument that the limited number of flights requested would have very little impact on the environment of the United States, Kaufman declared. There was no national rule that would bar the Concorde from commercial service in the United States; there was no international standard that the aircraft did not meet. Britain and France were ready to participate in an international program to monitor and control the many effects on the stratosphere; "Your environment is our environment. Your ozone layer is our ozone layer." Secretary Coleman asked both Kaufman and Abraham a question that was to prove significant: were they aware of any agreement between anyone in their governments and anyone in the United States that said the Concorde would have an absolute right to land in the United States? No, they were not. The French official went on to stress the importance of U.S. approval: "The objectives of the Concorde cannot be reached unless we fly commercially to the United States. Service to the United States is essential if we are to realise the benefits of the resources we have invested." Among the points emphasized by other speakers in the team were the small incremental effect of the Concorde on the cumulative noise exposure at the two airports, the uncertainty of the effects on the ozone layer, the exhaustive flight-testing program (more than 5,000 hours, far more than any other commercial aircraft), and the safety of the turn after takeoff from Kennedy runway 31L, as confirmed by FAA and airline pilots.

"The anti-Concorde team will now have an hour of time," intoned the hearing officer. "The first witness will be Mr. Bert Rein, Aviation Consumer Action Project." Rein argued that the Concorde should be treated as if it were an American aircraft. Its foreign origin should not cause the United States to discriminate against it, but "nor should an abstract recitation of foreign relations considerations cause us to discriminate in its favor against the health and welfare interests of our own citizens, and millions of other people throughout the world." Beware the European aerospace challenge, he warned: "we are dealing here, not with a question of biting the hand that has fed us, but really of feeding the mouth that seeks to bite us." Dr. Maurice A. Garbell, representing cities near San Francisco Airport, had an equally picturesque turn of phrase. The EIS claimed that the Concorde would cause no problem in air traffic control because it would be treated like an ordinary subsonic machine; that, Garbell opined, was like saying a tiger cub would not claw up the sofa and the drapes, because we were going to treat it as an ordinary pussy cat. The Concorde should use military airfields that had special high-speed routes for climb-out and descent.

Colorful religious fervor was supplied by the first British anti-Concorde witness, the purple-clad Right Reverend Hugh Montefiore, Bishop of Kingston-upon-Thames, speaking not for his diocese but as president of the Heathrow Association for the Control of Aircraft Noise. "The noise from Concorde is not hell because, after all, hell goes on forever. It is more like a secular form of purgatory. I can best compare it to the inflamed gall bladder. The pain is intermittent, but it can inhibit speech." The Concorde decision was not a matter of political trade-offs; it was a matter of moral principle. Another British opponent, Andrew Wilson of *The Observer* newspaper, here representing the British Conservation Society, dismissed as ludicrous the "vague threats" of possible retaliation if the Concorde were denied U.S. entry. A third well-known British campaigner, Richard Wiggs of the Anti-Concorde Project, also urged Secretary Coleman to deny the application. Kenneth Warren, Member of Parliament and chairman of the U.K. Conservative parliamentary aviation committee, reinforced his political opponent Mr. Kaufman's case for approval, arguing that the Concorde represented a satisfactory compromise between technology and the environment. From here on, it would be a normal evolutionary process to improve SST technology as public environmental expectations rose in parallel.

Two U.S. senators presented opposing views—Barry M. Goldwater of Arizona in favor, James L. Buckley of New York against. Senator Goldwater, a pilot for 45 years with 12,000 hours (including supersonic hours) in his logbook, was caustic: never had so much misinformation been put out; the SST was charged with causing everything but ingrown toenails—"And I will be surprised if the misinformers do not find a way to do that." The threats offered against the Concorde were so ill-founded on theoretical uncertainties and unsupported by facts that the Europeans could justly interpret a decision against the Concorde as being based on nothing more than economic protectionism. Not so, argued Senator Buckley: the noise around Kennedy Airport already was seriously affecting job performance, school work, family relationships, and human health. How could a government that was actively engaged in reducing noise levels even consider granting landing rights to an aircraft that generated two to three times as much noise as the subsonic aircraft that were already stretching the limits of what could be considered tolerable?

Members of the House of Representatives, also, were present to give Secretary Coleman the benefit of their views. Congressman John W. Wydler, whose fifth district of New York adjoined Kennedy Airport, reported strong public opposition to the Concorde, which he described as "a flying mess" that was already obsolete. The bicentennial year of 1976 might be an appropriate time to "declare ourselves independent of this British noise machine, because certainly the SST Concorde is an aircraft whose time has passed." Congressman Joseph L. Fisher reported similarly from the tenth district of Virginia, whose Fairfax County and Loudoun County residents were exposed to the noise of aircraft using Dulles Airport. "Opposition in northern Virginia to allowing the Concorde to land at Dulles is overwhelming," he claimed. "The views of the thousands of people who reside in the sound footprint of the Concorde should be heeded." These views of representatives of the people of New York and near Dulles were hardly surprising, but another New York congressman, Samuel S. Stratton, dared to be different. "I believe that the arguments against the Concorde have been greatly exaggerated," he commented, "and it is time to inject some perspective and commonsense into the discussion." The congressman urged Coleman to permit the limited Concorde flights for a reasonable trial period so that U.S. officials could collect relevant environmental data.

Congressman Lester L. Wolff of the sixth district of New York, an acknowledged anti-SST activist, raised allegations of future noise ("Concorde will blanket nearly half a million of my friends and neighbors on Long Island with 90 EPNdB [effective perceived noise decibels]") and past skulduggery ("The British Air Registration Board tried to kill the sales of Lockheed Constellations and Boeing Stratocruisers because they were not British-made"). Another New York congressman, Richard L. Ottinger, suggested the aircraft should be renamed the Discorde, defined in the dictionary as "harsh noise, clashing sounds, want of harmony between notes sounding together." In short, he said, the Concorde was a flying environmental nightmare. It was a flying white elephant, opined Congressman John D. Dingell of Michigan. Other congressional Concorde opponents included Sidney R. Yates of Illinois and James V. Stanton of Ohio. The objections of Governor Hugh Carey of New York state were conveyed by Raymond L. Schuler, his secretary of transportation. Other anti-Concorde groups represented at the hearing included the Center for the Study of Noise in Society, Environmental Defense Fund, National Parks and Conservation Association, D.C. Committee for Wilderness, Friends of the Earth, and Airport Operators Council International.

Local groups opposed to the aircraft included Howard Beach Association, Queens, New York; the National Council of Jewish Women, Peninsular Section, Long Island, Evening Branch; Spring Park Civic Association; Arlingtonians for the Preservation of the Potomac Palisades; Fairfax County Park Authority; Fairfax County Board of Supervisors; Lawrence Central Council PTA; Metropolitan Washington Council of Governments; Alden Manor Civic Association; and Loudoun County Board of Supervisors. Ernest H. Major spoke not only for Brookfield Citizens Association, Greenbriar Civic Association, Reston Garden Club, Deepwood Homeowners Association, and Golf Course Island Cluster Association but also with the endorsement of Centreville District Council of Citizens' Association, Brookside Homeowners' Association, Country Club Manor Civic Association, Reston Democratic Club, and the Ad Hoc Committee to Keep Reston Reston (all located in Fairfax County, Virginia). The target of many objectors, including Edwin Krawitz, principal of Lawrence High School on Long Island, was the intolerable existing noise from jet aircraft using Kennedy Airport. The prospect of the Concorde, Krawitz said, was an abomination that reached indescribable heights. The language used by the objectors ranged from the formal resolution:

> Whereas, the Fairfax County Federation of Citizens Associations has in the past opposed development of an SST, and whereas this opposition is firmly rooted in concern for the quality of life in the vicinity of Fairfax County airports; and whereas the Department of Transportation is considering granting test flight privileges to an SST; and whereas data has been published which raises severe concern about the adverse noise impact of the Concorde;
> Therefore, be it resolved: that the Fairfax County Federation of Citizens Associa-

tions urges Secretary of Transportation not to authorize further flights of Concorde SST into Fairfax County airports.

to the emotional plea (in this case, from Carol Berman of the Emergency Coalition to Stop the SST):

> We are pleading with you for our homes, for our children, for our lives. I would like to add that the people who live in our area consider themselves Americans, entitled to the same right to life, liberty and pursuit of happiness as our fellow citizens across the land. We believe in government of the people and by the people. That is why we came here today by bus, plane, car, at not inconsiderable difficulty and expense, middle-class, middle-American people. Please show us that it is also government for the people, so that we shall not perish from this earth.

Apparent inconsistencies in the views of the Environmental Protection Agency were explored by Coleman in his cross-examination of Roger Strelow, an assistant EPA administrator. The agency's present view, it emerged, was against approval, for environmental reasons. Dr. Richard L. Garwin of the Federal Energy Administration's Environmental Advisory Committee said that the argument that it would be unfair to require the Concorde to meet the requirements of FAR-36, as if it were a subsonic aircraft, ignored the fact that it was FAA inaction that had created the lack of an SST rule. He added that this reminded him of the story of the young man who murdered his parents in cold blood and then threw himself on the mercy of the court because he was an orphan. Morton Haves, president of the Five Towns Real Estate Brokers Association, had a simple message: stop the development of Kennedy Airport and "let this missile go to the Kennedy Space Center, where it belongs."

Fewer organized groups but a respectable number of individuals appeared before Secretary Coleman to urge approval of the Concorde operations. Groups such as the U.S. Council of the International Chamber of Commerce, Citizens for a Better New York, the British-American Chamber of Commerce, and the Committee for Dulles emphasized the business and commercial benefits. The U.K.-based Campaign for Action on Supersonic Engineering (CASE) drew a parallel with the acceptance by the British and French authorities in the late fifties of the Boeing 707 and Douglas DC-8 jet aircraft, both of which were novel in design, did not hold U.K. or French certification, were noisier than any previous civil aircraft, lacked nonstop transatlantic range, and required a surcharge on fares. The Pacific Legal Foundation supported the application after consulting experts and weighing the conflicting factors. A Texan trio—the mayors of Dallas and of Fort Worth and the executive director of the Dallas–Fort Worth regional airport board—extolled the virtues of their airport, which had been designed with SSTs in mind, and extended a hearty southern welcome to the Anglo-French machine.

Individual supporters included John Shaffer, former FAA administrator; William Magruder, former DOT SST director, now executive vice president of Piedmont Aviation; John R. Wiley, former aviation director of the Port of New York Authority, now a visiting professor at MIT; and Richard FitzSimmons, director of advanced supersonic aircraft at McDonnell Douglas. Dr. Fred Singer, professor of environmental sciences at the University of Virginia, concluded that the Concorde services would have a negligible influence on ozone: "Whatever objections one may raise against the Concorde, stratospheric pollution should not be one of them." Wiley said he was speaking for the silent majority, whose overall interests were best served when the frontiers of science and technology were encouraged to expand through research and then to be proven by practical operating experience. He was responding to the sad reality that this democratic principle of the greatest good for the greatest number was sometimes overrun by the well-organized expression of a vocal, directly involved minority.

Secretary Coleman's long day's hearing had enabled everyone who had wished to express a view to do so—about 70 in all, metaphorically voting about 40 to 30 for the motion that the Concorde should not be allowed into the United States. All the issues raised in the secretary's prehearing questions had been addressed, but the greatest single objection of the opposers had concerned noise. The Concorde issue gave people living near Kennedy and Dulles airports an opportunity to voice their strong feelings about their existing noisy environment, and it was hardly surprising that they grasped the opportunity—and hardly surprising that their elected representatives reflected those feelings. The Concorde team's greatest single selling point was the small number of proposed flights, leading to their assertion that the environmental impact would be small. Their second main plank was the sensitive issue of international relations and perceived unfair discrimination in the event of a refusal. The hearing had been a window on the wide landscape of written facts, figures, assertions, opinions, and feelings that made up Secretary Coleman's voluminous docket on the Concorde affair.

Rehearsal at the Rotunda

Members of the Concorde team recall vividly a dress rehearsal for the Coleman hearing, held the previous Sunday in the rotunda of the British embassy on Massachusetts Avenue. One key player was William D. Ruckelshaus, former administrator of the Environmental Protection Agency and former U.S. deputy attorney general (who had resigned in October 1973 in the so-called Saturday-night massacre after refusing to obey an order from President Nixon to remove Watergate special prosecutor Archibald Cox). Ruckelshaus was practicing law in Washington and had been retained by the British government; in parallel the French government had retained another lawyer, former senator Charles Goodell. At the mock hearing, each played the part of Coleman, with Ruckelshaus questioning the French witnesses and Goodell the British team. "This was done to avoid alienating our own clients," Ruckelshaus explains.[11] Clearly the two lawyers played their parts well—too well, at one stage, according to the former deputy attorney general: "We expected the hearings would be rough, and therefore attempted to make the mock hearings equally contentious. At one point, the French became so exercised at my questions that they stomped out. Upon my reassuring them nothing personal was intended, they came back and resumed the testimony."

The initiative for the mock hearing came from Ruckelshaus, Goodell, and DGA International, a Washington public relations firm of which the former senator was chairman. (The name of the firm came from the initials of its founder, Donald G. Agger, previously involved in the SST debate in the Department of Transportation.) The significant roles played in Concorde affairs by Senator Goodell and the ubiquitous DGA are described in the following chapter.

DECISION AND DISSENSION | 9

William Coleman's decision and the exhaustive investigation leading up to it remain an outstanding example of American federal executive action at its best—not only in reaching a fair and prompt decision but also in adopting a clearly defined process and in explaining that process to the American people and the world.[1] The decision, in essence, was to permit the requested Concorde flights for an experimental period of up to 16 months, subject to certain restrictions. The decision as published was supported by a detailed consideration of the legal framework (both domestic and international), the policy framework, the environmental consequences, and the benefits of the Concorde in terms of technology and international relations. The text of the decision and of the international relations section of the supporting argument are reproduced as appendix 6.

Coleman concluded that the Concorde's impacts on air quality, low-frequency noise vibrations, and the stratosphere were not sufficient to justify a ban. He was troubled by the aircraft's relative fuel inefficiency, but it was no reason to dictate to other countries how they should allocate their fuel resources. The theory of ozone reduction and the associated increase in nonfatal skin cancer was of concern, but the stratospheric impact of the 16-month demonstration would be minuscule. Also, there were other U.S. releases into the stratosphere that unquestionably were more damaging than the limited Concorde emissions.

The most serious immediate consequence of the Concorde operations was noise, Coleman noted, although the limited number of flights would have little impact on the total noise exposure at Dulles and Kennedy airports. The Concorde's unique noise characteristics and the attendant publicity might well aggravate the community's initial response, and a controlled demonstration period would enable assessments to be made of both the subjective response and the measured noise levels. Although deeply concerned by the additional irritation that the Concorde flights might cause for some people near the two airports, the secretary believed that the environmental cost was outweighed by the benefits to the American people. Nevertheless, it was a difficult and close decision, he admitted—difficult because the benefits could not easily be quantified. Tangible benefits included the significant speed increase for transatlantic travelers, so facilitating international commerce and trade and cultural exchange. He added:

> In addition, extension to the Concorde of the opportunity to prove itself will be an expression of international cooperation and good will between the United States and two of our closest allies with whom we share a substantial cultural heritage. . . . It will be an important reaffirmation of the mutual reciprocity that has enabled the United States to benefit so substantially from the export of its aeronautical products for the past 30 years.

Secretary Coleman was well aware that a decision to ban the Concorde would be popular and widely acclaimed. "Perhaps I would even be depicted by the press, however mistakenly, as the man who stood up to some undefined but sinister pressure to let the Concorde in—however absent such 'pressure' has in fact been. But I have struggled to discount such considerations and searched instead for a better sense of historical perspective from which to resolve my dilemma." Limited approval would leave open the opportunity for further executive assessment and public scrutiny. The benefits of new technologies were not always readily apparent at the time they were introduced. Any new technology brought with it a degree of risk and some public concern. If the SST did become the aircraft of the future, that would be because technology would have been developed to enable it to meet environmental standards while competing effectively in the marketplace. If the Concorde were banned, that further technological advance would be delayed for decades.

Thus the demonstration period would enable the United States to evaluate whether the SST was commercially viable, whether the traveler would pay the extra cost for the reduced travel time, the extent to which fatigue and jet lag were reduced, and the advantages for international commerce. It would also enable further assessments of the environmental impact to be made. It would give both the French and British governments and U.S. private industry the opportunity to consider whether the development of cleaner, quieter, more fuel-efficient SST technology was a sound capital investment. It might well be that further development of this technology was not economically sensible at the present energy-conscious and environmentally conscious time. If so, then the Concorde would fail because it was an anachronism, and its failure would be recognized as such rather than attributed to an arbitrary, protectionist attitude of the United States.

> Thus, I have concluded that the benefits of an environmentally sound, commercially viable SST would be substantial. I am also convinced that we do not yet have sufficient information upon which to make a judgment about whether such an aircraft could be developed. Given the substantial effort by the French and British to initiate this technology, and the fact that United States participation may well be essential to the commercial success of the SST, I believe this demonstration is needed to determine whether a commitment to this new technology should be embraced.

A Prior Commitment?

Coleman's account of the reasoning behind his decision, generally welcomed as fair, honest, and comprehensive, was not accepted by all. In Congress, the House Committee on Government Operations had been investigating the Concorde issue, and on 26 May 1976 a joint hearing of subcommittees of that committee and of the House Committee on International Relations recalled Secretary Coleman to give further testimony.[2] His leading critics were Lester Wolff and Bella Abzug, who alleged that Coleman had misled Congress and that foreign policy aspects had interfered with U.S. domestic policy-making. In particular, the Nixon letters of 1973 to the British prime minister and the French president aroused their suspicion; the "secret concessions" in those letters, they alleged, were given only after the British and the French had gone to the Nixon White House and exacted them. The Nixon letters represented the tip of an iceberg in the files of the executive branch, Wolff said, which if fully explored would reveal depths of diplomatic involvement in the domestic decision-making process that clearly contravened the intent of Congress. "I agree that we should recognize our debt to the French during this bicentennial year, but really the Concorde decision goes too far," Wolff declared. "As for the British, Robert Morley says we can come home, all is forgiven. I should think so, Mr. Secretary, I should think so." (Wolff was referring to a "Come to Britain" television advertisement presented by the British actor.)

Prior to Secretary Coleman's involvement, Wolff alleged, the British and French were consistently able to head off potential problems by exerting sufficient diplomatic pressure to block promulgation of U.S. aircraft noise and related environmental standards. Coleman vigorously refuted the suggestion that there was any secret agreement, citing the specific denials at his hearing by Gerald Kaufman and Claude Abraham. The only State Department input to his decision had been the letter that Henry Kissinger had written at Coleman's request (reproduced in appendix 5).[3] And, he reaffirmed, his decision had been based only on public information—the EIS, the public hearing, and other written material submitted for the record.

State Department interference in the deliberations of the Port Authority of New York and New Jersey, proprietor of Kennedy Airport, had been alleged one year earlier, when a press report to this effect was cited in the House of Representatives.[4] James Lowenstein, deputy assistant secretary for European affairs at the State Department, had written to Ogden Reid, New York state environmental conservation commissioner (and Concorde critic), with a warning: "As you know, the sponsors of the Concorde are increasingly concerned that even though the aircraft may meet the current noise regulations in effect at Kennedy Airport, those regulations might be altered specifically to exclude it. Any discriminatory action against the Concorde by the operators of Kennedy Airport would adversely affect our relations with two important allies and be contrary to the foreign policy interests of the United States." Another State Department official allegedly had written along similar lines to Governor Brendan Byrne of New Jersey and Governor Hugh Carey of New York.

While denying any commitment prior to 1976, Secretary Coleman admits to knowing of a memorandum, signed either by President Nixon or his aide John Ehrlichman, which said that the Concorde issue should be decided not by the secretary of transportation but by the White House.[5] "When I became secretary I felt that that had no authority under President Ford, though I never went over and told the president, 'There's this memorandum in the files.'. . . I said [to President Ford], 'This is a decision I think I should make. I realize that ultimately you have the last call on it, but I would advise you that you are probably better off if you stayed the hell out of it, because I know you have other things to do, and if I'm wrong, you can just fire me.'"

Unquiet Takeoff

Following the Coleman decision, scheduled Concorde services to the United States began on 24 May 1976, with Air France and British Airways flights into Dulles Airport, Washington. The first departures of the Concordes from Dulles the next day provoked a flurry of protest, accusations of cheating, and an early-morning summons for Sir Peter Ramsbotham, the British ambassador. The two parallel main runways at Dulles are aligned along 010 degrees and 190 degrees, that is, roughly north-south. When used for a northward takeoff or landing, they are known as runways 01 left and 01 right (01L and 01R); used in the opposite direction the same runways are known as 19R and 19L. On 25 May the Concordes were expected to take off from runway 01L, but a change of wind direction forced a change to the opposite runway direction. News cameras and mobile noise monitors were moved from 01L to 19L, where the Air France machine took off first. The French captain elected to boost power (and noise) by keeping his Concorde's engine afterburners on, in order to gain height rapidly before passing over the town of Chantilly. Captain Norman Todd, captain of the British Airways Concorde, elected to use runway 19R.

The British aircraft was advised that "all the TV and cameras are set up for one nine left takeoff," but the copilot, Captain Brian Calvert, told ground control that 19R was preferable for community noise reasons. Accusations of cheating and evading the noise monitors followed. In the 26 May congressional hearing, New York representative James H. Scheuer accused his British cousins of not playing according to the Marquis of Queensberry rules. Five years later, Captain Calvert wrote, "The FAA knew we would use this runway as often as possible, simply because its departure route took us over fewer communities." He added, "Secretary Coleman was embarrassed and issued a public rebuke. . . . No harm was meant—we were simply doing our best."[6] In an interview in 1986, William Coleman recalled, "The British guy cheated and changed the runways. . . . I got on the phone and called the British ambassador, Sir Peter Ramsbotham, who was a good friend of mine, and told him to be in the office at six-thirty the next morning, which he was. I said I was going to stop it if the guy did anything like that again. After that there was never any problem."[7]

Ken Binning, leader of the British team campaigning for the Concorde in the United States, could not have attended Headmaster Coleman's study even if summoned. Having completed his tour as director general, he was heading for pastures new aboard Concorde G-BOAC as it took off from runway 19R on the inaugural service from Dulles. Looking down, he perhaps noticed the angry U.S. officials who, Brian Calvert avers, were up to their waists in poison ivy at the end of runway 19L.

The Lobbyists

During 1975–1977, as an accompaniment to the formal processes of seeking approval for the Concorde, the Anglo-French team of the two governments, four manufacturers, and two airlines mounted a campaign to present the general case for the aircraft to as wide an American audience as possible. At the very least, they had to counter the efforts of the organized antisupersonics campaigners, who had gained their battle honors fighting against the proposed American SST at the beginning of the decade and who were now determined to overcome the new foe—the Anglo-French SST. Eventually the pro-Concorde effort became a truly concerted campaign, but for a long time there was a marked difference of opinion between the French and the British sides on the best strategy and tactics to adopt.

In essence, the French government and Aérospatiale took advice from a group of high-powered U.S. public relations experts, who recommended a high-powered U.S. public relations campaign. The British team believed the port authority ban in New York that followed the Coleman decision was illegal and should be challenged in the courts. Also, 1976 was a presidential election year, which compounded the uncertainties.

Under the Foreign Agents Registration Act of 1938, organizations and individuals in the United States who represent overseas interests and who disseminate "political propaganda" are required to register as "foreign agents" with the U.S. Justice Department and to file regular reports of their activities. The three main organizations involved in promoting the case for the Concorde on behalf of Aérospatiale were DGA International, Daniel J. Edelman Inc., and International Public Relations Company (IPR). Also listed as French agents in 1976 were Rogers and Wells, lawyers, and Rinfret Associates, consultants, for Air France; Hydeman, Mason, and Goodell, lawyers, for the French government; John S. Meadows, political consultant, and European Aerospace Corporation, marketing advisers, for Aérospatiale; Robert B. Meyersburg Company, consultants, for European Aerospace Corporation; and W. A. Reynolds of Oklahoma City, public relations representative, for Aérospatiale Aircraft Corporation of Washington, D.C. The British case for the Concorde was presented by British Aircraft Corporation (U.S.A.) Inc., representing both the parent U.K. company and the British government (Department of Industry).

DGA International got off to an unfortunate start with the Justice Department when it forwarded a copy of its agreement with Aérospatiale in October 1975. The text of this agreement provided for bonus payments of $500,000 if authorization for the Concorde services was obtained.[8] Such contingent fees relating to U.S. government actions are illegal, and the Justice Department promptly filed a civil action against DGA complaining that the firm was violating Section 8(h) of the Registration Act in the way it was attempting to "prevail upon, indoctrinate, convert, induce, persuade or in some way influence" an agency or official of the U.S. government in "formulating, adopting or changing the domestic or foreign policies of the United States with reference to allowing or not allowing the Concorde

SST to obtain landing rights in the United States."[9] Also, the department filed similar actions against IPR, which had a similar agreement, and against the Edelman company, which had neglected to register as a foreign agent and to label its congressional material accordingly.

After an interim injunction, District Judge Charles Richey handed down his final judgment at the end of December.[10] Under the terms of the consent decree, to paraphrase the legal language, all three defendants agreed not to do it again, while not admitting that they had done anything in the first place. The revised DGA-Aérospatiale agreement went some way to mollify the Washington lobbyists, however: the bonus clauses contingent on U.S. approval for the Concorde were deleted, but the agreement was reworded to increase the payment to DGA in other ways.[11] First, DGA's hourly rate for 1976 was to be increased from $70 to $100. Second, an extra $200,000 was to be paid to DGA "to insure that top professional talent of DGA shall be available." For the benefit of the Justice Department, the agreement added, "Such sums are payable absolutely without regard to the occurrence or non-occurrence of any action by the U.S. Government."

The sums paid to DGA by Aérospatiale during the Concorde campaign were substantial. In the 24 months from November 1975 to October 1977 they amounted to more than $2.64 million, of which almost $480,000 was passed on to Edelman and more than $560,000 to the Washington law firm of Hydeman, Mason, and Goodell. This latter connection raises two intriguing aspects of the total lobbying effort. First, that firm's efforts were specifically on behalf of the French government. In addition, the other main participants—the British government, the four aircraft and engine manufacturers, and the two airlines—each engaged other law firms to pursue their interests. Whatever dire effects on the American environment the opponents of the Concorde might forecast, the supersonic machine was certainly good business for the American legal profession. The second element illustrated by the Hydeman, Mason, and Goodell connection could be considered a "top professional talent" issue, since the third-named was Charles Goodell, former U.S. senator and thus the possessor of more than average influence in Washington, D.C. Goodell was also chairman of DGA International. There were other influential names on the pro-Concorde team, including the former assistant secretary for international affairs in the Department of Transportation, Donald Agger (founder and president of DGA); William Ruckelshaus, former EPA administrator and deputy attorney general (a partner in the law firm of Ruckelshaus, Beveridge, Fairbanks, and Diamond, representing the British government); and William P. Rogers, former U.S. secretary of state (senior partner in Rogers and Wells, legal counsel for Air France). In New York, Richard R. Aurelio, former deputy mayor of the city, was hired as a consultant.

DGA's fees and expense reports to the Justice Department showed a regular pattern of consultancy fees, salary shares of senior DGA executives, and normal business expenses.[12] Regular meals at the Palm Restaurant were featured, and hotel bills included those of the Ritz-Carlton and Waldorf Astoria. In March 1976 Richard Aurelio collected $8,280, in April 1976 a luncheon meeting at the Smithsonian Institution cost $167, and in June 1976 DGA paid 15 cents for a copy of the *Washington Star* (and $19,749.80 to Hydeman, Mason, and Goodell). In November 1976 Thomas Scambos received $27 for airplane gas. Lloyd Preslar spent a modest $2.75 on a meal in March 1977, only to be outshone in frugality the next month by M. Gautier with a 97-cent meal (the same month, Hydeman, Mason, and Goodell services cost $30,336.40). In May 1977 a sum of $81.25 went for flowers from Palace Florists; in September 1978 a modest $31.52 was attributed to entertainment aboard the Dandy River Boat.

What was DGA trying to achieve? In general terms, quite clearly, to help to secure landing rights for the Concorde in the United States. The specific goals varied to reflect immediate challenges. Thus in 1975 and early 1976 the main aim was to lobby against proposed anti-Concorde legislation in Congress and in New Jersey, Virginia, and Fairfax County. In 1977, following the Coleman decision, DGA told the Justice Department that it was working with legal counsel in connection with the action brought by Air France and British Airways against the Port Authority of New York and New Jersey.[13] "Contact was maintained with the Executive Branch with respect to the litigation and with respect to a notice of proposed rule making on further extension of Concorde landing rights in the United States. Conversations were held also with staff and members of the port authority and other government officials in the New York State and City governments. There was continued contact with the Federal Aviation Administration in monitoring noise and community reaction to the flights operated into and out of Dulles airport." A list of contacts indicated the level at which former senator Goodell was operating; his appointments had included meetings with the chairman of the port authority, the secretary of transportation, and the assistant legal adviser at the State Department.

The role of the Edelman organization was primarily that of influencing members of Congress and their staffs, coupled with arranging talks and press conferences by Concorde spokesmen. In the first half of 1976, Edelman reported, company president John Martin Meek and Michael Scanlon had spoken to a large number of senators and representatives, and in opposing proposed anti-Concorde legislation, Edelman had furnished Concorde information to "the offices of virtually all Members of the Senate and House of Representatives."[14] Prior to the votes on two anti-Concorde amendments, "Edelman personnel telephoned the offices of virtually all Members of the Senate and House of Representatives to indicate Edelman's availability to respond to questions about the Concorde, and to ask for Members' consideration of the Aérospatiale position." Public events ranged from a news conference for French officials in December 1975 at the Sheraton-Carlton Hotel to a talk by Tim Stevens of British Airways to Fairfax and Vienna Lions Clubs at Bob's Beef House in Fairfax in May 1976.

The third main player for the French in the Concorde team, IPR of New York (operating as Concorde News Bureau) brought its local knowledge to bear on the difficult task of promoting a noisy aircraft in a very noise-sensitive city. According to its public-relations agreement with Aérospatiale, IPR was to work under DGA's leadership with the New York business community, with the media, and to perform ad hoc public relations tasks, in return for $5,000 a month plus expenses.[15] Its brief included distributing a steady stream of newsletters and news releases covering positive aspects of the Concorde and arranging for appearances by Concorde spokesmen on radio and television programs. The radio appearances, for example, included Dewi Rowlands of BAC on *UPI Roundtable,* Richard Aurelio on *The Arlene Francis Show,* Leo Schefer of BAC on *The Barry Farber Show,* Charles Carroll of DGA and Sandy Gordon-Cumming of the British embassy on *Let's Find Out,* and Gordon Booth, British consul general, on *In the Public Interest.* When newspapers prepared special Concorde reports, Robert T. Souers of IPR was available to argue the Anglo-French case in print, as in a comprehensive supplement to the *Queens Tribune* ("Concorde: Falcon or Turkey?") on 8 March 1977.

Sir Peter Ramsbotham, the British ambassador in Washington, was more actively involved in high-level lobbying for the Concorde than was normally an ambassador's lot. He cultivated the support of U.S. senators and dealt with the White House chief of staff in the Carter administration. William Coleman was a personal friend, but Ramsbotham's relationship with Jacques Kosciusko-Morizet, the French ambassador, could have been closer than it was. Sir Peter recalls the complications of the fight for approval:

> The French connection was unique, in my experience, in that we were not alone in presenting the British interests. The British interests themselves were complicated enough: we weren't just the Foreign Office arguing the political issues for Britain; we had at least two other elements, the company and the aviation ministry—who knew more about it than we did in one sense. And yet it became an international issue, and the Foreign Office in a sense was in charge. My instructions came from the Foreign Office, and the same thing was going on on the French side. But their pattern of government is different and so, because of this complication, more unexpected issues arose and instructions kept changing.
>
> We should have totally coordinated the two sides, but this proved a very difficult

thing to do. The French ambassador and I didn't really confide very much, though our ministers knew each other and acted together, as did those on the civil aviation side. I could never get close to my French colleague, and that made the work harder. One did one's best, but he and I should have been closely in touch throughout.[16]

William Coleman says that Sir Peter was a good friend and a wonderful gentleman, but that he "never came in to try to unduly influence me."[17] Did the Washington lobbyists approach the secretary? "They tried to approach me, but I wouldn't let them. That's why I had the public hearing. I said, 'Anything you say, put it on the record.'" Secretary Coleman answered specific questions on this point at the congressional joint hearing in May 1976:

> Mr. Gilman: Mr. Secretary, did you at any time meet with any of these gentlemen, Mr. Ruckelshaus, Mr. Rogers, Mr. Goodell, Mr. Clifford, or Aurelio, to discuss the decision prior to making the decision?
> Mr. Coleman: No. In fact, just to complete the record, there was one occasion when I was invited to the theater by Mr. Goodell. I did not know that he had any representation at all, and I found out another way because of a court proceeding involving a lobbyist matter. I then called him, or had my secretary call him. I rejected the invitation. I think I ended up paying for myself to go see Katharine Hepburn.[18]

Sir Gordon Booth, at that time the British consul general in New York, says that the battle for approval in that city presented a totally different dimension from Washington, and "the battle raged up many hills and into many valleys" before it was agreed that lobbying would not work and only a decision in the courts would remove the log-jam.[19] One reason lobbying would not work was that no local politician could possibly vote for noise. Sir Gordon recalls conversations with many people in New York and New Jersey who privately accepted that the Concorde noise impact would be minimal. "But," they added, "you cannot get us to go out, face our voters, and say we're voting for foreign noise." Other obstacles included the cancellation of the American SST, the U.S. airlines' cancellation of their Concorde options, and the country's determined move toward quieter aircraft engines. "We were becoming increasingly isolated," the former consul general says. Nonetheless an immense effort was mounted by the Concorde team, arguing from the Coleman decision, to try to convince New Yorkers that the aircraft should be allowed in.

The danger of a basic conflict between the hard-hitting efforts of the French-financed publicists and the work of the manufacturers' technical teams was recognized early on, at least by the engineers. Robert McKinlay was the U.K.-based (but frequently U.S.-flying) leader of the British Aircraft Corporation team, with

Bernard Brown and Dewi Rowlands of BAC (U.S.A.) as the main local contacts with the FAA. One of their problems, Brown and Rowlands recall, stemmed from DGA's aggressive approach to a number of U.S. government agencies.[20] "We tried to keep them well away from the FAA, because we at BAC had developed a very good relationship with that agency and we didn't want that to be upset. The FAA people have a reputation of being very impartial, and the lobbying effort was impinging on their impartiality." (Other aspects of the conflicts between the Concorde partners are noted in chapter 10.)

With hindsight, Lloyd Preslar, formerly with DGA, says bluntly that the biggest problem in obtaining Concorde landing rights in the United States, for those in the front line, was to keep the Anglo-French team together and on target.[21] Inevitably, the large number of institutions on the team led to problems of coordination, as individual agendas had to be reconciled. Preslar and others give Ken Binning and Michel Lagorce much of the credit for patiently achieving consensus, and DGA's working relationship with the British officials was closer than it was politic to make known at the time. As for the value of the public relations campaign, though the key decisions were those of Secretary Coleman and the New York courts, Preslar argues that the main public relations contribution was to help to achieve the objective while leaving "virtually no blood on the floor"—in other words, to leave relations between Britain, France, and the United States intact.

The Opposition

In the United States, the environmental lobby that had helped to force abandonment of the U.S. supersonic transport in 1971 had swung into renewed action four years later to resist the Anglo-French machine, first at the FAA hearings, again at the Coleman hearing, and, above all, in the battle for New York. In Britain, the Anti-Concorde Project had been campaigning since 1967 and in the seventies took its case to the United States, speaking before Coleman and at other hearings. One of the most persistent and influential of the American protesters was Dr. William A. Shurcliff, a physicist at Harvard University's Cambridge Electron Accelerator, who together with Professor John T. Edsall, a Harvard biochemist, and others in 1967 had formed the Citizens League against the Sonic Boom. Operating from a room in Shurcliff's home at 19 Appleton Street in Cambridge, this was a better class of protest: from the start the league insisted on "accuracy, politeness, and avoidance of colorful language."[22] The Harvard scientists presumably were somewhat embarrassed by the highly colorful language used by the Coalition against the SST, with which they were associated, in a full-page advertisement in

the *New York Times* on 5 March 1970, which proclaimed, "SST. AIRPLANE OF TO-
MORROW. BREAKS WINDOWS, CRACKS WALLS, STAMPEDES CATTLE, AND WILL HASTEN
THE END OF THE AMERICAN WILDERNESS."

Significantly, one of the most effective collaborations against the Concorde was
the close association that developed between Shurcliff and Richard Wiggs,
founder of the Anti-Concorde Project in Britain. The two men exchanged letters,
information, and moral support and generally cooperated in presenting the case
against the supersonic transport to as wide a public as possible. Both had been
strongly influenced by papers written by Bo Lundberg, director general of the
Aeronautical Research Institute of Sweden and an early SST opponent. Shurcliff
had little difficulty in raising money to support his cause, and from time to time
part of this largess was passed on to the less-affluent British group. Typical of many
letters from Shurcliff to Wiggs was a succinct note in 1970, which read in full:

> Dear Dick,
> At yesterday's meeting of C.L.A.S.B. members it was unanimously voted that you
> and your group are doing a marvelous and indeed crucial job and that I was to send
> you a check for $1,000.00 forthwith.
> Herewith.
> Sincerely,
> Wm A. Shurcliff[23]

To an exuberant "Success!" note to members on the demise of the American SST
in April 1971, Shurcliff added a postscript: "I will be writing to you in a few weeks
as to our revised aims, foremost of which is to stop the Anglo-French Concorde."[24] He advised Senator William Proxmire that the league was now focusing
its efforts on "shooting down the Concorde."[25] And not only the Concorde, he
reported later in the league newsletter: members had voted unanimously to
continue to work to help stop both the Anglo-French machine and the Soviet
Tu-144.[26]

The Citizens League proved a catalyst as Shurcliff encouraged other environmental groups to join the protest movement, first against the American SST and
then in opposing the Concorde's entry. In 1970 a group of 14 organizations, including the league, the Sierra Club, the Consumer Federation of America, Friends
of the Earth, the National Wildlife Federation, and the Wilderness Society, came
together to form the Coalition against the SST. On closing down the Citizens
League in November 1978, William Shurcliff distributed the league's bank balance
among four worthy causes: $100 each to Friends of the Earth and the Environ-
mental Defense Fund, $200 to Citizens against Noise—and the remaining $495.14
to the Anti-Concorde Project in Britain.

Talking in Trenton

Meanwhile, in March 1976, the New Jersey Legislature was considering the use of Kennedy Airport by the Concorde. Ken Binning and Michel Lagorce visited the State House in Trenton to argue their case informally. At a public hearing before a State Senate committee, A. R. "Sandy" Gordon-Cumming, civil aviation counselor at the British embassy ("When the British were in Trenton some 200 years ago they did rather badly"), and his opposite number at the French embassy ("My name is Léonce Lansalot-Basou, very unusual even in French") reviewed environmental and international factors.[27] Newark Airport in New Jersey was designated a possible alternative airport for Concorde flights to Kennedy, but the number of occasions when Newark would be used was likely to be no more than one or two a year, Gordon-Cumming suggested. Charles Carroll of DGA International, representing Aérospatiale, dealt with legal issues, and in particular whether New Jersey should join New York state in introducing a bistate bill that sought to bar the Concorde. The bill was discriminatory and unconstitutional, Carroll declared.

John D. Caemmerer, chairman of the New York State Senate Committee on Transportation, urged the New Jersey legislators to pass a bill identical to that enacted by New York. "Please join New York State in protecting your neighbors who face the threat of Jet Alley becoming a supersonic freeway," he declared. The committee declined to do this, concluding in their report that the Coleman decision was correct and that the proposed Concorde flights would not harm the environment, would only minimally affect the noise problem at Kennedy, and would not adversely affect New Jersey and its citizens.[28]

Fairfax County et al.

The Commonwealth of Virginia, in the person of Wayne A. Whitham, transportation secretary, had taken a pro-Concorde stance at the Coleman hearing, mainly because of "the importance we place on Dulles as Virginia's international gateway." This support reflected a joint resolution, approved by the Virginia Senate, which approved the Concorde trial operations and wished success to the operators of the Concorde. But members of the Fairfax County Board of Supervisors, and others, protested strongly to their representatives in the state legislature, and the resolution was defeated in the House of Delegates. Though the legislature's Concorde discourse was taken seriously enough by British and French officials—who addressed the House and lobbied individual members—the defeat of the pro-Concorde resolution was significant only in its psychological impact, for Virginia had no direct authority in the matter. The indefatigable Board of Supervisors of Fairfax County, however, kept up the pressure, first joining with other county bodies to take FAA administrator John McLucas to court to have Concorde operations at Dulles "enjoined" (prohibited) until SST noise regulations were promulgated. When this move failed, the board passed an amendment to its own local noise ordinance that in effect banned the Concorde because it could not meet the FAR-36 limits, and affirmed its intention to enforce this rule. This, a student of local politics observed, suggested that "the British and French emissaries on the maiden Concorde flights would upon disembarkation be met by the Fairfax County sheriff and promptly arrested."[29] When this move, predictably, also failed, Fairfax County supervisors resorted to a symbolic protest, hanging three red lanterns on the eleventh floor of the county office building to warn citizens that the British were coming again, this time by air.

Throughout 1976, as the petitions by Fairfax County and others for review of the Coleman decision progressed through the D.C. District Court and the Court of Appeals, submissions by British Airways and Air France formed part of the legal proceedings. The airlines were acting as "intervenors," in effect supporting the respondents McLucas, the FAA, Coleman, and the Department of Transportation in a group of cases—the other petitioners were Loudoun County, Virginia; Nassau County, New York; the state of New York; and the Environmental Defense Fund—that were considered together.[30] In November the Supreme Court declined to consider the combined case, so confirming the appeals court ruling in favor of the FAA-DOT.[31] The two airlines intervened also in another *Fairfax* v *McLucas* case; again most of the action took place in 1976, but the proceedings dragged on until 1979, when Judge Barrington D. Parker of the D.C. District Court dismissed the case as moot.[32]

A Change of President

Speaking in August 1976, Democratic presidential candidate Jimmy Carter had opposed U.S. landing rights for the Concorde. Writing in February 1977, President Carter stated that his administration would reaffirm the 16-month trial period set by former secretary of transportation Coleman, without prejudice to what should happen after the trial period.[33] Concerning landing rights at New York, the president stated that he could not direct the port authority or the governor of New York to reach a decision that was theirs alone. The occasion was reminiscent of the

Nixon letters four years before; the president was replying to messages of concern from the British prime minister and the French president—now James Callaghan and Valéry Giscard d'Estaing.

The French reaction to President Carter's February message was the subject of urgent State Department telegrams from the embassy in Paris. Reporting back on comments made by Prime Minister Raymond Barre at an Anglo-American Press Association lunch in Paris, Ambassador Kenneth Rush quoted Barre as saying that French and British public opinion would not understand how the United States, which preached free enterprise and fair competition, could adopt measures that "regardless of the pretexts that might be invoked," would appear designed to avoid fair competition in international air transport.[34]

The next day, Ambassador Rush filed another message, giving news of an Anglo-French write-in campaign to support Concorde.[35] The campaign had been launched by a Toulouse-based group with the support of newspapers in Bordeaux, Toulouse, and Bristol, which were inviting their readers to sign and send in for forwarding to New York a printed form inscribed, "Let it land—*Laissez-le atterrir.*" Earlier, the American Chamber of Commerce in France had sent a message of support for the Concorde to Governor Carey in New York, to which the governor had replied with a terse reaffirmation of his opposition. George Ras of the Bordeaux newspaper *Sud-Ouest* then consulted the American embassy in Paris on the possibility of a letter-writing campaign to influence the New York decision. "We told him embassy was certainly not in position to counsel him or other French interests on means of bringing pressure to bear on U.S. authorities," Ambassador Rush properly noted—but the embassy could make some general observations. French citizens were not the constituents of elected or appointed authorities of New York State, and all the letters from France would be expected to be pro-Concorde anyway. The ambassador concluded by advising Washington:

> Comment: The write-in campaign that has now been launched reflects the frustrations of Concorde supporters among French public opinion. In the face of a situation at New York that they deplore, that they cannot fully comprehend, and that they have been powerless thus far to influence in any decisive fashion, they must do something. Doing anything is better than doing nothing. We have no illusions that the write-in campaign, even if the volume of responses is really overwhelming, is going to influence anyone in New York. There is, however, the danger that if the New York decision is negative next month after *Sud-Ouest* and the other newspapers have helped the populace to get a good head of steam up over Concorde, then the counter-reaction in France could be just that much worse. Hell has no fury like a woman scorned. Rush.

THE BATTLE FOR NEW YORK | 10

The Coleman decision had enabled British Airways and Air France to begin supersonic services to Washington with little delay, since Dulles Airport was operated by the Federal Aviation Administration. But Kennedy Airport was operated by the Port Authority of New York and New Jersey, and the port authority chose to delay Concorde services there very much indeed. Though the reason was simple—politically, the authority did not wish to appear to be imposing more aircraft noise on the long-suffering residents of New York City—the legal issues were complex. One of the key questions concerned an issue that went back to the founding of the republic 200 years before: whether a federal decision should overrule, or preempt, a state or local one. William Coleman had been careful in the wording of his decision to leave this question open.

Another key issue with historical resonance was the division along national lines within the Concorde team over the best strategy to adopt in order to win the day. The battle for New York was just as much a battle between the French and the British as it was a battle with the port authority, suggests William C. Clarke, British Airways' U.S. counsel at the time.[1] Clarke was an outspoken hawk, arguing for immediate litigation rather than further lobbying, in the joint strategy meetings that were periodically held in the rotunda at the British embassy in Washington.

> The British and French sides of the Concorde team had serious differences about how to proceed. The French, following the advice of the former Senator Charles Goodell and his lobbying team at DGA International, did not want to force action

119

by the port authority, arguing that we should take more time in reasoning with them and, especially, trying to bring political pressure to bear on them from federal and state government officials. They did not want to precipitate a negative decision by the port authority, and they did not want to risk losing a law suit. This strategy seemed to me (and to our lawyers, British Airways management, and eventually the whole British side of the team) to be fundamentally flawed.

Clarke's reasoning ran as follows. In the Coleman decision the federal government had done as much as it was going to do on the Concorde approval issue. Neither Gerald Ford nor Jimmy Carter would risk offending voters in the key state of New York. And since the federal government had so far escaped any liability in airport noise litigation, there was an ingrained bureaucratic inclination in the FAA and DOT not to interfere on that issue. Among the active Concorde opponents were Governor Hugh Carey of New York, leaders of the state legislature, and the mayor and city council of New York City. The port authority was not going to oppose the state governor on a question affecting a New York airport, particularly as it was the airport proprietor who would be liable to noise damage claims. The governor of New Jersey, though well enough disposed toward the Concorde, would not interfere in a matter that primarily affected New York. Opposition to the Concorde was a no-cost option for the politicians and for the port authority.

None of that was likely to change in the foreseeable future without some external stimulus. Fortunately such a stimulus was at hand, in the form of litigation, a time-honored way of breaking political gridlock in the United States. A federal judge's decision could let public officials off the hook. The port authority could face no possible liability for noise damage—and its political masters could face little criticism—for obeying a court order, hence the British conclusion that the route through the courts was the one to take. A cynic might have speculated, and some did, that the French preference for continued lobbying might have been inspired by the mercenary instincts of their lobbyist advisers. William Clarke's theory is that "it was simply incomprehensible to the Gallic mind that a lone district court judge sitting in lower Manhattan could cut right through an issue that the president of the United States and the governors of New York and New Jersey, not to mention the U.S. Congress and the two state legislatures, were unwilling or unable to resolve."

The Port Authority Ban

"RESOLVED, that the Port Authority deny permission to operate any supersonic aircraft, including the Concorde, at Kennedy International Airport, until after at least six months of operating experience has been evaluated, after a report on such experience has been made to the Board and pending further action thereon by the Board." This resolution by the port authority board, passed on 11 March 1976, triggered the long and costly process of gaining access for the Concorde to New York.[2] The authority's noise limit for Kennedy was 112 perceived noise decibels (PNdB), and the board knew that the two airlines claimed that the Concorde could meet that requirement. But the board was concerned about the Concorde's low-frequency noise and the "expected aggravated community response" to it. Also, New York governor Hugh Carey had signed proposed legislation that would direct the port authority to refuse entry. (For this direction to take effect, concurrent legislation by the state of New Jersey was required.) The port authority board directed its aviation director to analyze six months of Concorde operations at Dulles, Heathrow, and Charles de Gaulle Airport in Paris.

The ban had been triggered by a decision by the Concorde team, made at a strategy meeting following the Coleman decision, to advise the port authority that British Airways and Air France intended to begin Concorde service to Kennedy Airport on 10 April 1976. The aim was to force the authority to act and, if landing rights were denied, immediately to challenge that action in the federal district court. Accordingly, a letter from the airlines was delivered to the port authority board for consideration at its 11 March meeting, whereupon the board responded by adopting the resolution to ban.

In challenging the ban, the immediate legal action taken by the airlines was less than wholehearted. At French insistence, it was agreed that the lawyers would initially file only a bare complaint, seeking a declaratory judgment and an injunction. They would not take the normal actions that would lead to a prompt decision, such as seeking a summary judgment. In effect, this was no more than a legal warning shot across the bow of the port authority, as the political advisers continued to pursue their persuasive arts. This warning shot was fired on 17 March 1976, when the two airlines filed their complaint in the district court and the matter was assigned to Judge Milton Pollack. More than a year passed before the case came before Judge Pollack—by which time the United States had a new president, Jimmy Carter, and a new secretary of transportation, Brock Adams.

The event that appeared to trigger the court case was the port authority's reaction to a telegram sent on 7 March 1977—three days before the authority was due to make its final decision on the Concorde—by Charles Goodell on behalf of the French minister of transport.[3] "The airlines reaffirm in the strongest possible way that it has been indisputably demonstrated by the manufacturers' tests at Toulouse and Casablanca that Concorde can meet the Port Authority noise regulations for operations at Kennedy Airport as they are applied to all other aircraft," Goodell began. The airlines believed that the noise impact could be further reduced by concentrating their takeoff operations on runways 31L and 22R, at weights significantly lower than maximum, and stood ready to discuss these new procedures further with the authority.

The port authority's immediate response was to announce the indefinite postponement of its Concorde decision, ostensibly to allow further consideration of the proposed new noise-abatement procedures.[4] Goodell's response to this response was to send another telegram, declaring, "We cannot accept any further postponement of a decision. . . . This is an issue of monumental importance to the French Government and the French people. . . . The Port Authority has available to it all the evidence necessary to make a decision at its meeting on Thursday, March 10. If the issue of Concorde landing rights is not decided, we will have no alternative but to pursue the matter in U.S. District Court on March 15 and we intend to do so. . . . Our patience has run out."[5] As will soon become clear, it was not only Senator Goodell's patience with the port authority that had run out; also expired was British Airways' patience with Senator Goodell.

Concorde 1

The Concorde's legal fight for New York rights was a four-round event. Four court cases were needed to dissect and decide the complex legal issues involved—two district court cases, known colloquially as Concorde 1 and Concorde 2, each followed by an appeal. The sequence began on 11 May 1977 before District Judge Milton Pollack.[6] British Airways and Air France claimed that the port authority ban conflicted with international treaties and agreements and illegally invaded an area of regulation that was preempted by the federal government, and they asked the court to declare the ban invalid. The port authority asserted that in the absence of a specifically stated federal preemption, it had the right to investigate the noise of the Concorde at Kennedy and in the meantime to exclude the aircraft from operating there.

The case raised a straightforward question of federal supremacy, Judge Pollack ruled. A 1968 addition to the 1958 Federal Aviation Act established the federal government's responsibility for noise abatement, though the FAA could delegate authority to regulate noise to local airport proprietors. Actions taken under this local authority were subject to any overriding federal action, must not impose an undue burden on interstate or foreign commerce, and must not unjustly discriminate between different categories of airport users. Since 1951 the port authority had had a regulation stating that no jet aircraft should land at Kennedy without permission. The Department of Transportation had considered but had rejected full federal preemption of aviation noise abatement, believing that the control of aircraft noise must remain a shared responsibility among airport proprietors, airport users, and governments. Though the airport proprietors were in the best position to assess a local noise problem and to determine how to respond to it, they were not always in the best position to judge the effect of a noise reduction proposal on national and international air transport systems. The federal government was obliged to ensure that airport actions to meet local needs did not conflict with national and international purposes. Federal action would, under the supremacy clause of the American Constitution, invalidate local action where the two schemes of regulation were in conflict. So, was there a conflict between the Coleman decision and the port authority resolution banning the Concorde?

Judge Pollack reviewed the statutory aspects of the Coleman decision in detail. The secretary certainly had statutory authority for his decision, and it was not necessary for him to state specifically that he was preempting any regulation of the port authority (whose only avowed noise regulation was the one requiring the permission of the authority for jet aircraft to land at Kennedy). The subject of the port authority resolution was noise around Kennedy, and the authority had stated that its role was limited to the question of whether the Concorde could meet the Kennedy noise criteria. The secretary had concluded that noise and other environmental impacts were not significant reasons for denying limited operations, that the environmental cost was outweighed by the benefits that would accrue to the American people from observing at first hand the application of the technology and obtaining actual noise data during the trial period.

Self-evidently, Judge Pollack concluded, the port authority resolution conflicted with the federal decision, and so the resolution must give way under the supremacy clause of the Constitution. The port authority resolution was void, and the two airlines were entitled to the injunction they had sought. The judge added that the other ground on which the airlines had argued their case—that of conflict with international treaties and agreements—was not relevant since the proposed services were "experimental tests."

Thus, in the first round of their fight through the courts, British Airways and Air France won on a principle that had been spelled out in the American Constitution. Judge Pollack had ruled in their favor because an authorized federal decision—the Coleman decision—overruled a conflicting decision by an airport proprietor—the Port Authority of New York and New Jersey. But the judge had not accepted the airlines' contention that international agreements applied to the proposed services. Back in the two airline offices, the general managers celebrated in stereotypical style (if the front page of the *New York Times* was to be believed): Roderick Wilson of British Airways with a cup of tea, and Antoine Girot of Air France with a bottle of Moët et Chandon champagne. Their joy was premature.

Concorde 1 Appeal

The port authority's appeal against Judge Pollack's decision, heard at the beginning of June, introduced a new factor into the case—not because of anything the plaintiffs or the defendants said, but because of a point made in an amicus curiae ("friend of the court") brief submitted for the United States by the acting assistant attorney general. Amicus statements may be made by anyone with an interest in the subject of the case; they were filed on this occasion for Friends of the Earth and other organizations, the British government, the French government, New York state, California, the town of Hempstead and other municipalities, and individuals. But the amicus brief for the United States had been requested by Chief Judge Irving R. Kaufman, and it was to prove a turning point in the Concorde approval process.

Fifty years ago, Judge Kaufman recalled, Charles Lindbergh had crossed the Atlantic to Paris in the *Spirit of St. Louis* in thirty-three and a half hours.[7] Now, as the result of an expensive joint venture, France and Britain offered a return voyage of only one-tenth that time. Unfortunately, instead of engendering closer ties, the Anglo-French Concorde had thrown traditionally staunch allies into legal warfare. "As in so many cases in which a political solution is preferable," he added pointedly, "the parties find themselves in a court of law."

The port authority took pride in its tradition of noise regulation. The two airlines claimed that the Concorde could meet the Kennedy standard and sought to prove this in actual operation there. The Coleman decision had recognized the right of the port authority to refuse landing rights to the Concorde. Secretary Coleman, his successor Brock Adams, and President Carter had all affirmed that the Coleman decision did not preempt the port authority's right to exclude the Concorde on the basis of a reasonable, nondiscriminatory noise regulation. "We need not tarry long over the issue that heretofore has occupied center stage in this litigation," Judge Kaufman went on. Judge Pollack's argument that the Coleman decision preempted the conflicting exercise of power by the port authority was "untenable and erroneous." The Coleman decision was never intended to deprive the port authority of the right to impose reasonable noise regulations for the use of Kennedy by the Concorde.

However, an associated point was raised for the first time in the amicus brief: whether the port authority's delay in evaluating the Concorde's operating experience and in taking further action was reasonable. Thirteen months had elapsed since Concorde operations began at Dulles. "Implicit in the federal scheme of noise regulation, which accords to local airport proprietors the critical responsibility for controlling permissible noise levels in the vicinity of their airports, is the assumption that this responsibility will be exercised in a fair, reasonable and non-discriminatory manner." But that point was not a matter for the appeals court, as the district court had not considered it.

(The amicus brief for the United States, after arguing that there had been no federal preemption, stated, "However, we do believe that the Port Authority is obligated to conduct its proprietary determinations in a reasonable manner and one that is not unfair or discriminatory. There is evidence that this is not the case. Specifically, the Port Authority has ignored its own resolution of March 11, 1976, to assess and report in a timely fashion upon Concorde noise as that data became available from operations elsewhere. Also, it has given no reason why the Concorde is not acceptable under standards generally applicable to other aircraft operating at Kennedy."[8] The brief concluded, "The Port Authority may have exercised its proprietary powers in such a manner that its ban against the Concorde could not survive judicial scrutiny. We believe its actions have been unfair, dilatory, arbitrary and unreasonable.")

The regulation of aircraft noise had traditionally been a cooperative enterprise, Judge Kaufman continued, involving both federal authorities and local airport proprietors. But the scope of the port authority in this enterprise was limited: the authority's power was simply to promulgate reasonable, nonarbitrary, and nondiscriminatory regulations to establish acceptable noise levels. The port authority accepted that its power to set noise rules was subject to the proviso that the rules must be reasonable.

Also, U.S. treaty obligations were relevant. Equal treatment of domestic and foreign air commerce was the touchstone of the complex network of agreements regulating international aeronautical traffic, of which the United States was a major beneficiary. The two airlines argued that the port authority's ban was not a valid and enforceable regulation under the bilateral agreements; it was an ad hoc measure directed solely against them and preventing them from demonstrating that the Concorde was environmentally acceptable. If the ban were to be found arbitrary and capricious, it would raise the serious question of its compatibility with American treaty arrangements.

So, the result of the appeal was a reversal of Judge Pollack's ruling that the port authority ban was preempted by the Coleman decision, but a new question—whether the 13-month delay in promulgating reasonable SST regulations represented unfair discrimination—was passed back to the district court to decide. Chief Judge Kaufman was in no doubt about the urgency of the matter. While appreciating the pressures that had been brought to bear on the authority by the interested governments, the state of New York, and segments of the public, he urged the port authority to "conclude its study and fix reasonable noise standards with dispatch."

Concorde 2

In August, the district court's reappraisal of the port authority ban concentrated on the detail of the authority's actions rather than on general principles.[9] What emerged was a damning account of time-wasting and inconsistency in dealing with the Concorde question. The court ruled in favor of the airlines, on the basis of the following findings as outlined by Judge Pollack.

In essence, the port authority's avowed purpose in imposing its ban was to have an opportunity to set noise standards that would apply to supersonic transports. It had not done so. Instead, the ban had been extended indefinitely, ostensibly to permit further research and analysis. The scope of the further studies was nebulous, and nothing had been undertaken or funded. Meanwhile, the Concorde was being deprived of a chance to prove itself environmentally acceptable at Kennedy.

The court went into some detail on the characteristics and measurement of aircraft noise. Psychoacoustic measures such as perceived noise decibels took into account the different perceived noisiness of different frequencies. Measurements in effective perceived noise decibels reflected both the frequencies and the duration of the sound. Such levels could be plotted as noise contours around a specific airport to show an aircraft's noise "footprint," so enabling comparisons to be made of the relative effects of different types of aircraft. These so-called single-event measures represented the noise made by a single takeoff or landing, but a further measure could be applied to indicate the noise experienced over a 24-hour period. One such measure was known as the noise exposure forecast (NEF). NEF contours enabled the incremental effect of additional noise—such as that caused by four Concorde flights a day at Kennedy—to be seen in relation to the existing level of noise at that airport.

At the time of the authority's ban, the FAA's final environmental impact statement had presented single-event and NEF contours, which gave a comprehensive picture of the likely noise impact of the Concorde at Kennedy Airport. The EIS also covered likely vibration effects. Thus a vast quantity of relevant scientific data was available. Since then, the port authority had employed two consultants—Dr. Karl Kryter of Stanford Research Institute, a psychoacoustic expert, to assess the validity of the EIS; and Dr. Aubrey McKennell, a British social psychologist, to survey the reactions of people living near Heathrow Airport. Kryter had taken measurements and recordings at Kennedy, Dulles, Heathrow, and Charles de

Gaulle airports and had developed a "vibration rattle index," which could relate low-frequency vibration to noise levels. But there remained the problem of "additivity"—how could the combined annoyance of noise plus vibration be calculated and compared for different aircraft? In February 1977, he told the authority, it could not; further research was needed.

On 7 March 1977, the airlines requested permission to present to the port authority new Concorde operating procedures, designed to reduce the aircraft's noise impact at Kennedy. This caused the authority to delay further a decision on the Concorde. On 1 April the British and French airlines and aircraft manufacturers submitted a written report on the new procedures and their predicted effect, including NEF contours showing almost identical noise footprints for the Concorde and the Boeing 707-320B. At the request of the port authority, BAC and Aérospatiale sought FAA confirmation that the report was technically valid.[10] On 14 April the FAA confirmed that the Anglo-French analysis was technically sound and that, if the assumptions were borne out in practice, the indicated noise reductions would be realized.[11]

Kryter apparently was assigned to assess the impact of the new procedures. On 7 July he presented his final report to the port authority board, but there was some uncertainty about the assessment. The board reviewed the reports of the two consultants; according to the minutes of the meeting, the reports showed that the proposed Concorde operations could be expected to result in "significant annoyance and complaint activity." A vibration rattle index was being further studied, but more research and analysis were needed. Thus the board resolved to continue in force the ban on Concorde operations at Kennedy.

Judge Pollack went on to summarize the port authority's activity since March 1976. The authority had been "re-ploughing old ground and doing re-reviews of scientific and theoretical data previously available." Its consultants had undertaken vibration tests at Dulles and Kennedy airports and community-response tests at Heathrow. It had had monthly federal reports on Concorde operations at Dulles and reports of the NASA vibration studies. These reports had yielded no index by which vibration could be measured as additive or unique in terms of the noise spectrum. The port authority had confirmed that the Concorde could meet the 112 PNdB noise regulation at Kennedy. It had no evidence that the community effects of the limited test operations as federally authorized were rationally unacceptable or that the operations would appreciably worsen present conditions. Secretary Coleman had found that low-frequency vibrations would be slight, brief, and barely perceptible, presenting no danger of structural damage and little possibility of annoyance. The research that Kryter and McKennell undertook for the port authority appeared to be redundant and irrelevant.

The conclusion is inescapable from the evidence presented to the Court, and the Court finds that the Port Authority has no intention of taking the responsibility of setting the present or another noise standard applicable to the Concorde. Its failure and excessive delay in doing so are unreasonable, discriminatory and unfair and an impingement on commerce and on the national and international interests of the United States.

Under the circumstances, Judge Pollack concluded, the ban on the Concorde's transatlantic services at Kennedy was an undue interference with the achievement of congressional and national objectives. The airlines were entitled to proceed at Kennedy under the existing regulations. The port authority regulations of 11 March 1976 and 7 July 1977 were unlawful and void. That appeared to be clear enough: the 17-month delay by the port authority was unreasonable, discriminatory, and unfair. It was not at all clear to the port authority, however, whose chairman, Alan Sagner, promptly declared the authority's intention to appeal the decision.[12]

Concorde 2 Appeal

Between the arguments before the appeals court trio of Chief Judge Kaufman and Judges Walter R. Mansfield and Ellsworth A. Van Graafeiland on 19 September 1977 and their decision ten days later,[13] the Carter administration published a notice of proposed rule-making for the operation of supersonic transport aircraft. Transportation Secretary Brock Adams announced also that pending the issuance of permanent SST noise regulations, the Concorde operations at Dulles would be allowed to continue. The administration continued to support also the proposed trial Concorde services into Kennedy Airport, subject to court action. Giving his decision in the appeals court, Chief Judge Kaufman was highly critical of the port authority.

Reviewing the facts of the case, Kaufman noted that the port authority had been advised over seven years previously that Concorde services were desired at Kennedy. The director of aviation had replied that SSTs would "be required to meet the same noise levels as will be demanded of subsonic aircraft." The Concorde manufacturers were well aware that its noise posed a serious problem, and had spent almost $100 million on noise abatement. Tests had shown that the aircraft could consistently meet a standard of 109 PNdB. NEF contours considered by former secretary Coleman had indicated that the impact of the proposed Concorde services would be negligible, but he recognized that a testing period of actual Concorde operations was necessary; raw data alone could not forecast community response. "The 16-month demonstration ordered by Coleman was thus a crucible in which to assay the subjective attitudes of airport neighbors and our willingness to fairly assess the issue of supersonic transportation."

While technicians strove to project scientifically the community response to Concorde noise, Judge Kaufman commented, local leaders on the political scene lobbied to prevent the aircraft's use of Kennedy. At the Coleman hearing and again before the port authority's operations committee, New York state commissioner Raymond Schuler conveyed Governor Carey's unqualified opposition to the Concorde. The impact of these actions on the port authority commissioners was not known, but the authority's ban followed soon thereafter.

When the authority's consultants reported in March 1977, Kryter noted the unsolved additivity problem, but the port authority refused to fund any further research on it. "Thus it is not at all clear to us how the port authority intends to solve this additivity dilemma, if indeed it ever expects or wants to do so," the chief judge noted. McKennell reported that his Heathrow study on the whole was inconclusive. Although the port authority's March 1976 ban had been set to apply for up to six months, the authority ultimately established 10 March 1977 as the date by which it would reach a definitive decision. Much relevant information was available by that date, but the authority had responded to the airlines' further submission by postponing a decision until "a later date." No wonder the airlines told the port authority their patience had run out.

Tracing the port authority's response to the Concorde 1 case, Chief Judge Kaufman recalled that on 7 July the authority had indefinitely extended the "temporary" ban imposed 16 months earlier. The authority had now grasped another excuse for nonaction; it would await a final federal compilation of Concorde data, due in late September. This was puzzling in light of the authority's repeated rejection of earlier federal studies favorable to the aircraft. Even more perplexing, since the work of its consultants had ceased four months earlier, was the authority's statement that "a vibration rattle index is being further studied." On 15 September Transportation Secretary Adams declared that it was unnecessary to define a vibration-rattle index before taking regulatory action on new noise standards and indeed had reported that the Concorde vibrations were no greater than those induced by such subsonic aircraft as the Boeing 747 and the Douglas DC-10, both of which had been flying into Kennedy for several years with no apparent rattle problem. Thus the 23 September decision that the existing 16 Concordes could fly into 13 U.S. cities, including New York, involved no further vibration research. The chief judge continued:

> The law simply will not tolerate the denial of rights by unwarranted official inaction. . . . If ever there was a case in which a major technological advance was in im-

minent danger of being studied into obsolescence, this is it. There comes a time when relegating the solution of an issue to the indefinite future can so sap petitioners of hope and resources that a failure to resolve the issue within a reasonable period is tantamount to refusing to address it at all. The same is true of studying the question in such a manner that the issue will disappear by sheer frustration or the assumption by another institution—in this case the courts—of the task of deciding a charged dispute whose resolution otherwise is the duty of the agency. The hour is at hand for the Port Authority's indefinite ban on Concorde flights to be recognized as an abdication of responsibility. The airlines should no longer be forced to suffer the consequences of such illegal delay.

The appeals court had urged in the Concorde 1 case that the port authority expeditiously establish reasonable, nonarbitrary, and nondiscriminatory noise regulations at Kennedy. "This it has not done. Rather, the Port Authority has steadfastly refused to accord landing rights to an airplane that is capable of meeting the rule that has consistently been applied to all other aircraft for nearly 20 years—112 PNdB." Accordingly, the chief judge ruled, the court confirmed the order of the district court in dissolving the port authority's ban—but left it open for the authority to adopt a new, uniform, and reasonable noise standard in the future.

Not every point in the chief judge's announced decision was unanimously agreed. In a minority comment, Judge Mansfield agreed with the main ruling, to confirm the abolition of the port authority's ban. But he could not agree with his colleagues that the port authority had acted in bad faith. He agreed that a continued ban could not be justified—not because the authority was at fault but because "there comes a time when the hourglass runs out and even a public agency must 'fish or cut bait.' That time has now passed."

The port authority was not convinced. In a last-ditch attempt to postpone fishing a while longer, the authority appealed to the U.S. Supreme Court to allow the ban to remain. The Supreme Court refused.[14] The port authority announced that Chairman Alan Sagner had expressed "extreme disappointment" at the news.[15] The authority's obligation to develop and promulgate new noise regulations remained, he said, despite the Supreme Court's decision. The Supreme Court decision finally cleared the way for Concorde services to New York to begin, which they did on 22 November 1977.

Discord in the Concorde Camp

Though the Anglo-French team had presented a united front in public in arguing the Concorde case, there was a sharp division of opinion behind the scenes between the British and the French on how the task should be tackled. As noted earlier, the British side, in particular British Airways, favored the route through the courts, while the French put their trust and much money into a substantial campaign of public relations and political lobbying. The long delay in coming to court in New York reflected this dichotomy. Gordon Davidson, British Airways Concorde director at the time, recalls, "We in British Airways said right from the start the only way to achieve success was to do what any domestic U.S. airline would have done and take the matter to court. The French did not agree. They felt that high-powered diplomatic action up to presidential level was needed to see the way clear."[16]

Captain Brian Calvert of British Airways, in his book published in 1981, revealed that Senator Goodell's approach (the so-called Goodell initiative) to present new procedures to the port authority in March 1977 had been made without consulting British Airways, "who were horrified by the whole business."[17] This led to "some acrimonious discussions" between the two national groups, but it did, finally, produce a resolution of their disagreements—not only a resolution but also a bluntly enforced deal, according to Gordon Davidson. Again referring to the Goodell approach, the former Concorde director comments:

> Since we did not support this proposal, and Goodell had not obtained my approval to include British Airways in the request, we had finally acquired the necessary leverage to impel the French into court alongside us. In brief, to avoid embarrassment, we attended the port authority presentation on condition that the French would come to court.

Accordingly, when the Goodell initiative failed to produce any action, Air France agreed to join British Airways in filing a motion for summary judgment, leading to the series of court cases.

This example of lack of communication between the U.S. legal adviser to the French government and the British airline, leading to the bizarre contretemps described above, serves to illustrate also a wider, continuing problem faced by the Anglo-French team. As mentioned, there were many players on this team, and the problem was to accommodate and coordinate their various aims and activities. There was a general suspicion on the British side of the French public relations efforts, though individual British officials speak highly of DGA and its people. To such questions as "Who was in charge?" and "How was the effort coordinated?" different participants give different answers.

Back home in Britain and France, the strategic decisions for the Concorde program, including the moves to gain U.S. approval, were made by the Anglo-French

Concorde Management Board, and so were joint decisions. But in fighting the battle in the United States, it was logical for cultural and language reasons that the British should take the lead. Indeed, Ken Binning recalls, "It was actually agreed as a formal minute, which said that the Brits take the lead in the U.S. and that the co-ordinating responsibility is with the British director general, Concorde."[18] Binning describes Sandy Gordon-Cumming, the civil aviation counselor at the British embassy, as his chief of staff. "He would put together something that looked like the next tactical move. It was my job to get it cleared with the French— and with many of the Brits, because the technical arguments that were being produced were arguments which had implications for other aspects of government. And Sandy worked hand in glove with Chick Carroll of DGA."

Binning and his French opposite number, Gérard Guibé, were alternating chairmen of the Concorde Management Board, which was at the same time struggling among other things to ensure that the two countries picked up equal shares of the total Concorde costs. Binning speaks highly of the contribution made in the United States by Michel Lagorce, Guibé's right-hand man, and by Léonce Lansalot-Basou of the French embassy. For the British Foreign Office, Binning points out, the main policy interest in the Concorde issue in the United States was the status of the international agreements. Another diplomatic concern was to maintain Britain's reputed special relationship with the Americans, "and the notion that we might ruffle their feathers was one about which they were very concerned."

How were the efforts of the motley crew of officials, diplomats, technicians, managers, publicists, and lawyers coordinated? "With great difficulty" appears to be the answer. The main task, in general successfully accomplished, was simply to keep in touch. Some speak of regular meetings, but the process appears to have been more a series of ad hoc attempts to inform and discuss the next step. Asked whether it was difficult to coordinate the activities, Gordon-Cumming replies, "No, it wasn't difficult. It was impossible."[19] He credits Eileen Denza of the U.K. Foreign Office as the key coordinator on the legal aspects of the campaign. Alan E. Clarke, Binning's assistant director (development), was responsible for technical aspects throughout the process, including liaison with the FAA and the port authority. The close working relationship that developed between Gordon-Cumming and his opposite number at the French embassy, Lansalot-Basou, was a critical factor in helping to ease the frictions that arose.

Sir Gordon Booth, British consul general in New York, recalls vividly the problems caused by the large number of players— "a cast of thousands"—on the Concorde team.[20] "It could not be assumed that if there was a rope which appeared to be the one on which you were pulling, everybody had his hand on that rope. The agenda was not necessarily the same for everybody the whole time, and because of

the large size of the cast it became an infernally complicated process to make anything move." As New York became the focus of the battle, it became clear that
some form of coordinating mechanism was required. A group was set up to address
this need. Known as the Concorde Committee for New York, it was chaired by Sir
Gordon.

Leo Schefer, former head of public relations at BAC (U.S.A.), spells out the basic difference in the French and British approaches, as he saw it at the time:

> Basically the British approached it on the basis of technical fact and stayed away
> from politics, and said we've got a treaty on these issues, that's the way to go. The
> French said this is Washington and we'll go buy the Congress, and they set out to do
> it that way, and we all had to work together. And they rolled around in limousines
> and we rolled around in compact cars. I believe the British government were at first
> embarrassed by the French consultants and then enamored of them. We felt the
> French spent far too much money, and indeed their overzealous lobbying became
> an embarrassment once or twice. But, in terms of working the system and helping
> to smooth the way, I think the consultants were very helpful.[21]

Also helpful was the generally open attitude of the U.S. administration, which led
to effective informal contacts. The British embassy in Washington, for example,
had its own Deep Throat informant at senior level in the Department of Transportation. No deal was, nor could have been, concluded via this channel, but it
suited both sides to exchange confidential information on the various moves that
were afoot.

As for what might be termed the out-of-court case of *Air France* v *British Airways*
(fought largely in the British embassy rotunda in Washington), which preceded the
case of *Air France and British Airways* v *the Port Authority of New York and New Jersey*
(fought in the U.S. District Court for the Southern District of New York and the
U.S. Court of Appeals for the Second Circuit), William Clarke offers a wry
comment:

> In five months from the time the airlines finally got around to filing their summary
> judgment motion, the matter was fully and favorably resolved in the courts. I could
> say "I told you so," but my friends on the French side would probably counter that
> the port authority's unconscionable delay was the winning argument in the end.
> And I do have to credit them with doing so very much to facilitate that delay—a
> brilliant strategy they no doubt had in mind all along.[22]

Also, he recalls, another aspect of the legal battle concerned the port authority's
handling of the matter. At the time, it was suggested that this was so pathetically in-
ept as to constitute taking a dive in the federal court. There's devious.

11 | THROUGH THE POLITICAL SOUND BARRIER

The orderly progress of the Concorde issue through the courts had not been taking place in a vacuum. Outside the courts, the proponents and opponents of the Anglo-French SST were not sitting back quietly and awaiting the outcome. Throughout 1977, they continued to fight a somewhat disorderly battle in which the leaders of the opposing armies, as depicted in the steady stream of press reports of the many engagements, appeared to be New York governor Hugh Carey and French president Valéry Giscard d'Estaing. The Concorde affair was not just a legal tussle between the French and British airlines and the Port Authority of New York and New Jersey; since the issuing of the environmental impact statement and the Coleman hearing it had grown into a headline political issue, not only in New York City but also at the state level, at the U.S. national level, and in the international arena. Also, behind the headlines, another aspect of the affair was being pursued: certification of the Concorde for U.S. airline use.

Controversy in Public . . .

The flavor of the battle for New York in 1977 is well reflected in table 4 in a brief selection from the many hundreds of engagements reported in the *New York Times*.

French Concorde supporters took their fight into the heart of enemy country; the pro-Concorde petitions reported on 13 March were delivered to Governor Carey's Manhattan office by a delegation from the Concorde Support Committee

134

Table 4

Selected News Items, 1977

Date of Publication	Event Reported in *New York Times*
January 30	Vice President Walter Mondale warns that French president expects approval*
February 3	New Jersey Senate committee votes in favor
February 10	New York Senate votes against
February 17	Concorde flights backed by Carter
March 5	Giscard calls Carter on Concorde
March 8	French parliamentary leaders plead with U.S. envoy for Concorde
March 9	Effort on Concorde pledged by Giscard
March 10	New Jersey senator urges Newark Airport for Concorde
March 12	Carter and Callaghan discuss Concorde
March 13	Carey given petitions by Concorde backers
March 14	Mayor of Newark urges Newark Airport for Concorde
March 29	Carey suggests use of Stewart Airport
April 3	Giscard warns
April 5	Carey reiterates opposition
April 6	French march down Fifth Avenue proposed
April 13	Foreigners support Queens on SST
April 17	Opponents ignore injunction in effort to mount motorcade at Kennedy
April 18	600 cars snarl traffic at Kennedy
April 23	Briton links air treaty to dispute on Concorde
May 9	Giscard deplores Concorde ban
May 10	French discuss retaliation
May 16	SST demonstrators tie up traffic at Kennedy
May 22	New York police deploy tow trucks
May 23	Turnout increases in car protest against Concorde
June 9	Congress ban attempt fails
June 28	New York Assembly says homeowners can sue
July 6	New Jersey governor says he will veto ban
July 6	Balloon protest
July 7	Philadelphia should have "bad neighbor" award for wanting Concorde, says N.J. representative
July 9	Tass accuses port authority
September 3	U.S. cabinet meeting on Concorde classified secret
September 16	French prime minister Barre tells Carter Kennedy landing rights are vital
October 10	Protesters slow traffic
October 12	Carey threatens to veto no-ban decision
October 13	Carey says Supreme Court cannot overrule him
October 18	Carey says he will abide by Supreme Court ruling, reiterates opposition to Concorde

(Continued on next page)

Table 4 *(Continued)*

Date of Publication	Event Reported in *New York Times*
November 21	250-car protest
November 23	Scheduled services to Kennedy begin
December 15	Port authority adopts noise rule that would ban Concorde from 1985, subject to veto
December 28	Governor Byrne vetoes port authority noise rule

★ "Approval," "in favor," "ban," and "against" refer to Concorde rights at Kennedy Airport.

in France. The heading to the 6 April A.P. agency report from Paris was "Allons, enfants, a la 5th Avenue": Hector Rolland, a Gaullist legislator, had called on his colleagues to join him in a march down Fifth Avenue to press for Concorde landing rights. But collaborators were active, also, as reported on 13 April. Two anti-Concorde rallies organized by local groups were to be attended by activists from Europe, including Catherine de Couan of the French Friends of the Earth and Richard Wiggs of the British Anti-Concorde Project.

July, as reported in the *New York Times,* was a particularly interesting month. On 6 July a photograph carried the caption

> A stuntman hanging from a balloon piloted by Ronald Di Giovanni during a flight over Queens yesterday protesting landings by the Concorde SST at Kennedy Airport. Mr. Di Giovanni and Jerry Hewitt, the stuntman, took off at about 8 a.m. near Flushing Airport and were chased by police helicopter to St. John's University, where they landed in the football field. Mr. Di Giovanni was issued summonses for unauthorized landing, unauthorized advertising (a "Ban the SST" poster hung from the balloon), flying over congested areas and reckless endangerment. Mr. Di Giovanni was cited for a similar flight in December.

On 7 July the paper reported that Representative James J. Florio of New Jersey had called Mayor Frank Rizzo of Philadelphia "a prime candidate for the bad neighbor of the year award" for suggesting the Concorde should land at Philadelphia International Airport. On 9 July the news was that Tass, the Soviet press agency, had entered the fray, accusing the port authority and "influential American circles" of maintaining a "deliberately hostile, discriminatory and intolerable attitude towards the Concorde."

The French president's many blunt expressions of his country's forthright views on U.S. approval contrasted sharply with the understated public utterances of the British, at times so understated as to be virtually inaudible. This was but one example of the national differences characterizing the joint Anglo-French promotion of the Concorde in the United States. In a magazine interview, Giscard d'Estaing said that serious damage had already been done; America's "fierce resistance against a limited European technological breakthrough" appeared to be quite out of proportion.[1] The role of New York authorities was not the issue; "There comes a time when political leaders must see the issues on a loftier level." A permanent negative decision, the French president warned, would trigger a reaction. "I am not brandishing any threats," he concluded, "but no country can accept passively what it regards as a violation of its rights."

. . . And on Capitol Hill

A simple, authoritative answer—"No"—to the question of whether the Concorde should be allowed to land at Dulles and Kennedy could have come from the United States Congress. Representatives and senators on Capitol Hill could have passed a law to deny the aircraft access to the United States. They had cut off funds for the American SST in 1971 and had since passed legislation prohibiting commercial supersonic flight over the United States. They never did enact a permanent ban on the Concorde, but several attempts were made to introduce legislation that would have had the same effect. Among a number of bills introduced in 1975 were identical ones by Senator William Proxmire and Representative Lester L. Wolff, which would have prohibited Concorde landings unless the aircraft complied with the FAR-36 noise standards. This it clearly could not do. No congressional action was taken on those bills, but in July 1975, during the House passage of the appropriations bill for the Department of Transportation, Representative Sidney R. Yates proffered an ingenious amendment. It would have prevented the use of FAA funds for air traffic control of supersonic aircraft that did not comply with the subsonic noise standards. A nice try, but the amendment was rejected by 214 votes to 196. In the Senate, a similar amendment by Birch Bayh also was rejected, but by a majority of only 2 votes, 46 to 44.

The first successful attempt in either chamber to deny landing rights to the Concorde came in December 1975, during passage of routine legislation to extend federal aid to airports and other aviation projects. After a failed attempt in committee to deny funds to any airport accepting any civil supersonic transport that exceeded the FAR-36 noise standards, the House of Representatives accepted an amendment to the airport aid bill unequivocally banning all supersonic transport aircraft from U.S. airports (except the federally owned Dulles) for six months. Originally the period of the ban had been a full year, but it was reduced in the light of Secretary Coleman's promise of a decision on the Concorde by the following February. The amendment passed by 199 votes to 188 in the House but later was rejected by the Senate.

In February 1976, Congress responded immediately to the Coleman decision. One day after the transportation secretary had announced his approval of Concorde services on a trial basis, attempts to overturn his decision were rejected by the Senate Commerce Committee. Discussing the airport aid bill, the committee first rejected (14 votes to 4) an amendment to ban the Concorde until it could meet the FAA noise standards, and then went on to reject, by the narrowest of majorities (10 votes to 9), an amendment to ban the aircraft altogether. (Also in February, the committee called Secretary Coleman to testify at an SST oversight hearing, as did the House Committee on Government Operations.)[2] The following month, three anti-Concorde amendments to the airport aid bill were easily defeated. In passing the bill, the Senate also rejected the House-passed ban on Concorde landings in the United States. Later that year, further anti-Concorde amendments were rejected as Congress passed the transportation appropriations bill. The following year, renewed anti-Concorde amendments were rejected even more decisively during passage of transportation appropriations. At that time, the fate of the Concorde in the United States already was being decided not in Congress but in the courts.

Airworthiness

In parallel with the airlines' struggle to obtain approval for Concorde flights to the United States, a rather more orderly if protracted process was under way to obtain another type of approval. This was the issuance of an American "type certificate" for the aircraft. While the French and British national certificates of airworthiness for the Concorde enabled the two national airlines to operate the aircraft, an American type certificate, issued by the FAA, was required before any U.S. airline could do the same. The long path to U.S. approval of Concorde airworthiness went through three stages: early informal transatlantic discussions, an attempt to agree on standards of airworthiness that would apply both to the Concorde and to the U.S. supersonic transport, and the final, formal, type-certificate procedure.

Anglo-American talks on safety aspects of supersonic transports had begun even before the launch of the Concorde project. In April 1961, at the request of the British Air Registration Board (ARB), officials of the board met with FAA staff in Washington to discuss potential problem areas.[3] Since design features of the aircraft were unknown at that time, only general discussion was possible. Once the Anglo-French agreement to develop a supersonic transport had been signed, Sud and BAC lost no time in considering airworthiness certification, both to coordinate British and French requirements and to plan how U.S. certification should be tackled. In December 1962 in Paris, the SST committee of directors of the two companies decided first to agree on a joint Franco-British approach on regulations, after which discussion with the FAA should begin.[4] In the meantime, contact with the FAA should be maintained to ensure that "nothing detrimental to us was being done."

This contact included further consideration of the sharing of information between the British Ministry of Aviation and the FAA. In January 1963 Lucian Rochte, SST program manager in the FAA, warned that care should "be exercised in selecting the specific areas for exchange of technical information," since the British officials might be able to speak for their manufacturers in making such commitments, which was not the case in the United States.[5] In April the framework of discussion was widened, with the first conference between officials of the FAA, the ARB, and the French Secrétariat Général de l'Aviation Civile (SGAC) aimed at developing international certification standards for supersonic transport aircraft.[6] Chairman of the meeting was George C. Prill, the FAA's newly appointed assistant administrator for Europe, Africa, and the Middle East. One of Prill's principal tasks in his new post, the FAA stated, was to deal with certification questions arising from the Anglo-French effort to develop the Concorde.

The pace quickened during 1964, when much effort went into two joint meetings: an Anglo-American one in Washington in March and a tripartite one in Paris in June. At the Washington meeting the supersonic transport was one of three items on the agenda.[7] Najeeb Halaby and Julian Amery cochaired the final plenary session, at which Gordon Bain reported on SST working-group discussions on the exchange of information on economic analyses, operational factors, and public reaction to sonic booms. The meeting agreed to the exchange of noncompetitive information and to a further meeting, probably in May 1964. This tripartite meeting slipped to June and was held in Paris. The purpose of the meeting, the U.S. delegation was told, was to exchange views and noncompetitive information on airworthiness, "systemworthiness," sonic boom and airport noise limitations, and operational factors.[8] The FAA had earlier identified a number of special problem areas that were likely to arise, but the agency approach to the tripartite meeting was cautious. "The delegation will refrain from indicating firm views on any of the problem areas which are to be discussed at this meeting," the team was instructed.

This instruction was indeed followed by the U.S. delegation, which was heavily outnumbered by the British and French representatives—and also somewhat overwhelmed by the volume of working papers produced for the meeting by the host partners.[9] The Paris meeting was important in marking the start of a formal program, known as FAUSST (Franco-Anglo-U.S. SST), intended to unify certification requirements on both sides of the Atlantic. Timing presented an immediate obstacle, however. From the French and British view, firm design decisions on the Concorde were now due, and a number of TSS (Transport Supersonique) "firm standards" had been drafted by the regulators, who were pressing the FAA to indicate whether the United States would accept these standards as a basis for U.S. certification. The U.S. view was that no commitment could yet be made on standards; the FAA's own tentative SST airworthiness objectives and standards had yet to be discussed with U.S. industry. A program of further cooperative action was agreed on, and the FAUSST meetings continued over the next few years.

In September 1964 an FAA team led by Administrator Halaby spent a week in England for what he described as "intensive and extensive discussions" with senior government officials and industry managers involved in the Concorde program. On their return Halaby reported a disagreement between the officials and the companies—in both countries—over the wisdom of requesting FAA type certification of the Concorde.[10] While the companies required answers on important design features, Halaby noted, the ministries were reluctant to let the FAA have free access to design information. This disagreement had been resolved by 15 July 1965, when General André Puget and Sir George Edwards on behalf of their companies signed an official application to the FAA for a type certificate for the Concorde.[11]

Though the procedures for certification were essentially technical matters—the FAA had first to establish technical requirements and then be satisfied that the aircraft could meet them—General Bozo McKee, just sworn in as the new FAA administrator, was aware of the wider political issues the formal application raised. Thus he lost little time in warning the State Department that there were a number of potentially serious problem areas ahead in the Concorde certification process.[12] The State Department, after a more detailed briefing from the FAA, spelled out the implications in a letter to Charles Cary, the agency's head of international aviation affairs:

> There is no doubt that should the Concorde fail to qualify for a United States type certificate or should there be a great delay in receiving such certificate, the ire of the British and French would be great indeed. The political repercussions which would result from a United States refusal to certificate the Concorde after its having been certificated by the British and the French aviation authorities would undoubtedly be enormous, no matter how good our technical justification for such.[13]

Thus the FAA should stay closely in touch with Concorde developments, the department added, and the British and the French should be promptly advised of any Concorde characteristics that might prevent its qualifying for a U.S. type certificate. At this stage, America's views should be stated in a low-key manner.

It was Raymond Maloy, who had succeeded George Prill as the FAA's man in Brussels, who conveyed the low-key views to the British and French regulators in February 1966.[14] "It appears that we should now begin preparation for the first meeting on the Concorde certification," he advised. The FAA's list of "possible problem areas" had grown to 23 topics: cockpit view, emergency evacuation of passengers, runway length, fuel reserves, noise abatement procedures, center-of-gravity control, controllability, crashworthiness, reliability of systems, new materials, structural loads, speed margins, de-icing, and ten specific propulsion items.

A series of type board meetings (TBMs) to discuss certification issues continued throughout 1966 and 1967, and the FAA canvassed the views of U.S. airlines holding Concorde options. But at the rollout of the first prototype Concorde at Toulouse on 11 December 1967, Pierre Satre and William Strang complained to Maloy of serious problems in the FAA certification processes. The processes themselves were not clear, and as they stood they would delay Concorde development. Maloy agreed to set up a joint meeting in Brussels just one week later with the companies, the ARB, and the SGAC to discuss the problems.[15] At the meeting, Satre argued that the production design characteristics of the Concorde were already chosen, and since the first 18 aircraft (for Air France, BOAC, and Pan American) must all be to a common standard acceptable to the FAA, it was imperative that the final FAA requirements be made known as soon as possible. The FAA in turn complained about the slow progress in issuing the Anglo-French TSS standards, which the agency needed for comparison. Both sets of standards were continually changing, Maloy noted. After a wide-ranging discussion, they agreed on a six-point statement of ground rules that defined the schedule for the approval of standards. The unwritten small print of the six-point statement was interpreted in a follow-up letter from the ARB and the SGAC to Maloy, and honor was satisfied on both sides.[16]

FAA certification of the Concorde was to prove a long, drawn-out affair. In July 1968 Maloy reported on progress, adding a caustic comment on the practical problems facing the British and French in their efforts to complete the TSS standards:

> There has been evidence of inconsistent organization, overlapping, repetition, and the ever-present problem of translating the half that are in French into English. It should be borne in mind that, on the manufacturers side, the Filton Division of the British Aircraft Corporation has not engaged in a civil transport certification pro-

gram since the Britannia program in the mid-1950s, and Sud has not been involved in a type certification since the Caravelle was certificated in 1958, thus both companies show evidence of being out of practice. . . . This confusion is being augmented by the inputs of a number of committees, airlines, IATA [International Air Transport Association], IFALPA [International Federation of Air Line Pilots Associations], plus two ministries and three airworthiness authorities.[17]

An important milestone on the road to U.S. certification was the ninth type board meeting, held in Paris in December 1968. This meeting was particularly significant, Maloy reported, since it represented the completion of first-round evaluation of the Concorde and the presentation by the FAA of the proposed basis for Concorde certification to the French and British authorities.[18] The draft "validation program document" marked the start of the legal process of obtaining U.S. certification. At that time 27 fiches (technical problems) had been closed (i.e., resolved) and 29 remained open. The Concorde was about to begin to prove its airworthiness in an exhaustive flight-test program. The Soviet Tu-144 prototype was the first SST to fly, on 31 December 1968, and Concorde prototype 001 made its first flight on 2 March 1969.

Technical meetings between the FAA and the British and French Concorde makers and regulators continued to thrash out the details of the special conditions that were to be applied before the aircraft could receive its U.S. type certificate. Along the way, development of the United States SST was dropped in March 1971, and Pan American and TWA canceled their Concorde options in January 1973. As the airworthiness negotiations continued, the Flight Simulator for Advanced Aircraft at the NASA Ames Research Center in California proved an invaluable resource in exploring the performance of the aircraft, establishing appropriate standards, and assessing flight-test methods.[19] In the latter half of the seventies, the topic of type certification of the Concorde became entwined with the problem of U.S. noise regulations for supersonic aircraft. Thus to airworthiness was added what might be called earworthiness.

Earworthiness

In its prolonged efforts in 1976 and 1977 to ban the Concorde from Kennedy Airport on the grounds of noise, the port authority was at least being consistent. As early as January 1964 the port authority's chairman had told Najeeb Halaby at the FAA that the authority was "greatly concerned" about the noise problems that could be generated by supersonic transports.[20] In March 1968, Frank E. Loy of the State Department told the assistant secretary for international affairs at the Department of Transportation, "We understand that the Concorde engines may or will be very noisy."[21] Transportation agreed with State that the aircraft would be very noisy indeed, and added, "Meanwhile, it is obvious that the noise/sonic boom question, coming ripe with the approach of an operational Concorde, is a web of technical, legal, social, economic, and political issues."[22] In one of the more piquant examples of actors in the American Concorde story whose roles changed as the story unfolded, Loy's correspondent at Transportation was Donald G. Agger, later to weave a web of his own as founder and president of DGA International, the Washington public relations firm whose deal with Aérospatiale for promoting the Concorde attracted the attention of the Justice Department.

What was to be the final phase of the Concorde U.S. certification saga began in April 1977 when the Department of Transportation issued a draft environmental impact statement, prepared by the FAA, on "noise regulation and type certification alternatives for civil supersonic aircraft." This discussed the impact of alternatives ranging from no regulation to a complete ban on SSTs. Though all the U.S. Concorde options had been dropped, Braniff International Airlines had requested permission to operate leased Concordes between Washington, D.C., and Dallas–Fort Worth, Texas. Hearings on the draft EIS—covering both the type certification and the noise regulation issues—were held in Washington, Honolulu, and Los Angeles.

Under the U.S. Federal Aviation Act, the mechanism for introducing noise regulations is the submission by the EPA of proposed regulations to the FAA, which then publishes the proposals as "notices of proposed rule-making," for comment. Such notices had been published in March 1975 and February 1976. After the FAA considered the response to the notices and to the draft EIS, together with the record of Concorde operations into Dulles, the administration's decisions on SST noise were announced by Brock Adams, secretary of transportation, on 23 September 1977.[23] A notice of proposed rule-making would be issued, he said, that was "designed to protect the health and safety of the American people, set a fair and reasonable noise standard for SST operations, and strike a balance between legitimate domestic and international interests of the United States." The main effect of the rule would be to permit the 16 Concordes already completed or being built to operate in the United States, subject to a number of conditions. Secretary Adams announced also that Concorde operations could continue at Dulles, pending final SST noise regulations, and the administration supported the proposed trial flights into Kennedy—subject to court action.

The proposed rule, together with a supplemental draft EIS, was issued the following month. Included in the EIS was an analysis of the maximum possible Concorde operations at 13 airports: in addition to Washington and New York, they were Anchorage, Boston, Dallas–Fort Worth, Honolulu, Los Angeles, Miami, Houston, Chicago, Seattle, San Francisco, and Philadelphia. Further public comment was invited, a public hearing on both documents was held in Washington in December, and the final environmental impact statement was issued in June 1978.

For the final EIS the FAA studied nine alternative actions, ranging from the banning of all civil SST operations in the United States to the issue of a Concorde type certificate without establishing any noise limits. The agency's main conclusions were that all SSTs, except Concordes flying before 1980, must meet FAR-36 Stage 2 noise limits; noise-increasing modifications to Concordes were prohibited; and operating restrictions on Concordes should be maintained. For the 16 Concordes expected to be flying by 1980, the noise limit would be simply their de facto noise levels, but their U.S. airport operations must remain within the hours of 7 a.m. to 10 p.m.

The special treatment for the Concorde was explained in the noise-rule notice (and similarly in the EIS) as follows:

> The noise levels of the Concorde, which is the only SST for which application has been made for U.S. type certificate, would be limited to the minimum noise level that is technologically practicable and economically reasonable for that airplane type. Type certification for the Concorde was initially requested in July 1965. Because there is no known technology which would reduce Concorde noise levels, the noise limit would, at this time, be the current noise levels of that airplane rather than the noise limits of Part 36 in effect on January 1, 1977 ("Stage 2 noise limits"). Any Concorde that had flight time before January 1, 1980, would be "grandfathered" for operation in the United States.[24]

All other SSTs would have to meet the FAR-36 Stage 2 noise limits in order to operate in the United States. These limits were set in December 1969, when Concorde development was well under way. (A grandfather clause serves to exempt a group from a law because of previous circumstances.) There was a precedent for the special treatment accorded to the Concorde: the first generation of subsonic jet airliners, including the Boeing 707 and the Douglas DC-8, had benefited from similar grandfather rights in a postponement of their liability to the Stage 2 limits. The more stringent limits of FAR-36 Stage 3 were set for type certification of new aircraft in March 1977.

After further hearings in late 1977 and early 1978, which elicited more than 11,000 comments, the above principles were confirmed in a final decision on SST noise regulations announced by Brock Adams in June 1978, to take effect on 31

July. Those rules still apply today. The transportation secretary summarized the thinking that had led to the final rules:

> These are strong standards. They are meant to be. The public need for noise control at our major airports has been established. The public demand for such noise control has been made evident at several public hearings and through written comments. However, the Concorde is a good faith effort by two of our steadfast allies to develop a new generation of aircraft technology. There is no evidence that this technology, as limited by these rules, poses a threat to our public health and safety—and we have found no such evidence during 16 months of testing. Therefore, in the spirit of fairness the United States is applying the same principles used when jet aircraft were first introduced by admitting these first 16 Concordes.[25]

Aircraft Noise and the Congress

As in other aspects of Concorde acceptability in the United States, the official earworthiness steps noted above were not taking place in a vacuum. It was hardly surprising that the U.S. Congress was interested, and in February 1978 the House Committee on Government Operations published a report specifically addressing "aircraft noise and the Concorde."[26] The message of the report was clearly conveyed in a number of section headings:

> –The FAA has not been aggressive or successful in forcing reductions in noise from commercial aircraft.
> –EPA's enforcement has been slow, disorganized and less than effective.
> –EPA-FAA conflict has inhibited Federal aircraft noise reduction efforts.
> –The FAA has not acted favorably on most EPA proposals for aircraft noise.
> –Both fundamental conflict and petty bickering between FAA and EPA have reduced the effectiveness of the Federal aircraft noise program.
> –The Concorde supersonic transport is noisy, energy inefficient, and environmentally unsound; yet the Federal Government has taken no action to protect U.S. citizens from the Concorde.

In its emphasis on the general topic of aircraft noise, and on frictions between the FAA and the EPA, the report underlined that aircraft noise had become a major focus of national environmental concerns. Opposition to the Concorde was a token of those concerns. This was reflected also in an earlier report by the U.S. comptroller general, which concluded, "It appears that permitting the introduction of the Concorde or any other aircraft type that cannot presently meet noise standards or cannot be retrofitted to meet these standards is counter to the thrust of the national noise abatement effort."[27] This national effort was creating its own controversies in Congress and elsewhere in parallel with the Concorde arguments.

By the end of 1978—17 years after the first informal talks, 13 years after the application for a type certificate, and 10 years after the start of the formal legal process—all the technical problems raised by the FAA were finally resolved. On 9 January 1979 copies of the U.S. type certificate for the Concorde were handed over to Aérospatiale in Paris and to British Aerospace in London (BAC had become part of British Aerospace in 1978). Three days later, Braniff inaugurated its subsonic Concorde service between Washington and Dallas–Fort Worth as an extension of the British Airways and Air France London-Washington routes. Braniff continued this service until 1 June 1980, when it was abandoned as uneconomic.

FUTURES | 4

A SECOND GENERATION? | 12

In 1971, few mourned the death of America's supersonic transport program, though many Americans were uncomfortable with their country's abdication from such a leading-edge technology. Conflicting postmortems were held by interested parties, but other, more important issues were preoccupying the nation and the president. On the positive side, NASA had achieved John Kennedy's goal of landing men on the moon, to international acclaim. But no solution to the Vietnam war was in sight, and the White House style was setting the scene for the forthcoming Watergate scandal that would force Richard Nixon out of office. Nonetheless, in government and in industry, the question was being asked, would the United States be content to leave supersonic air transport to the Europeans and the Soviet Union, however questionable the economics and performance of the Concorde and the Tu-144? If not, what should be done? As it turned out, the first thing to be done was to begin to discard the term "supersonic transport."

An early discarder was the U.S. Department of Transportation, which in July 1971 argued that the "advanced high-speed commercial transport" should be assessed as one element in the wider challenge to the U.S. lead in air transport posed by Europe (in particular, by France) and Asia.[1] "The international competition that stirred President Kennedy to action in 1963 has grown in intensity in both Europe and Asia," the department declared, "while the economic health and technical superiority of our own aerospace industry has seriously eroded." Options for action included joining Britain and France in the expected Concorde 2 program and developing a competitor to the Concorde 2 in partnership with Japan or possibly Germany.

Neither of those options was taken up, but the following year the Nixon administration instructed the National Aeronautics and Space Administration to mount a focused research program designed to explore SST technology.[2] This program, known successively as Advanced Supersonic Technology, Supersonic Cruise Aircraft Research, and Supersonic Cruise Research (SCR), ran from 1972–1973 to 1980–1981 at an annual funding level of $8 million to $11.7 million. This was supplemented by a separate propulsion research effort to explore the technology of a promising concept known as the variable-cycle engine. Work by industry and in NASA research centers helped to advance the technology in most areas of supersonic flight, and tentative SST design concepts were examined. The designs included double-decker and twin-fuselage machines.

From the start, the NASA supersonic research raised questions in Congress and elsewhere on the real motive behind the program. Was it a disguised attempt to revive the canceled SST program? Senator William Proxmire, noted SST opponent and chairman of a subcommittee of the Joint Economic Committee, held hearings (which government departments and agencies and the aircraft companies declined to attend) and produced a report warning against any attempt to renew federal funding for an SST.[3] In March 1973 James C. Fletcher, NASA administrator, strove to clarify the agency's rationale: the aims of the program were simply to expand the technology, assess environmental and economic impacts, and ensure a sound base for any possible future SST consideration.[4] Though the NASA program fell short of any commitment to develop an aircraft, Congress remained skeptical, cutting the requested 1973–1974 appropriations for the program from more than $40 million to $10.1 million.

As the NASA research program continued, so also did congressional concern over its implications. In February 1975 the NASA administrator, in a reply to Senator William Roth, insisted, "The NASA supersonic research program is not oriented to the design or development of a supersonic transport, but is limited to the identification of the major problems and the development of technology which may provide for their solution."[5] Nonetheless, the agency was looking ahead and attempting to evaluate the post-Concorde SST market. In October 1976 a NASA headquarters estimate assumed this market to be 300 aircraft, costing $90 million each (in 1975 dollars), with U.S. airlines taking half the total.[6] In the best case (if the United States built all 300) about 55,000 jobs and a $16 billion positive balance of trade would be generated, and the United States would maintain its dominance of the world aircraft market. The worst case (if the United States built none) would result in a $16 billion negative balance of trade as U.S. airlines bought a foreign machine to remain competitive.

At a NASA conference at Langley Research Center in November 1976, progress toward three possible SST designs was reported.[7] Boeing had studied a blended wing-fuselage design with variable-cycle engines, Douglas an arrow-wing design using less-advanced engine technology, and Lockheed an arrow-wing design with engines attached both above and below the wings. A few months later, a flurry of congressional controversy surrounded plans for NASA's supersonics research. In a wide-ranging report on the future of aviation, the House Science and Technology Committee had earlier complained that the supersonic transport field had been left to the Europeans and the Russians; the United States could and should build a viable, advanced SST.[8] As the NASA authorization for 1977–1978 began its passage through Congress, the committee returned to the attack.

In its report on the bill the committee not only included $15.2 million to continue the supersonics research program but also expressed concern that a research base "adequate to permit development of an advanced supersonic transport (AST) in the foreseeable future" was not being developed. The committee directed the NASA administrator to prepare an overall program plan "with the goal of achieving technology readiness for such an aircraft by the early 1980s." During debate on the floor of the House, SST opponents—led by the New York City representatives who were fighting to ban the Concorde from Kennedy Airport—objected strongly. The House accepted a compromise amendment under which the funds could not be used for design or procurement of an AST prototype, and this was confirmed (together with the $15.2 million for research) following Senate debate and final conference discussion.[9]

The Prospects

Among the resources available to the U.S. Congress in analyzing complex issues are the Congressional Research Service of the Library of Congress and the Office of Technology Assessment (OTA). Both organizations contributed to the debates that followed the cancellation of the U.S. SST. In April 1978 the House Science and Technology Committee asked the OTA to examine whether the potential benefits of advanced supersonic transport aircraft justified an increase in federal funding for supersonic cruise research. Two years later the office published its response.[10] In essence, the answer to the specific question was that an increase in research funding was justified if Congress wished to preserve the supersonic option. But as the OTA's carefully argued case made clear, there were wider questions to be addressed. The line of reasoning ran as follows.

Barring some major disruption in the growth of the world economy, the total market for air travel should continue to grow substantially. Supersonic transports might satisfy a part of the long-range market, but the dominant share would be retained by subsonic types. The most compelling argument for an advanced supersonic transport was higher productivity, and the existing cost penalty of achieving this was likely to fall in the future as technology advanced. If an economically viable and environmentally acceptable AST could be developed in 1990–2010, its greater productivity could command about one-third of the anticipated total sales for long-range airliners through 2010. But there were major uncertainties, such as the future price and availability of fuel, the effect of noise regulations, and doubts whether industry could afford to adopt the advances in technology arising from NASA's SCR program. Foreign companies faced the same uncertainties but posed a potential future threat. Accordingly, the OTA concluded, a generic research and development program to preserve the supersonic option did appear appropriate, but the existing level of federal support was not adequate to accomplish that. R&D would shed no light, however, on the external factors governing the viability of an AST.

NASA's own technology assessments at that time included modest research contracts with Boeing, Lockheed, and McDonnell Douglas to explore further three broad SST concepts, based on speeds of Mach 2.4, 2.5, and 2.2, respectively.[11]

Meanwhile, in Europe, the Concorde partners had been assessing the prospects for an improved version of their pioneering SST. Throughout the latter half of the sixties, the threatened competition from a bigger and better version of the Concorde had loomed large in American thinking. At the beginning of 1965 Maynard Pennell of Boeing warned Najeeb Halaby at the FAA that the basic Concorde know-how could readily be applied to a larger, faster, and more economical version of the airplane. Such a machine would be far more competitive with the proposed American SST and would have serious implications for the U.S. program.[12] Six years later, U.S. State Department sources were forecasting that a Concorde 2 would be produced to follow the initial Concorde by two years.[13]

For the Anglo-French partners, other things being equal, the prospects for such an aircraft must have appeared better than those for the original Concorde, but other things—fuel costs, environmental pressures, route constraints—were rapidly becoming very unequal indeed. According to Gilbert Cormery of Aérospatiale, a study of a possible "Concorde B" was begun in 1974.[14] Improved engines, aerodynamic refinements, and a lighter structure would have helped to reduce noise and increase range. Cormery, writing in 1986, added, "Notwithstanding the relatively modest additional cost, the catastrophic market situation led to the decision to abandon this 'B' version in June 1976."

Also in 1976, Aérospatiale's British partner had begun to examine the longer-term prospects for a follow-on AST. In a paper written in May of that year, the month regular Concorde services to Washington began, Michael Wilde of BAC proposed an initial two-year study to establish the engineering and economic viability and the environmental acceptability of "an advanced supersonic transport for the 1990s."[15] The study would enable Anglo-French AST knowledge to be added to the Concorde experience "to provide a good bargaining position with other possible partners." For BAC and Aérospatiale, the preferred American partner at that time was McDonnell Douglas.

In January 1978 BAC became part of British Aerospace (BAe), and in December of that year the three companies—BAe, Aérospatiale, and McDonnell Douglas—published their shared views on "the prospects and problems of supersonic transportation up to the end of the century."[16] They concluded that an acceptable second-generation Mach 2 transport was feasible and could enter service as early as 1990, provided government support for R&D was provided. International collaboration was desirable if not essential. Earlier collaboration in the midseventies by British Aerospace, Rolls-Royce, and McDonnell Douglas had included the development of engine noise-reducing nozzles. They were tested in flight in Britain and in a large wind tunnel at the NASA Ames Research Center in California.

During the development of the Concorde, the use of NASA wind-tunnel facilities by the Anglo-French team was proposed and discussed, but not implemented. In February 1980 Alan Greenwood of British Aerospace approached NASA with a proposal in the reverse sense: that the U.S. agency should make use of an Anglo-French facility in its Supersonic Cruise Research program. The facility he was offering was a Concorde aircraft.

NASA was interested. Agency headquarters and research centers reviewed the proposal, and the centers identified a group of experiments that could be flown on the aircraft. In October that year teams from NASA and British Aerospace met at Bristol and came up with a group of six experiments suitable for an initial collaborative program involving in-flight tests and ground simulation.[17] The cost to NASA would be less than $500,000. The agency then set up an ad hoc subcommittee of its Aeronautics Advisory Committee to review the experiments. At the beginning of March 1981 the ad hoc group endorsed both the principle of cooperation and the specific experiments.[18] Unfortunately for both sides, the NASA aeronautics budget for 1981–1982 was cut in mid-March by the new Reagan administration, leading to cancellation of the SCR program and abandonment of the proposed Anglo-American joint project. A similar Russian-American proposal based on the Tu-144 aircraft was to be taken up in the mid-nineties.

Impetus for Action

Official U.S. interest in supersonic flight was rekindled in March 1985 with the publication by the White House Office of Science and Technology Policy (OSTP) of a report on national aeronautical goals.[19] Written by the office's Aeronautical Policy Review Committee, whose members came from government, industry, and academia, the report reflected the widespread concern that America's traditional leadership in aeronautics was being eroded. To arrest this decline, goals in three areas of technology—subsonic aircraft, supersonic cruise aircraft, and hypersonic vehicles—were identified. Development of the technologies needed for efficient, long-distance supersonic cruise aircraft had both military and commercial importance, the report argued, and a new-generation commercial SST would be particularly valuable in linking the United States and the Pacific Rim countries.

One result of the OSTP report, and of President Reagan's announcement of the National Aero-Space Plane (NASP) in his State of the Union message to Congress in February 1986, was an unusual initiative intended to stimulate international interest in the possibility of moving ahead toward a second-generation supersonic airliner. The initiative came from Battelle Memorial Institute of Columbus, Ohio, an international technology consultancy, and it was launched at a symposium in Columbus in October 1986.[20] This event was intended to be more than just another conference at which technical papers on ASTs were presented (there had been many such conferences and papers in the 15 years since the cancellation of the American SST); it aimed to explore much broader issues. Earlier that year Battelle had set up a center for high-speed commercial flight "as a rallying point for manufacturers, operators, and other parties as they pursue the design, development, and marketing of a new high-speed commercial transport under U.S. leadership," no less, and the symposium was cosponsored by the institute and the U.S. Department of Commerce.

Not surprisingly, the symposium raised more questions than it answered. More surprising was the emphasis on Mach 5 hypersonics rather than supersonics, following President Reagan's linking of the NASP program with a possible "Orient Express" hypersonic airliner. Crawford Brubaker, deputy assistant secretary for aerospace in the Department of Commerce and a member of the OSTP committee, warned, "There is no current consensus on the need for a civil long-distance supersonic cruise airplane." Najeeb Halaby also was skeptical, drawing on his FAA and Pan American experience and urging those present to beware the technology zealots. Focus on Mach 3, he advised, and look to Japan for a consortium partner. Halaby's aim was to bring the discussion down to earth, in more ways than one, as he asked, "What in the world are we doing, going to Mach 5 when we can't even get an average speed to the airport of 25 miles an hour?"

In late 1986 and early 1987 NASA and the White House both returned to the supersonics scene, prompted by forecasts of long-range international travel that could imply a substantial market for supersonic transports in the first quarter of the twenty-first century. In the hope that euphemism might help to erase bad memories, NASA renamed the supersonic transport the high-speed civil transport (HSCT) and launched a round of HSCT studies—funded jointly by the agency and the companies—with Boeing, McDonnell Douglas, General Electric, Pratt & Whitney, and Aerojet. Initially, the range of speeds to be considered was from Mach 2 to Mach 12 (the higher-speed vehicles being expected to draw on NASP hypersonic technology), but the upper limit was later reduced to a more realistic Mach 5. The studies, which continued for two years, indicated that aircraft cruising at between Mach 2 and Mach 2.5 were most likely to prove economically viable and environmentally compatible.

The White House returned to the subject in February 1987 in a follow-up report by the OSTP committee.[21] The report proposed an eight-point plan of action to help achieve the goals set two years earlier. The first three points called for increased, innovative R&D in industry, aggressive pursuit of the National Aero-Space Plane program, and the development of a technology, design, and business base for a long-range SST "in preparation for a potential U.S. industry initiative." The national supersonics goal remained a "great market-driven opportunity," the committee affirmed, and a coordinated approach by government, industry, and academia was needed to develop the technology and to mobilize the large capital resources required for full-scale development. The topic was to be taken up by Congress as a firm proposal for action was put forward by NASA.[22] (The resulting research program is described in the next chapter.)

Battelle's Battle

Battelle Memorial Institute had not been idle since its 1986 HSCT symposium: four working groups, consisting largely of experts from outside organizations, had been active in exploring further aircraft R&D, operations and markets, consortia and financing, and institutional concerns. Their findings were presented in October 1988 at a second symposium, which the institute hoped would mark the end of talk and the start of action.[23]

The working groups concluded that the target for the introduction of an acceptable HSCT was the year 2010. From the user's point of view the aircraft should be able to carry 300 passengers over 6,500 nautical miles (12,000 kilometers), cruising at a speed—between Mach 2 and Mach 3—that would cut long-haul travel times in half. The market would be from 250 to 350 aircraft if a "modest premium" over subsonic aircraft fares was required, or up to 700 aircraft assuming no fare premium. International collaboration would be essential and would demand exceptional cooperation between governments. But nothing would happen unless the private sector initiated and led the program. A three-phase program could begin with two to three years for evaluation and planning, costing $10 million–$12 million; five to seven years for "technology maturation," costing up to $3 billion; and about seven years for preliminary design, development, and production, estimated to cost from $10 billion to $20 billion.

Thus the groups wisely had abandoned thoughts of hypersonics to concentrate on a Mach 2–3 supersonic craft. The NASA-funded HSCT studies were described at the symposium by Louis J. Williams, at that time the agency's assistant director for aeronautics, and industrial work also was reported. Despite generally positive views on likely advances in technology, the symposium was realistic in facing up to the problems. The project would be very difficult to finance: it needed a lot of money, it depended on a series of technical breakthroughs, it had significant political risk, and it demanded a long-term commitment.

Regardless of technical and economic issues, the symposium was told, an HSCT program would need political support and public acceptance. "With the exception of special groups like ours here today," warned Michel Lagorce of the French Directorate-General of Civil Aviation (a veteran of the U.S. Concorde approval campaign), "commercial supersonic flight has not captured the imagination of anyone except the small and prosperous elite and the occasional technocrat. An HSCT would require development of a broad base of public understanding and support."

Battelle's initiative provided a valuable stimulus for preliminary joint studies on key aspects of supersonic air transport. But it was ahead of its time; the institute's hoped-for launch of an actual international consortium failed to take off. James P. Loomis, director of the high-speed commercial flight center, sought firm commitments from manufacturers and airlines in Japan, Europe, and the United States during 1989; participation from all three areas was judged essential for the program, which would have been coordinated by Battelle. Though positive responses were obtained from Japan and Europe, U.S. manufacturers declined to participate, leading to the collapse of the proposal and the end of Battelle's active interest in supersonic air transport.

A European Conference

In November 1989 a major European symposium provoked renewed interest—at least, technical and operational interest—in supersonic (and, alas, hypersonic) transportation systems.[24] Organized in Strasbourg by the French and West German aeronautical societies and cosponsored by the Royal Aeronautical Society, the symposium covered the Concorde experience in airline service as well as future engineering prospects. Though most participants were from European manufacturers, airlines, and government agencies, a number came from the United States and from Japan. In general the papers and discussions reflected the technical interests of the organizing professional societies, but environmental topics and the problems of international collaboration also were addressed. The main omission, as a member of the Royal Aeronautical Society pointed out later, was that costs and economic objectives were largely ignored.[25]

Japan's active interest in advanced supersonic and hypersonic transports was reported at the symposium: after a two-year preliminary study of market prospects and key technologies, three new joint industry-government programs were being started in that country. They comprised a three-year feasibility study of supersonic and hypersonic transport development and two eight-year research studies into propulsion systems and materials. The symposium concluded optimistically that Concorde experience plus later work gave confidence that a transpacific-range SST could indeed be built to go into commercially viable service soon after the turn of the century.

Tentative Togetherness

A number of national and collaborative study programs were under way toward the end of the eighties. These included moves toward a joint European approach and a first attempt at a wider international grouping. British Aerospace and Aérospatiale, partners in developing and producing the Concorde, had each continued a modest program of advanced supersonics research, and in May 1990 they announced an agreement to conduct joint preliminary studies into a second-generation supersonic airliner.[26] Their earlier individual efforts had been focused on outline designs known respectively as the Advanced Supersonic Transport and Avion de Transport Supersonique Futur. Now they were to embark on a joint five-year program to determine the technical, environmental, and commercial viability of an as yet unnamed son of Concorde. Henri Martre, Aérospatiale president, suggested that "a further ten years will be needed to design and build such an aircraft," leading to a possible in-service date of 2005.[27] "The two partners will explore together wider international cooperation which will be necessary for the commercial success of a project of this magnitude," the two companies concluded.

Only two weeks later, a separate move toward wider international cooperation was announced. Aérospatiale, British Aerospace, and Deutsche Airbus (part of Deutsche Aerospace) in Europe joined with Boeing and McDonnell Douglas in the United States to form an international study group to explore the potential for next-generation supersonic transports.[28] These joint studies were to focus on general topics—environmental, certification, market, cooperation, and business compatibility issues—and would complement those being pursued by the individual companies and by the Anglo-French partners. The group set up two working groups, one concerned with business issues and the other dealing with technical and marketing questions.

At the Paris air show in June 1991 the group declared that substantial progress had been achieved and that the Society of Japanese Aerospace Companies and Alenia Aeronautica of Italy had joined the studies.[29] Several companies displayed "brochure SSTs" at the show, including Aérospatiale, whose own design was now called Alliance. The French company continued its superactive promotion of supersonics by proposing a timetable for an international SST project, leading to aircraft certification in 2005. Aérospatiale's enthusiasm extended to its market estimates, which ranged from 500 to more than 1,000 aircraft. In September 1991 the international group welcomed a new member, the Tupolev Design Bureau of the Soviet Union, and agreed to extend its studies for 12 months.[30] The studies were further extended and were still going strong in 1996.

The Technological Challenge

Supersonic air transport as one part of the technological challenge in aeronautics facing the United States in the nineties was reviewed in 1992 in a wide-ranging report written at the request of NASA by a committee of the aeronautics and space engineering board of the U.S. National Research Council.[31] This report, which was influential in shaping the aeronautics policy of the incoming Clinton administration, set the scene—in great detail—for NASA's supersonics research in the nineties.

The starting point for the committee's assessment was erosion of the U.S. market share in aeronautics. Though the current effect was most marked in subsonic airliners, the report noted, U.S. participation in the important future market of supersonic transports could well be forfeited if research into environmental and economic factors was neglected. NASA's priorities in advanced aeronautics should be (1) advanced subsonic aircraft, (2) supersonic aircraft, and (3) short-haul aircraft. Advanced subsonic aircraft would continue to provide the bulk of the future market; nevertheless, the potential future HSCT market was significant.

The report recommended that NASA increase its atmospheric research; develop propulsion technology that would reduce emissions and engine noise; ensure that the HSCT program adequately covered propulsion, aerodynamics, structures, materials, and overall vehicle management and control technologies; and continue to investigate ways of reducing sonic-boom levels. These aims set the guidelines that NASA was to follow in the mid-nineties in its pacesetting High-Speed Research program.

13 | ONCE MORE, WITH HINDSIGHT

Once more, in the decade of the nineties as in the fifties and sixties, the prospects for a supersonic transport are seriously being assessed—by NASA, by companies, by groups of companies, by countries. These players and groups of players have different agendas, but it is generally agreed that it will take until the turn of the century to determine whether a second-generation SST could make environmental, technological, and economic sense. As the millennium approaches, it is possible to trace the early results and point to likely future directions.

Exploring the Science

In 1989, the results of Boeing and Douglas HSCT studies were reported to NASA.[1] Both firms gave promising market estimates for an economically viable, environmentally acceptable aircraft, with Boeing forecasting best prospects for a machine cruising at Mach 2 to 2.5 over water and Mach 0.9 over land. (Douglas had examined higher speeds, focusing on Mach 3.2.) A three-class aircraft, seating 250 to 300 passengers and having a range of 5,000 to 6,000 nautical miles (about 9,000 to 11,000 kilometers), could justify a total fleet size of more than 1,200 machines between the years 2000 and 2015, the Seattle firm declared.

The reports of these studies laid the foundation for the major NASA research program that is now under way—and which will continue to keep the agency and the industry busy until the year 2000. In turn, this decade-long effort, known as the

High-Speed Research (HSR) program, is laying the foundation for any U.S. supersonic transport that might be developed in the future. In the first phase of the new program, NASA focused its research on three major environmental issues: atmospheric effects, airport community noise, and the sonic boom.[2] The most serious atmospheric effect to be explored was the possibility that engine emissions might deplete the ozone layer. If the public is to accept an HSCT, it will have to be no noisier than subsonic transports. As for the sonic boom, NASA was reluctant to assume that the boom must continue to rule out supersonic flight over land, and so was exploring whether the boom could be softened to an acceptable level.

In a bid to preempt the sort of environmental arguments that had helped to kill the U.S. SST program in 1971, NASA set up a stratospheric-effects advisory committee containing some of the world's leading atmospheric scientists—including Michael Oppenheimer of the Environmental Defense Fund, a leading opponent of the SST in 1971. This committee performs assessments and guides the research program to validate the assessments and improve the mathematical models of the atmosphere. Nitrogen oxide, which acts as a catalyst to destroy ozone, is regarded as the biggest threat to the ozone layer. Here the target was to develop engine combustors that emit no more than five grams of nitrogen oxide per kilogram of fuel burned—about one-tenth the level previously attainable.

Noise research included the obvious but notoriously difficult target of reducing engine noise at its source. The goal was at least to meet FAR-36 Stage 3, the current noise standards for subsonic airliners. In addition, aerodynamic improvements to the aircraft might allow less engine thrust to be used for takeoff, and special operating procedures (shades of the Concorde at Kennedy) were being explored.

The third part of the phase 1 program posed the question: Could the boom intensity be lowered sufficiently to allow supersonic cruising flight over land? If not, could an HSCT be designed that would cruise relatively efficiently at subsonic speed when over land? If not, were there enough overwater routes for economical HSCT operation? Wind-tunnel tests, flight testing, and human-factors work in a sonic-boom simulator led to the early conclusion that the answer to the first question was probably no—hence an emphasis on improving the subsonic efficiency of the HSCT. Besides the normal sonic boom that is trailed continuously by an aircraft cruising at supersonic speed, focused (louder) booms may be heard when the aircraft is accelerating, decelerating, or turning; and secondary (quieter) booms may be caused by reflection from upper layers of the atmosphere in certain weather conditions.

Atmospheric assessment in phase 1 was encouraging. If the target of five grams of nitrogen oxide per kilogram of fuel burned could be achieved, the calculated effect of a fleet of 500 aircraft cruising in northern latitudes at Mach 2.4 at a height of 18 kilometers would be a decrease in ozone of only 0.1 percent. That, according to Louis Williams, now NASA director of high-speed research, is within the natural variation of the atmosphere.[3] International agreement on acceptable levels of nitrogen oxide for future supersonic transports has yet to be negotiated. In the meantime, the uncertainties of theory and prediction are being reduced by atmospheric measurements from aircraft and spacecraft.

NASA's direct attacks on the problems of emissions, noise, and sonic boom are being supplemented in the HSR program by work on an aerodynamic technique that, if successful, could indirectly contribute to the solution of all three problems. This technique, known as laminar flow control, is a means of smoothing the flow of air over the wing so that the drag caused by friction is reduced, enabling the weight of the aircraft and its engines to be reduced. Smaller engines mean less noise and lower emissions, less fuel means more payload, and a lighter aircraft means a softer sonic boom. Against this, the potential benefit of laminar flow on an SST is relatively small, and the practical design difficulties are great.

In parallel with the HSR program, a separate research effort was mounted to stimulate advances in engine materials suitable for use in supersonic transports. In an unusual partnership between General Electric and Pratt & Whitney, normally fierce competitors in the aeroengine market, the two companies merged their work on high-temperature composite materials for use in HSCT engines. This project, known as the Enabling Propulsion Materials program, is managed by the NASA Lewis Research Center in Cleveland, Ohio.

Tackling the Technology

The environment-oriented phase 1 of the High-Speed Research program began in 1990 and was due to continue until 1996. But by 1993 the positive research results had convinced NASA that the environmental problems could be solved, and so the agency lost no time in moving into phase 2, the development of technology items that are critical to HSCT success. NASA chose its words carefully—and its sales estimates optimistically—in April 1993 in describing the strategic importance of phase 2:

> Phase 2 of the High-Speed Research Program provides needed high-risk, long-term research and technology development that is currently beyond industry's investment reach. The potential payoffs for the country are substantial: positive balance of trade ($200–350 billion of sales), creation of about 140,000 high-value jobs and preserving the general strength of the U.S. aerospace industrial base for civil and military applications.

The required investment for HSCT technology development is large: an estimated $4.5 billion prior to an industry go-ahead decision leading to certification and production. The current technical, environmental, economic and political uncertainties are too great, however, for industry to make major funding investments in the very early stages of technology development.

The $1.5 billion proposed Phase 2 of NASA's High-Speed Research program provides a public-sector catalyst by addressing the highest-priority, highest-risk technology. Industry has indicated it will provide additional parallel investments along a schedule consistent with the progress and success achieved in the NASA program. It is a commitment that reflects the above uncertainties and that it will be at least 15 years before the manufacturers begin receiving income based on future aircraft and engine sales. . . .

The goals in each technology area are very challenging and high-risk—but attainable. If it appears that it is not possible to achieve the environmental or economic success requirements, the program will be reassessed and redirected or canceled as appropriate.[4]

In other words, this is no rerun of the SST prototype development program canceled in 1971. No decision to build another supersonic transport has been made, and any such decision will be made by industry, no earlier than the turn of the century. But it is in the U.S. national interest to mount a major government-industry effort to try to build the required technology base by the year 2000. If the attempt to achieve the environmental and economic targets fails, there will be no HSCT.

Three broad areas of technology are being tackled in the phase 2 program: airframe, propulsion, and flight-deck systems. Earlier flight-deck research had pointed to a radical change that, it appeared, could improve the performance of any future supersonic transport: abandon the droop-nose feature as used on the Concorde to improve visibility on landing and takeoff, and switch to artificial vision.[5] Instead of looking out through the windshield, the flight crew would look into electronic displays (presenting information from advanced sensors based on military aircraft technology). The main reason for making this change, if approved, would be to save weight.

The goals of the phase 2 program are challenging. Aerodynamic improvements are aimed at obtaining a 33 percent increase in range and a 50 percent reduction in the noise footprint of the aircraft. Advances in airframe materials and structures are aiming at a weight reduction of 30 to 40 percent. These lighter materials will have to withstand temperatures up to 350 degrees F on the wing surface for a lifetime of 60,000 hours. Thus, not only is it necessary to develop the materials themselves, but they will also need to be incorporated in structural components and tested to prove they can meet those stringent conditions.

In the propulsion area, also, new and improved materials are essential if the desired performance is to be achieved. But the key propulsion question is the choice of the type of engine that will best satisfy the conflicting requirements of reduced noise on takeoff and increased efficiency in supersonic cruise. In March 1994 NASA announced that the "mixed flow turbofan" and the "fan on blade" (Flade) concepts had been chosen for further research.[6] Both designs cut noise on takeoff by mixing air with the engine exhaust. In the mixed-flow turbofan the ambient air is brought in behind the main engine, while in the Flade design it is introduced near the front of the engine. European work is described later in this chapter.

Explaining the Rationale

"It's time to go supersonic," declared Daniel Goldin, NASA administrator, writing in a Smithsonian Institution journal in the summer of 1993.[7] No single program would have such an impact on America's efforts to "regain its share of the aviation market, produce manufacturing jobs, and reassume the leading edge in aeronautics" as to develop the technology for an environmentally friendly, economically successful HSCT. Goldin developed his argument in testimony before a congressional subcommittee in February 1994.[8] Research leading toward the next-generation supersonic transport was industry's top priority, he told the subcommittee. Supporting the agency's request for $221.3 million in High-Speed Research funding for 1994–1995, Wesley Harris, associate administrator for aeronautics, underlined the importance of the program and its promising initial results. Phases 1 and 2 together, he stated, represented "the complementary and necessary technologies for HSCT development and production decisions by U.S. industry." Russia might contribute to the U.S. research program, Goldin suggested; in particular, the Russians possessed the Mach 2.1 Tu-144 aircraft. Later that year, a deal to use the Russian aircraft was confirmed.

International Studies

European collaboration on supersonic transports advanced somewhat in April 1994, when Aérospatiale, British Aerospace, and Deutsche Aerospace agreed to mount a joint research program.[9] This extension of the Anglo-French collaboration to include the German company is known as the European Supersonic Research Programme. The combined studies are intended to be funded equally by the three countries and aim to develop and verify key SST technologies. In assessing the feasibility of a possible future SST, the studies assume a Mach 2, 250-passenger, three-class machine having a range of 10,000 kilometers or about 5,500 nautical miles. The European group is convinced that Mach 2 is the right speed.[10]

If, at the end of the century, an international collaboration is mounted to develop and build an SST, the consortium to do it will emerge from the present seven-nation study group. The group's aim in essence is to determine whether the joint development of an SST—the group's appellation is Supersonic Commercial Transport (SCT)—is viable. Two types of viability are involved: a viable product, implying a viable market, and a viable collaboration. Overall market viability remains an open question, but the group is convinced that there will be room for only one supersonic airplane in the market.

Since the member companies are both collaborators and competitors, the SST studies raise sensitive issues of markets and technology. Each of the companies has its own in-house SST design studies, which are not part of the joint work, and each of them—in their own right or, in the case of the European firms, through Airbus Industrie—has existing and planned subsonic airliners that will form part of the competition for any future SST. Also, the involvement of Boeing and McDonnell Douglas in the NASA High-Speed Research program adds its own complications, since HSR information is restricted to the U.S. firms. On the technical side, according to Michael Henderson, HSCT program manager for Boeing, the partners are remarkably close in their view of the aircraft requirements, apart from differences on the cruising speed.[11]

If the international group does eventually embark on the development of a supersonic transport, other sensitive issues will arise: who will lead the project, for example, and how will it be organized? According to Malcolm MacKinnon, HSCT chief engineer at Boeing, three things are needed for the supersonic enterprise: a solid technology base, strong manufacturing resources, and a lot of money.[12] The extent to which individual partners can meet these requirements will determine, as in any consortium, who the major player and the minor players will be.

Very Fast or Very Large?

One of the key questions affecting prospects for the next-generation supersonic transport concerns the impact of the next-generation subsonic transport—a very large aircraft carrying 600, 800, or even 1,000 passengers. By its very size the aircraft will be limited in its possible routes, but it could be competing for investment and resources with the supersonic machine. This competition for resources is more significant than the overlap in the market, according to Michael Henderson of Boeing, who describes as "inconceivable" the thought that both a brand-new large airplane and a supersonic machine could be absorbed by the aircraft industry or the airlines at the same time.[13] Thus the question is, which comes first, the very fast airliner or the very large one? Because of the long period of technology development needed before the viability of a supersonic transport can be assured, then to be followed by the actual aircraft development, Boeing and NASA see the year 2005 or 2006 as the earliest in-service date for a supersonic airplane. Hence, if the market were to demand a large subsonic aircraft before that date, the vast cost of such a program to both manufacturers and airlines inevitably would delay the introduction of any supersonic machine.

For what is being called the Very Large Commercial Transport (VLCT) airplane, yet another international study group was formed to examine prospects. Partners in this enterprise were Boeing and the four Airbus companies: Aérospatiale, British Aerospace, CASA of Spain, and Daimler-Benz Aerospace (formerly Deutsche Aerospace). In July 1995, after two and a half years of study, the five firms announced that they had confirmed the technical feasibility of such an airplane.[14] "However," they added, "market studies do not indicate sufficient volumes to justify the launch of the programme today." The companies vowed to continue to monitor market conditions and to review prospects for a development program later. Alas, by early 1996, market realities had overcome any thought of collaboration. The VLCT study group was dissolved, leaving Boeing and the Airbus partners to go their separate ways. Clearly, the time is ripe for neither a supersonic transport nor a very large subsonic one. But the answer to the basic question, as seen in 1997, must be: very large first, very fast later.

Problems of Power

In the Concorde and in any future supersonic transport, the powerplant is the key to the performance of the aircraft. In providing the thrust to propel the vehicle at supersonic speed, however, it provides also the noise and the emissions that must be reduced if ever a second-generation SST is to take to the air. As well as solving those two problems, which are severe, the SST engine designer faces two further obstacles: the engine must be efficient both in subsonic flight and in supersonic cruise (normally these are mutually incompatible requirements), and the powerplant and the airframe must be integrated to an unusual degree. Thus the SST studies and the tentative moves toward collaboration by the aircraft companies were accompanied by parallel actions by the engine firms, notably one joint effort by Rolls-Royce and SNECMA, partners in the Olympus 593 powerplant for the Concorde, and another, unprecedented collaboration between the two main U.S. engine makers, General Electric and Pratt & Whitney.

Toward the end of 1989, after separate studies, Rolls-Royce and SNECMA agreed to collaborate in surveying the SST market, identifying feasible engine concepts, and defining key technologies and test facilities for joint investment. This Anglo-French team was expanded two years later to include Fiat Avio of Italy and MTU of Germany. Rolls-Royce and SNECMA (together with the two main U.S. engine firms) also joined the significant propulsion R&D program for supersonic and hypersonic transports launched by Japan in 1989.

Rolls-Royce also was pursuing an unusual third line: together with the Lyulka Engine Design Bureau in the Soviet Union, the British firm was working on the preliminary definition of an engine to power the proposed U.S.-Soviet supersonic business jet aircraft proposed by Gulfstream Aerospace Corporation and the Sukhoi Design Bureau. This project, announced in 1989, was later abandoned, but not before Sukhoi had flight-tested a powerplant fitted to an adapted fighter.

SNECMA also was cooperating with the Soviet Union on SST propulsion at this time, in a joint project with the Central Institute of Aviation Motors in support of Aérospatiale-Tupolev SST discussions. Apart from the business jet, the main thrust of the engine firms' work related to what might be termed the mainstream SST concept, for an aircraft that would cruise at Mach 2-plus, carrying 250 to 300 passengers over a range of about 11,000 kilometers. Rolls-Royce was interested also in examining the prospects for a smaller SST that would carry 70 to 100 passengers—in effect, an improved Concorde that might represent a more readily affordable program—but concluded later that the economic prospects for the smaller aircraft were not good.[15]

In the United States, the partnership between General Electric and Pratt & Whitney began in 1990 with feasibility studies of powerplants for civil transports cruising at speeds from Mach 1.5 to Mach 3.5. By 1994 the choice of possible engine concepts had narrowed to the mixed-flow turbofan and Flade designs, one of which will be chosen for full-scale tests of components in the later years (1998 to 2001) of the HSR program. The European firms also have narrowed their possible designs to two, one of which—the mid-tandem fan—is the preferred choice. The alternative is known as the mixer nozzle ejector layout and is similar in principle to the U.S. mixed-flow turbofan. Whatever the design, experience has shown that only when a demonstrator engine has been built and flown can the true performance and noise levels be established.

The Critics

As the SST studies advanced in the mid-nineties, it was not surprising that the voice of the critics was raised once again. In Britain, old-time Concorde opponents Richard Wiggs and John Connell fired warning shots on environmental issues to the press.[16] Other people had other objections. One such is R. E. G. Davies, curator of air transport at the National Air and Space Museum of the Smithsonian Institution in Washington. Davies, a former market researcher in the aircraft industry, first in Britain and later in the United States, is a long-time opponent of supersonic transportation. His opposition is based quite simply on his calculations of the likely future market for the SST, which point to a requirement of no more than 40 (first-class only) aircraft at most. Since no realistic market exists, he argues, no SST can possibly be justified and so the environmental objections do not arise.

Davies has consistently advocated this view; he says that his own low estimates of the SST market made while working as a market analyst for Douglas Aircraft Company in the late sixties were suppressed by company management in favor of higher figures.[17] In a paper presented in 1992, Davies quoted 36 aircraft as the total market he had estimated for the Concorde 25 years previously, and the same total (though based on different assumptions) for either a Mach 3 SST in the nineties or a Mach 5 hypersonic transport in about 2005.[18] In 1994 he repeated categorically that his calculations demonstrated that there was simply no market for a supersonic airliner of any kind.[19]

Davies attacks the industry's "top-down" approach to SST market estimates, in which the potential first-class market is taken to be an arbitrary (and arguably high) percentage of the total forecast traffic, as grossly overoptimistic. "People do not fly on percentages, they fly on routes. The basis of all SST calculations must be to identify the routes that can or could generate sufficient traffic in total to justify an assumption of an adequate percentage of travelers who would pay the high fares necessary to produce a yield that would cover the high operating costs." There are very few such routes, he insists. Also, in assuming three-class supersonic travel, the industry figures "have to assume operating costs for, say, a 300-seat SST to be on a par with those of a subsonic super-747 or super-Airbus with 700 or 800 seats. And this is clearly impossible."[20]

Toward a World SST?

In 1997 the world's most comprehensive SST research effort remains the NASA-industry High-Speed Research program in the United States. Boeing and Mc-

Donnell Douglas are leading the industry team on HSR phase 2 technologies, under an eight-year, $400 million NASA contract. Honeywell also is working on avionics and flight-deck systems. By completion of the program the cost to NASA is expected to be almost $2 billion—plus perhaps $4 billion from U.S. industry by about 2001, when a decision to develop an HSCT might be made.[21] Europe's embryonic joint research program is small by comparison, but it can draw on the experience of the only aircraft makers in the world to have built a successful operational SST. Japan continues its interest in future high-speed flight, including hypersonics. But the future of commercial supersonic flight is set to be shaped in large measure by the work of the international study group, embracing all the above interests and more. So, what is the group's basic raison d'être, how might it develop, and what are the chances of a truly global enterprise being launched to develop the next supersonic airliner?

Toward the end of 1994, at another European conference, this time in Toulouse, the international group put forward its considered case for global cooperation on a supersonic commercial transport.[22] Why cooperate? The prime reason, the group members agreed, was to share the risk. The next SST would involve a higher risk than any project in commercial aviation history, and a strong partnership would help to reduce that risk.

Next, how to cooperate? This question raises many more: What form of management structure? How will decisions be made? What form of legal entity? How will work be allocated? Where will the final assembly line be located? How will the aircraft be sold and supported? Earlier international projects have used a variety of mechanisms. The Concorde project involved separate companies in a joint venture. Airbus Industrie is a "grouping of economic interest" in which the partners accept joint liability and pool their resources. Panavia, Eurofighter, and International Aero Engines are examples of limited-liability companies set up to manage joint programs. The Boeing 777 is produced by a lead company with risk-sharing partners and subcontractors. Nobody—certainly nobody who experienced the trials and tribulations of the Concorde program—is suggesting that collaboration is easy. But this time around, in the climate of the nineties, unlike that of the sixties, absolutely nobody is discussing going it alone.

Within Europe, the loudest voice in favor of substantially strengthening the European SST research and development effort, not surprisingly, is that of Aérospatiale. Both at the 1994 Farnborough air show and at the Toulouse conference, Louis Gallois, chairman of the French company, was concerned to ensure that the continent that had produced the Concorde should not be relegated to a minor role in any second-generation SST program. Opening the Toulouse conference, he noted that the existing European budget for SST research was about $15 million a year, tiny compared with $187 million in the United States and $55 million–$60 million in Japan. Europe should commit itself to a minimum of about $100 million a year, he argued, not simply to work toward a next-generation SST but as a "technology engine" for the European aircraft industry and in order to reestablish Europe's credibility in the field.[23]

LESSONS AND PROSPECTS | 14

More than twenty years after its transatlantic debut, almost forty years after conception, the Concorde remains a unique and controversial airplane. It remains at once an engineering triumph and an economic disaster. Only the small number of Concordes in regular service (one dozen) prevents its being described as an environmental disaster also. The Concorde remains an outstanding example of how *not* to develop and build a supersonic airliner—or any other high-technology product. Both the Concorde and the abortive U.S. SST demonstrated a unique interplay between technical, industrial, political, and economic factors. What lessons can be drawn from the experience of these aircraft, both as projects in their own right and in their transatlantic interactions?

Consider the origins of the two contenders. In Europe, the stimulus for action came primarily from the government scientists at Farnborough, backed by the U.K. aeroindustry and reluctantly endorsed by the Macmillan cabinet, and from their French opposite numbers, drawing on the British Supersonic Transport Aircraft Committee (STAC) report and with wholehearted government backing. In the United States, the initial push came primarily from industry, drawing on NASA research and enthusiastically embraced by President Kennedy's aviation adviser, Najeeb Halaby. In each case, public funds were to support the development of the aircraft, after which the manufacturers would fund production. In each case, the airlines were reluctant customers, but for competitive reasons the major ones took options on both types, until the fragile edifice of options collapsed under the weight of economic reality.

Once locked into the Anglo-French agreement, the Concorde nations were doomed to struggle on to completion—of 16 airplanes only. Realistic joint assessment of prospects was minimal, such were the political imperatives of the time. Costs rose inexorably. In the United States, the SST was examined and reexamined repeatedly and critically, as government agencies and individuals put their conflicting stamps on the project. At the second attempt, a practical design appeared to be emerging, but public opposition led to its cancellation by Congress.

Progress on one side of the Atlantic was marked by naïveté, conflicting concepts of European unity, a tradition of government support for the aircraft industry, arguments between partners, and a lack of economic realism. In the New World, meanwhile, the nation was accepting the concept of government involvement in a hitherto commercial area in the perceived national interest, but with strict conditions attached. Underlying the U.S. SST effort was America's easy assumption of its natural, national superiority (or arrogance, as seen from across the water) in matters technological.

In the climate of the time, cancellation of the American SST was inevitable. Survival of the Concorde was not inevitable, but was secured by a combination of French determination and American justice. The U.S. approval process was a complex and wholly exceptional experience, its outcome decided by the Coleman decision, the port authority's procrastination, and a helpful amicus brief from the attorney general's office—all in all, a remarkable piece of aviation history.

Key Lessons

Some of the key lessons of Concorde technology and organization were identified in this writer's previous book on the aircraft by a number of those personally involved.[1] Sir James Hamilton, director general for the Concorde from 1966 to 1970, concluded that "a single man in government and a single man in industry" should have held responsibility for the technical direction of the project. Dr. William Strang, deputy director of engineering on the combined Concorde team, quoted two basic lessons that could not have been assumed at the start of the project: that a supersonic transport really could be made to work and that international programs of this complexity were possible.

Ken Binning, director general from 1973 to 1976, stressed the hazards of forecasting both technological and sociological changes. It was difficult to predict the response of the population to the environmental effects of the aircraft. Also difficult to predict was the future pattern of air travel and the constraints that would affect supersonic transports. As the Concorde issues proceeded through the U.S.

public hearings, British officials swiftly had to learn another lesson: how to present and defend their case effectively against an active, highly vocal, and less than scrupulous opposition ("Many of the people who gave evidence had remarkably little regard to the scientific fact," Binning commented).

British officials recall and savor the irony of testimony at public hearings in Faneuil Hall, Boston, where anti-British revolutionary town meetings were held some 200 years earlier. "Here both before and during the revolution were held many patriotic meetings," a plaque inside the hall declares, "which kept alive among the people the fires of freedom and stirred them to greater deeds, from which fact the hall became known as the Cradle of Liberty." This location, and the historical resonance of the first battle of Concord not many miles away, gave the men from the ministry food for thought and the opposition a ready analogy with the past. Once more the message to loyal minutemen was "The British are coming"—this time supersonically, and with the French on their side.

Thus there were clear lessons to be learned in effective international collaboration on high-technology projects, in orderly design development, and in the perceptive assessment of broader societal trends and influences. Certainly many of the mistakes of the Concorde have been corrected in the organization of later international ventures, notably the four-nation Airbus Industrie consortium, which has grown from nothing to give Europe a significant share of the world airliner market.

With hindsight, and for Robert McNamara with foresight, neither the Concorde nor the American SST could have been a commercial success. President Johnson's right-hand man recalls:

> I was absolutely convinced in my mind that the Concorde wouldn't be commercially viable for the British and French, and the SST wouldn't be commercially viable for the U.S. either. On technology, I must say that Britain and France did a superb job on the aircraft, but it was predictable then that the technology could not produce a commercially viable airplane because the payload was so very small in relation to the fuel requirement.[2]

Many of the mistakes that were made in the Concorde program stemmed from the sacrosanct nature of the Anglo-French agreement—a point that was missed in most of the ongoing American assessments of Concorde options. Under the agreement, the two countries were locked into the project with no provision for unilateral withdrawal. That leads to the lesson that perhaps must top the list of lessons: do not sign agreements that do not have an escape clause. It is hardly a new thought, but research for this book has shed new light on the implications. Amazingly, the terms of the 1962 agreement seemed a good idea at the time. Speaking in 1976, Julian Amery, the British minister who signed the deal, explained why: "If you commit that amount of brainpower and that amount of money to a particular project, you can't be at the mercy of your partner running out after two, three or six years."[3] Amery's concern in 1962 was that the French might run out; two years later, it was the British who tried to escape.

Michel Lagorce, a forceful French member of the Concorde team fighting for U.S. approval in the mid-seventies, was equally forceful in drawing realistic lessons in 1988. Optimistic and flawed SST market studies were not evaluated critically, he admitted, because of the conviction that a European SST should be built simply because it was technically possible to do it.[4] French national pride and a lack of business experience in the defense ministry, at that time responsible for aviation issues, were two other reasons the program gained irresistible momentum in Paris, according to the French official.

A Not-So-Special Relationship

Going back to the beginning, what are we to make of the abortive efforts to launch an Anglo-American SST program? An FAA historian has put forward a reductionist reason for the failure of the proposed deal: quite simply, the United States, unlike Britain, had no need of a partner.[5] Najeeb Halaby, the man who politely but firmly resisted the British overtures then, demurs: there would have been benefits, but they were outweighed by the perceived problems. As a former assistant secretary of defense for international security affairs, Halaby had enjoyed working with the British. As a former test pilot on the early jet aircraft, he recognized the technology contribution that the United Kingdom could bring to the table. Thus reasons of international diplomacy, plus the benefits of cost-sharing and potentially easier agreements on landing rights, favored a joint venture. Against that, the United States was more advanced in materials technology and so was not restricted to light alloys and Mach 2, and there would have been major problems in linking publicly subsidized British companies with a private American company. Halaby adds:

> There were also competitive industrial factors that said, not only we can do it better, but we should do it as an American aircraft as we have done the DC-8 and the 707 and so on. We wouldn't be constrained by the government bureaucrats in Britain and France. . . . In general, I guess it's fair to say we were still in a superpower, near-monopolistic, aggressively competitive frame of mind at that time, and there weren't too many saying "go multilateral."[6]

In fact, after leaving the FAA, where he had fended off the British advances in the sixties, Halaby in the seventies had appeared to favor transatlantic collaboration on a super-Concorde. In 1976 he recalled proposing that Britain and France should build "only enough Concordes to do the service testing across the Atlantic," after which collaboration with the United States on a super-Concorde could result in a bigger, faster SST. The three governments—or possibly the European Community and the U.S.—might provide enough research and developmental support to enable the fuel cost problem, the airport noise problem, and the alleged ozone-layer problem to be solved.[7]

Denis Haviland, a senior British official during the 1960–1962 Anglo-American SST talks, has consistently maintained that the failure to launch such a joint venture was a "world tragedy in aviation."[8] His recollection, unsupported by available contemporary papers, is that at an early stage—before the U.K.-French talks that led to the Concorde—a deal with Boeing on an "interim" Mach 2 machine was close to approval. American interest suddenly waned in 1961, apparently because of technical doubts about the feasibility of the Mach 2 design approach.

Sir George Edwards and others identify the obvious sticking point: the conflicting national preferences for Mach 2 and Mach 3. "The biggest hurdle to a joint American-European programme then was the determination on the part of the Americans, both industry and NASA, to do a steel/titanium aeroplane cruising at Mach 3," Sir George writes, "and to regard the Concorde as an interim aeroplane."[9] Sir James Lighthill, who was director of the Royal Aircraft Establishment when the STAC report was published, agrees:

> In retrospect I feel that there was never any realistic prospect whatsoever of a joint supersonic transport aircraft [STA] project between the U.K. and the U.S.A. On the contrary, the U.S. were determined that if a supersonic transport aircraft emerged it would be American. They believed, furthermore, that their imagined technical superiority would ensure the development of a better STA design which would be competitively an overwhelming winner. Here, of course, they were mistaken, because they underestimated the immense amount of effort that had been put into the STAC report.[10]

For Aubrey Jones, the British minister who started the supersonic ball rolling in Macmillan's cabinet in 1958, there is a wider political message. In his view, the history of the Concorde epitomizes the history of Britain since 1945.[11] "The country has remained slung uneasily between the U.S.A. and Europe, unable to let go its wartime remnant of glory with the United States, and nervous over seeking a new glory through Europe." Certainly Britain's role in Europe remains a controversial political issue in the nineties, as the federal implications of a potential United States of Europe provoke continuing conflicts, both within Britain and between the United Kingdom and its continental partners.

Impacts and Approval

"The Franco-British Concorde program . . . sets the pace, poses our problems and defines the competitive and technical necessities of the United States supersonic transport," wrote Eugene Black and Stanley Osborne in December 1963. Indeed, there can be no doubting the enormous influence of the Concorde program on U.S. SST planning. This influence was characterized by the overuse of the foreign-threat argument by the SST protagonists, a healthy skepticism of Anglo-French claims by the opponents, and a continuing search for accurate Concorde intelligence. In the reverse direction, the influence of the American SST program on the Concorde was simple: a strong pressure to move ahead as fast as possible—resulting in at least some of the mistakes that were made. Equally, the cancellation of the American program in 1971 had an effect on the Concorde program that was not readily appreciated at the time. It left the Anglo-French machine in an exposed position as the only western SST under development. As long as both the Concorde and the American SST were in business, supersonic transports were in a sense respectable—or relatively so. With the U.S. machine out of the race, all the environmental and other opposition would be focused on the Concorde. Also, the Anglo-French team feared that an anti-Concorde campaign might be mounted by American industrial or political interests based simply on the airplane's non-American origin. No evidence of any such campaign, other than isolated comments in Congress, was found during the research for this book.

As for the approval process, behind the bare bones of the decisions by William Coleman, Judge Pollack, and Chief Judge Kaufman lay a number of crucial legal and political issues. Though Judge Pollack's ruling that the Coleman decision preempted the port authority's ban was reversed on appeal, there was no doubt that the transportation secretary had the power to preempt. Foreign relations and the regulation of international air transport are clearly a responsibility of the federal government, and any action by an individual state—or a bistate agency such as the port authority—that conflicts with federal government policy is unconstitutional. The other side of this coin is that if the federal government does act to preempt local actions, it is responsible for the consequences. Thus, in the case of the Concorde, the federal government would have been legally responsible for noise damage claims, and President Ford (or his successor, President Carter) would have been politically responsible for imposing the environmentally controversial Concorde service on the voters of New York state.

Thus the dilemma for the Ford administration was whether to incur the wrath of Britain and France or offend New York voters and possible plaintiffs. In resolving this dilemma, Secretary Coleman trod a narrow, slippery path, authorizing the demonstration services while remaining equivocal on the question of preemption. Indeed, his decision mentioned the possibility of a refusal of landing rights by the airport proprietor at New York. In other words, a federal decision appeared to contemplate some scope for contrary state action. According to a key participant, this is sometimes known as "tap dancing" (your feet never quite stay on the ground), and in his Concorde decision William Coleman proved to be a veritable Fred Astaire.[12]

Thus the matter had to be resolved in the courts. Though the final ruling against the port authority was not made on the preemption issue per se, it was still very much a preemption decision. Chief Judge Kaufman held that the port authority's action had exceeded the bounds of the federal policy to permit reasonable and nondiscriminatory local noise restrictions.

Since the federal government possessed the power to preempt local actions, it was hardly surprising that President Giscard d'Estaing's repeated efforts to have the ban overturned were directed at the U.S. president. The French were placing political blame for the situation, correctly, on the executive branch of the federal government, which had decided to risk a rupture with Britain and France rather than take the domestic heat of a decision to order the port authority to admit the Concorde. On the other hand, as seen by their British partners, the French appeared unable to recognize the politically face-saving role that the federal courts could, and ultimately did, play in resolving the dilemma.

The equivocal Coleman decision was presented in such a way that the New York issue was virtually certain to go before a federal judge for final resolution. That route offered a new avenue for the U.S. government to help the Concorde proponents, one that proved decisive, in the shape of the amicus curiae brief in the appeal. In this brief, for the first time, the U.S. government stated that unreasonable or discriminatory action by an airport proprietor would violate federal policy and would be unlawful.

Airline Service

The real aim of the Concorde program was not simply to design and develop a supersonic airliner, or to occupy scientists, engineers, managers, and civil servants, or to promote togetherness between Britain and France. Those were means to an end, and the end was to provide airlines with an aircraft that would carry passengers routinely and profitably in regular service. The lessons of airline service, therefore, are particularly important. An early lesson was that most airlines chose not to buy Concordes, since on normal commercial grounds the aircraft would have been unprofitable to buy and to operate. This left Air France and British Airways as the only Concorde operators, the purchase of their aircraft having been largely financed by the two governments. In other words, the lesson of the market was that this airplane was not economical to buy or to operate.

The positive lesson of airline service is that this airplane flies well, is liked by its crews and passengers, and fills a market niche for regular transatlantic first-class travel and a range of worldwide charter operations. Capital costs having been written off, this airplane shows an operating profit—at fares on scheduled services about 30 percent above normal first-class fare. On the other hand, it needs—and receives—above-average care and attention.

In the air, the Concorde gives passengers the obvious benefits of supersonic speed and comfort. On the ground, it gives airline maintenance staff the headaches and high costs associated with complexity and sixties and seventies technology. Maintenance costs per flying hour are about four times those of the subsonic Boeing 747. In return for this careful grooming, the Concorde delivers an unmatched operational performance, in terms of reliability and punctuality as well as sheer speed. The safety record of the Concorde is excellent: no fatalities or injuries, though four major incidents were experienced between 1979 and 1993 (one tire burst on takeoff, causing wing damage on landing, and in three cases rudder sections broke off in flight).

The Concorde is likely to remain in service for a long time. In this respect as in others, it differs from the typical subsonic airliner. Normally, an airline is keen to fly its aircraft as intensively as possible, to gain the maximum annual utilization during the lifetime of the aircraft, which normally is determined by the approach of a successor promising better economic performance. Since Concorde regular scheduled routes are few and frequencies low, the annual utilization of the aircraft is much less than for typical subsonic airliners—about 1,000 hours per aircraft, compared with more than 4,000 hours for a subsonic 747. And there is no immediate successor in view.

The safe life of the Concorde was established by testing two complete airframes in elaborate test rigs at Farnborough and Toulouse. In the Farnborough fatigue laboratory, supersonic flight was simulated by repeatedly applying combined cycles of heat and pressurization to represent typical Concorde flights. This testing continued to a total of 20,000 cycles, or simulated flights, equivalent to about 60,000 flying hours. Applying a safety factor of three, the Concordes are cleared to continue flying until they have each logged 6,700 supersonic flights. This approved life is being extended, initially to 8,500 cycles, through an agreed program of modifications.

Whatever the eventually approved life, however, this limitation is unlikely to determine the date when the Concordes will cease flying. According to Captain W. D. "Jock" Lowe, British Airways director of flight operations, his airline will continue to fly the aircraft "as long as it makes a profit."[13] Revenue can be expected to increase slowly in the years ahead, he argues, while the costs of maintenance and fuel are likely to rise more rapidly. Thus, at some stage, costs will exceed revenue and the aircraft will become unprofitable—but not until well into the next century. In January 1996, as the Concorde completed 20 years in airline service, British Airways confirmed that the aircraft could well remain in service for another 20 years. The condition of the Concorde was said to be comparable to that of a four-year-old subsonic machine, thanks to the lower rate of flying, periodic refurbishment, and the heat generated in supersonic flight, which keeps the structure dry and so inhibits corrosion.[14]

Captain Lowe bases his assumption of increasing revenue on two factors: the traveling public's increasing disposable income and the addition of new seasonal routes. Both have been demonstrated by British Airways, which in addition to the year-round New York service flies scheduled services at certain times of the year to Barbados, Canada, and the Middle East. The Barbados service is significant in that it is not primarily a business route; people are buying tickets with their own money to make vacation trips, and increasingly so. Concorde charter flights, offered by a number of travel companies, continue to supplement the scheduled airline services of both Air France and British Airways. A variety of exotic excursions are offered, including round-the-world tours, weekend trips to Cairo, packages in association with the *Queen Elizabeth* 2 ocean liner and the Orient Express train, and supersonic "round the bay" trips featuring Christmas lunch over the Bay of Biscay before returning to Heathrow. More than 160 destinations have been visited on these supersonic charters.

In broad terms the Air France and British Airways experiences of the Concorde have been similar, though the British airline's aircraft have been flown more intensively and profitably, in part because London generates more traffic. Operationally, the airlines' Concorde record is one of innovation and excellence. In their first two decades of service, the French and British Concordes flew almost 200,000 hours.

Uneconomy Class

The sorry story of Concorde economics, judged by normal airline standards, was the result of a combination of factors, many of which had nothing to do with the characteristics of the aircraft. In principle, the main benefit to airlines offered by supersonics is productivity. In practice, since the main benefit to passengers is convenience, productivity is constrained by the hours of daylight and the effect of differing time zones. Other external factors that worsened Concorde economics included the seventies energy crisis and the political impossibility of establishing a wider route network. The experience of BOAC (which merged with British European Airways to form British Airways in 1972) illustrates the complex issues involved.

In the late sixties and early seventies, BOAC faced a dilemma. The British government, having paid (with the French) for the Concorde to be developed and built, expected the national airline to order the aircraft in the national interest. But the airline, though a nationalized corporation, was expected to apply normal commercial judgment and, on that basis, could not justify the purchase of the Concorde. A compromise was reached: BOAC would order five Concordes but would expect the government to assist if Concorde operations worsened the airline's finances. The £115 million order was signed in July 1972; it covered the first five aircraft at £13.5 million each, plus £47.5 million for spares, equipment, and other costs (all at estimated 1974 prices).

In April 1974 the airline, faced with the worldwide energy crisis and holding Concorde operating rights for not a single route, estimated that supersonic service was likely to lose about £16 million in a typical year. Its provisional operating plan for 1977–1978 was based on service to New York, Washington, Tokyo via Novosibirsk, and Sydney via Bahrain and Singapore, and assumed an annual utilization of 2,826 hours per aircraft. The capital cost of a Concorde was quoted as £19.16 million plus £23.64 million for spares and support, and the operating cost per seat-mile was estimated at 5.12 pence (the same cost for a Boeing 747 was only 1.64 pence). By January 1976 the airline's £115 million total Concorde investment had risen to £155 million, mainly because of inflation, and the cost per aircraft had risen to £20.5 million.

For the first three years of its supersonic operations, British Airways included amortization charges (assuming a ten-year life) in its Concorde financial accounts. In its annual report for the year ending 31 March 1976, covering only the first 174 hours of commercial Concorde flying, a loss of £2.3 million was recorded. In 1976–1977 the operating loss was about £8.5 million, highlighting the fact that each Concorde was carrying passengers for an average of about one hour a day only. "In these circumstances, any aircraft would lose money," the airline noted. In 1977–1978, a Concorde fleet loss of £17 million (after providing for amortization of £15 million) was reported.

The airline and its supersonic losses could not go on meeting like this. In 1979, after a government review, a new deal was negotiated. British Airways was to be allowed to write off the cost of purchasing its Concordes, and the government would take 80 percent of the airline's future Concorde surpluses. No such surplus had materialized before another new deal was struck in 1984. In-service support costs incurred by the manufacturers had been borne by the government since airline services began in 1976, and in 1982 the government warned that it intended to pay those costs no longer. In March 1984 the deal was settled: British Airways would pay £16.5 million to acquire the existing stocks of spare parts, to be released from the 80 percent commitment, and as a contribution to the support costs for 1983–1984. Thereafter the airline itself would pay British Aerospace and Rolls-Royce for their continuing in-service technical support of the Concorde fleet. (The support costs are substantial, including not only spares but also the costs of the manufacturers' development and support teams and the expenses of the periodic restyling of cabin interiors and of upgrading the aircraft to meet the longer-life requirements.)

On that basis, with capital costs written off and the airline paying the manufacturers' support costs as well as the normal direct and indirect costs of operating the aircraft, British Airways' Concorde fleet has remained profitable since 1983–1984. In its budget plan for 1980–1981 British Airways had given a further set of comparative operating costs for the Concorde and the Boeing 747 on the London–New York route. Total cost per seat was £398 for the Concorde and £115 for the 747, i.e., the supersonic machine was almost three and a half times as expensive.

So much for the Concorde and the facts of its unusual economic history. As for a possible future supersonic transport, we are dealing not with facts but with speculation and uncertainty. The outcome will depend basically on whether a three-class supersonic machine is economically possible. The proponents claim that it is; the critics argue that it is not. Certainly the Concorde experience underlines the difficulty of achieving that target. It is true that technology has advanced greatly since the Concorde was designed, and will advance farther, but subsonic technology also is improving, so the goalposts for comparison and competition are moving. The proponents foresee a substantial SST market based on the forecast expansion of the total long-range market; the critics doubt whether SSTs will be appropriate for more than a few first-class routes. Who is right? Time will tell—but one may note that the proponents tend to be manufacturers, not airlines.

Over the Horizon

In many ways, for those of us old enough to recall the aviation scene some 40 years ago, the present discussions on a possible successor to the Concorde—let us call it an advanced supersonic transport, or AST—arouse a distinct sense of déjà vu. As with the Concorde, industry estimates are promising a market of 500 to 1,000 air-craft. As with the Concorde, the talk is of collaboration between companies and between countries in order to share the cost and risk. As with the Concorde, there is a difference of opinion between the United States and Europe on the appropriate speed—though this time the choice is closer, between Mach 2.4 and Mach 2. As with the Concorde and the U.S. SST, the United States and Europe are each talking in terms of maintaining or regaining aeronautical leadership. On all these points, we have been here before.

In other ways, the situation is very different indeed. First, we have the Concorde experience as a guide, albeit with some reservations. The airline experience is valid, since the Concorde is the only supersonic transport in service. But the development experience is artificial, since normal commercial practices were distorted by the political context in which the project was conceived, leading to the straitjacket of the Anglo-French agreement. Had normal practices prevailed, the project would have been canceled, if not in 1964 then in 1974, or indeed it might never have been started without much more thorough preparation. In essence, a superb supersonic flying machine was built for the wrong reasons. It was built for national, political reasons on the foundations of technological optimism. It was a high-risk project throughout, and the performance of the resulting airplane is a credit to those who designed, developed, and built it. But nobody would dream of launching a supersonic successor that way today. That which we have already seen is now being seen through a different lens.

Certainly the dream of a son of Concorde is alive, but the dream will not be translated into an airplane until the environmental requirements have been set, the technology is available to meet those requirements at reasonable cost, there is a market for the product, and adequate financing is available to enable that market to be served. NASA repeats the mantra "environmentally acceptable, economically viable," but that sine qua non is frequently ignored, whether deliberately or not, by both proponents and opposers. Opponents tend to protest too much and too soon; since no supersonic transport is being developed, their ire is premature. Enthusiasts tend to assume that what may be technologically possible will inevitably come to pass; there are no "show-stoppers" so far, they proclaim (referring not to spectacular performances but to insurmountable technical barriers). Neither are there any show-starters, they could add.

If NASA and the companies mean what they say, the environmental battle is over; the standards are to be agreed on internationally, and until they can be met there will be no AST. It goes without saying that there will be no AST until the "economically viable" part also is achieved. But, and perhaps this does need to be said, this time around there will be no AST, even an environmentally and economically correct one, until the airlines want one. Deadlines for decisions are inappropriate. In 1994 the International Air Transport Association reported that the world's airlines were emerging from "the longest and most damaging period of financial losses in their history"; they are hardly likely to be pressing for early supersonics to ensure their future financial health.[15]

Najeeb Halaby, archadvocate for the SST in the sixties, thinks differently in the nineties. Times were different, he stresses: then the United States had a balanced budget, interest rates were 2 to 3 percent, and America was going to the moon. Going supersonic across the Atlantic and the Pacific appeared better than going to the moon, in terms of relative national product. Now, he says he was ill-advised to push the SST as much as he did. "My view now is that we've got to be careful about making national judgments on major projects, and look not just at the politics of technology but at its cost-benefit in the broadest sense." For the future, an advanced SST probably will cost $15 billion or more to develop. "In the midst of a worldwide depression, to spend any more than a little research money on an SST seems to me to be imprudent."[16]

Risks, Costs, and Flimflam

If there is to be a new supersonic airliner, it will be civil aviation's riskiest project ever. It was this realization that brought the member companies of the international study group together, and it is the detailed assessment of the various risks involved that continues to occupy their attention. Compared with a subsonic project, an AST is more expensive, demands a longer investment period, involves a higher level of new technology, and carries its own peculiar ecological and market risks. To reduce those risks to an acceptable level before launching the program—acceptable, that is, to prospective sources of finance as well as to the aircraft designers—will cost much more than for a subsonic machine.

Any new AST must satisfy the needs of different groups. Airlines must find it profitable to own and to operate. Passengers must find it affordable. Governments must find it environmentally acceptable. Manufacturers must see an adequate return on their investment. Just how the present AST research can be translated into a firm project to develop and build a machine able to meet all these needs—and, indeed, whether it should be so translated—are moot points. But in theory the various national and regional research programs now under way could come together to form a coordinated global group of programs, leading to agreement on a predevelopment phase, leading in turn to the launch of a firm development program. In the hope of turning this theory into practice, the five founder members of the international study group—Aérospatiale, Boeing, British Aerospace, Deutsche Aerospace (now Daimler-Benz Aerospace), and McDonnell Douglas—have suggested a sequence that they believe to be realistic.[17] The present combination of independent and collaborative research, they suggest, could be followed in about 1998 by a commitment to partnership on a joint predevelopment phase. A decision to launch a firm development program could be made in 2000 or 2001, leading to a first flight in 2004 or 2005 and the environmental-impact processes in 2006–2007.

Realism or flimflam? As with the Concorde and the U.S. SST, the issues are many and complex. The global approach would remove any competition for national leadership, except in the context of project leadership. This could dampen motivation for the project, which could push back the target dates, which in any case must be regarded as highly optimistic. The global approach also would raise big problems in selecting and implementing an effective organizational structure. Could the Airbus style or the Boeing 777 style be extrapolated to encompass the large number of participants? If not, is a second SST race conceivable—the United States and partners versus Europe and partners? That way, sadness lies.

Times Have Changed

The world aviation scene has changed a lot since the fifties, when Britain's plans for a supersonic airliner were discussed by no fewer than seven indigenous aircraft firms and four engine companies, when the annual Paris and Farnborough air shows invariably displayed new airplane types, when technical innovation in aeronautics tended to be pursued at the expense of commercial realities, and when air transport was a minority interest. Forty years on, mass air travel is routinely expected to be cheap, safe, frequent, and accessible; and the manufacturing and operating industries serving this market are facing tough competition in a depressed economic climate. Britain has slimmed down to one major aerospace firm and one aeroengine company, while in the United States even the largest of aerospace companies are coming together in mergers and takeovers. Europe now has experience of a variety of cross-border collaborative projects in aviation, in missiles, and in space technology. Worldwide, the realities of profitable business dominate decisions on high-technology ventures.

Projects such as the Concorde and the American SST experienced another type of change, as noted by Mel Horwitch in his analysis of the U.S. SST program.[18] In the early sixties, the American program emerged from a confident, protechnology society. Decisions on projects were determined by a relatively small group of advocates from industry and government, and debate was confined to this supportive network. As the decade advanced, however, society changed, and the impacts of technology became matters of public concern, culminating in the defeat of the U.S. SST in March 1971.

Though the environmentalists took credit for the cancellation of the SST, this oft-repeated claim was not the whole truth. Certainly, perceived environmental dangers affected the decision to cancel, but so also did wider congressional concerns such as national priorities and the merits and costs of public investment in private-industry projects. Boeing's questionable commitment to the SST as cancellation loomed also has been noted.[19] But whatever the reasons, the SST cancellation—and the later fight for the Concorde to fly into New York—underlined the significant change that had taken place, at least in the United States. Expensive aerospace decisions were no longer the prerogative of the advocates; aviation interests had become engulfed in wider issues and were now a matter for society at large. Indeed, the SST debate was the harbinger of open debates on other technology issues, such as nuclear safety and the implications of biotechnology.

As examples of the impact of technology on society, the U.S. SST and the Concorde highlighted the general issues of environmental concern and the role of technology in national priorities. But they give no general answers, because supersonic flight is a special sort of technology, bestowing its benefits up to now on a limited group of affluent people—far different, for instance, from the revolutionary, all-pervasive impact of information technology and digital communications in the nineties.

Some national attitudes have not changed, including the French enthusiasm for the supersonic cause. In June 1993 Air France flaunted a word it would not have dared to use 16 years earlier in an American newspaper. In a nearly full-page advertisement in the *Washington Post,* a large area of white space was occupied only by a small sketch of the Concorde and the words "sonic BOOM."[20] The text announced, "No other upgrade makes this kind of noise," and went on to tell of a scheme to upgrade first- and business-class passengers to seats on the supersonic airplane. In September 1990 Aérospatiale had taken a full-page, full-color advertisement in the British press to declare "WE BELIEVE . . . IN THE NEW ADVANCED SUPERSONIC AIRCRAFT."[21] Telling the British public of the new international study group, the French company concluded, "AEROSPATIALE: BELIEVING MAKES IT HAPPEN." Alas, there are those, and not only in perfidious Albion, who doubt the truth of this Cartesian proposition.

As for the British view, the name "Concorde" continues to arouse conflicting emotions, from "scandalous" to "magnificent." Robert McKinlay of British Aerospace says he has tried repeatedly to explain that while the British establishment may see the Concorde as a national folly, "the rest of the world has no such hang-up, and sees it as a great technical and collaborative achievement, one which the U.S. industry is particularly envious of."[22] With hindsight, the French can be regarded as both the villains and the heroes of the Concorde story: they ensured the survival of the aircraft, to disastrous economic effect—but they also ensured Europe's place in aviation history as the birthplace of the world's first operational supersonic airliner.

Times have indeed changed. There are signs that some of the lessons have been learned and that the early steps that might lead to an AST are being taken with care. In the United States the High-Speed Research program is set on the right lines—though arguably based on suspect market estimates. In Europe and in the international study group, the industry is cautiously exploring the concept of collaboration a great deal more realistically than before. On the other hand, NASA and U.S. industry may be showing undue haste in starting to develop the technology (HSR phase 2) before the environmental studies (phase 1) are complete. And there are questions concerning the development content of the U.S. research program, at least as seen from Europe.

The prime objective of the U.S. program is to ensure that U.S. industry is well placed to take the lead in any future AST. Europe has no such publicly funded program, but the British and French companies are anxious to gain a place commensurate with their Concorde experience in any international effort. Despite the impressive facilities built up at Toulouse as a direct result of the Concorde program, however, there is little prospect of a next-generation SST being assembled anywhere other than Seattle.

So, any attempt by an outside observer to answer with any assurance the question "Will there be another SST?" faces many uncertainties. Just as many uncertainties face the SST insiders as they attempt to unravel the unique combination of technological, environmental, economic, and political challenges that the laws of nature, business, and society have posed. Not only is the jury not out yet, but the case has not yet reached the courtroom. For Aérospatiale and others, the answer lies in faith—"Believing makes it happen." Others reach a very different conclusion: all supersonic transports are nonsense. Between those two extremes lies the reality.

In 1989 Louis Williams of NASA answered the question "Is a second-generation supersonic airliner possible?" with a qualified affirmative.[23] "Yes—but it probably won't arrive by the year 2000; it will be a very difficult and high-risk undertaking; the current technology is inadequate; and the public will resist its development unless it is clearly harmless to the environment." Deleting the word "probably," his nutshell answer remains true today.

Allied questions pose new scenarios. Is it conceivable that there will be a gap between the end of the Concorde's operational life and the appearance of another, advanced supersonic? That one day early in the next century the transatlantic flight time will be three and a half hours and the next day it will be eight hours again? That transportation will advance by slowing down?

Yes, it is conceivable—and we should not be unduly concerned. After the glorious aberration, the magnificent anomaly of the Concorde, the next supersonic airliner will appear if and when the time is ripe, if and when the technology, the economics, and the environmental safeguards are good enough. None of the three SSTs that have been tackled so far has been totally successful. If we take the time to think it through, we may be able to get it right next time.

APPENDICES

APPENDIX 1

Supersonic Transport: American Cooperation

Paper by Morien B. Morgan, deputy controller of aircraft (research and development), U.K. Ministry of Aviation, 12 October 1960
SOURCE: U.K. PUBLIC RECORD OFFICE, AVIA 63/21-E46

The line of argument I would like to advance, as a covering note to DGSR(A)'s essay at Enclosure 2 [a paper by L. F. Nicholson, "The basis of British policy for supersonic transport"], is the following:-

(1) A wide body of opinion believes that in two or three decades from now the bulk of long distance passenger travel will be at supersonic speeds. If Britain is to retain its position as a leading aeronautical power, we cannot let ourselves be edged right out of the supersonic transport field by America and Russia.

(2) At the moment we have a two or three year lead on the U.S.A. in hard thought and supporting research on supersonic *transport* (not bomber) problems. They are in effect just considering setting up the equivalent of our STAC to steer research and project work. We did this over three years ago.

(3) In this country, even if adequately financed, we really couldn't cope by ourselves with a Mach 3 steel design except on a very extended time scale with years of preparatory R&D assessment. So this can be dismissed. On the other hand, if properly financed, we *could* deal by ourselves with a Mach 2 design in light alloy without seri-

ously unbalancing our industry. It would only mop up a portion of the resources of one of our large groups.

(4) All the present indications are that the Americans will, for prestige reasons, go for a Mach 3 steel machine. However, technical sense may in the end prevail, and they may veer round to a Mach 2 light alloy aircraft. According to Quesada they will not be in a position to go to industry and select firms for a specific task for another two years.

(5) DGSR(A)'s curves illustrating the influence of numbers built on direct operating costs suggest to me that once you have built about 30 light alloy machines the whole venture may be commercially viable even if you amortise fully your development charges. It would be nicer to build 80, but the variation of direct operating costs as between a build of 30 and 80 is quite comparable to the result of possible variation in the technical parameters such as structure weight, L/D [lift/drag ratio] and engine efficiency. I suggest that we should be able to sell 30 to BOAC, Transport Command, and a few friends, and that "going it alone" on a light alloy machine is not necessarily ludicrous. Anglo-American (and Anglo-French) cooperation can of course be explored. My point is that we would not be sunk if such cooperation was not achieved.

(6) If the Americans went ahead vigorously with a steel machine, I suggest that it would come out on the routes at least three years later than our light alloy machine; that its direct operating costs would be higher than ours, even if no development charges were included, and that its initial cost would be considerably higher. Very substantial subsidy would be needed for it to compete with ours. We will not know the precise form here for several years, but my estimate is that we could successfully "go it alone" on our light alloy machine even if the Americans settled on steel; provided, and only provided, we get moving quickly and don't abandon our lead time.

(7) If, after two years study, the Americans settle on Mach 2 light alloy, *then* will be the time for a straightforward commercial deal between our firm and the American firm to share the market, split design responsibility, and split production. This is bound to lead to inefficiency, but this may be the price to pay for not being forced right out by strong arm methods. If, as I suspect, there is a market for well over 100 aircraft, then it by no means follows that such cooperation is essential; but the case for it can be seen, although I do not think it is as strong as many people at present believe.

One fact is inescapable, however. Our bargaining position will be immeasurably increased if, during the next two years, we really have made substantial and sustained progress with an actual design. Resting on our STAC laurels would cut no ice at all.

(8) The moral of all this is that, even with the present policy thoughts on cooperation with U.S.A., not much detailed planning on cooperation can be done for the next two years until the Americans have completed their STAC type work and selected a firm; and that there is everything to be gained by really getting a move on at this end with our local Mach 2 project. In this context the £500,000 for the first year is on the thin side, but it will at least enable us to start getting up steam.

(9) Cooperation on such matters as certification, background research on airfield standards, noise, harmonisation of safety requirements, and so on is obviously desirable;

it may well be appropriate for our people to get together with the FAA chaps on this, as a follow-up to Quesada's visit, in the spring of next year.

APPENDIX 2

The Black-Osborne Report

Extracts from the report to President Johnson by Eugene Black and Stanley Osborne, 19 December 1963
SOURCE: LYNDON B. JOHNSON LIBRARY, PRESIDENT'S ADVISORY COMMITTEE ON SUPERSONIC TRANSPORT, BOX 69

<u>Should the United States now join the "Concorde" consortium?</u>
While the possibility may have existed some years ago that we could have joined, at least the British, in a joint supersonic transport development, this possibility does not seem to exist today, although from time to time there have been intimations that conversations might be renewed.

1. The Europeans feel that they are well on their way towards production, and that their designs for air frame and engines are sufficiently frozen to make United States technical collaboration somewhat too late and the possible input too complicated to be feasible.

2. The "Concorde" producers seems confident that their technology and production schedules are well enough in advance of ours so that, at least in the Mach 2.2 regime, they will be able to capture the market. This aircraft has been intended to be the tool in making Europe the dominant force in air transportation during the 1970s and beyond.

3. Our own manufacturers, wary of committee management inherent in consortiums, are even more hesitant of participating in one with foreign producers who have different technological systems and goals.

4. The only present feasible merging of interests would be through the contribution of funds to the "Concorde" development, and having one or more of our manufacturers acquire manufacturing licenses from the Europeans. This course would result in the necessary division of future markets, compromises on the part of the United States airlines on the first (and probably the next) generation of aircraft, and a marked slowing down of supersonic technological development within the United States. It would also probably make it impossible to proceed with any advanced aircraft, and might well freeze all supersonic transport development to a tripartite consortium for the foreseeable future.

Unless technological or time factors change current postures, we see neither an efficient nor a commercially possible way of forming a tripartite consortium.

5. The ideal solution for the Europeans would be for the United States to concede the first generation of supersonic transports to the "Concorde," and to proceed now with the development of a larger and faster, Mach 3.5 or upward, hypersonic plane,

which would follow the "Concorde" by seven to ten years. This we do not consider sound nor feasible, from an economic and technological point of view, and we will discuss this more fully later.

6. We are not that far behind our European friends to force us to trade money and market limitations for possible advanced technology, which we might think we do not possess. Nor will we lose the whole market if we complete a superior aircraft within a reasonable time after the "Concorde" is aloft in commercial service.

7. On the other hand, we should like to caution that under no circumstances should the United States assess its own future course by the conclusion that the "Concorde" will fail to be a good airplane, that it will not live up to its design characteristics, nor that it will not reasonably meet its time schedules. Advanced technology is not the property of any one nation as has been so vividly demonstrated in the past 20 years, and we are therefore confident that Great Britain's and France's technologists are knowledgeable, expert, and able to deliver on their promises.

It is our conclusion that it is not feasible to join the "Concorde" consortium and that we must "go it" alone or abandon the supersonic transport to Europe. . . .

How much delay in deliveries can a United States supersonic transport afford, compared with the "Concorde"?
While probably this subject should be discussed as part of the important discussion of "Program" below, we feel it is important enough to merit separate identification.

Based on the conviction that the United States should not race into a supersonic program just to be first or nearly so, at the cost of not having a sound, long-lived, and economic aircraft, we have studied the effect of a delayed delivery of a United States supersonic transport on its potential market.

The two most important factors in this situation are the rate of construction which the competitive plane will have, and the degree of obsolescence which a United States supersonic transport will bring upon the "Concorde."

(a) Even if the United States were only to produce a similar plane to the "Concorde," but with enough improvements to offset the cost/price differential, the projected construction rate of the European plane and the need of competitive airlines to get aircraft would permit the United States to lag behind on its first deliveries by about six months to a year and still have more than a reasonable chance to share the total estimated market of 200-400 aircraft in the 1970s.

(b) On the other hand, if the United States produces a definitely superior plane which incorporates greater range, higher speed, and better airline operating economics, plus the potentiality of "growth and development," we are persuaded that the United States can be as far back as two to three years and still capture the *bulk* of the supersonic transport market.

(1) The airline industry will probably not permit itself again to suffer the overnight obsolescence such as it had to undertake with the DC-7, and other advanced piston aircraft,

when the subsonic jets became operative. Therefore, if the United States can fly and demonstrate a prototype that answers the characteristics mentioned above, before orders have to be placed for the "Concorde," then no airline will permit more than an absolute minimum of planes to become obsolete.

(2) Unlike other planes, the United States supersonic transport will have a price of two to three times that of current jets, and should have a depreciable life of 12 to 15 years. This involves huge investments for the airline industry, and therefore the airlines cannot buy a fleet of an inferior plane, only to have it assuredly and rapidly obsoleted by a superior growth aircraft within the first 10%–20% of the fleet's expected life.

Therefore we conclude that with assurance that they can have distinctly superior aircraft available within two to three years, the airlines may buy a few "Concordes" to stay competitive on "blue-ribbon" runs, but will defer their major purchases for the United States supersonic transport.

These facts therefore lead us directly to the conclusions that:

1. The timing of the United States program need not be tied too closely to that of the "Concorde";
2. The United States program must be able to demonstrate to the airlines a qualified prototype at about the same time in which the "Concorde" is being demonstrated;
3. The United States cannot afford to build a copy of the "Concorde" but must, if it is going into the supersonic transport business, build a superior plane.
4. If a superior craft is built, the delay is not only agreeable to the United States airlines, but may even be for most others, including those airlines most closely related to the Governments of Britain and France.

APPENDIX 3

Concorde Impact on SST Schedules

Paper prepared by Dr. Stephen Enke for meeting of the President's Advisory Committee on Supersonic Transport, 9 July 1966
SOURCE: LYNDON B. JOHNSON LIBRARY, PRESIDENT'S ADVISORY COMMITTEE ON SUPERSONIC TRANSPORT, BOX 34

It is obvious that, rightly or wrongly, most persons in government concerned with the U.S. SST program have been influenced more strongly by the supposed Concorde "threat" than any other single factor. This has been true of Congressmen, two FAA Administrators, and some members of the PAC. It is therefore most regrettable that almost no analyses, quantitative or qualitative, have been made of the true nature of this threat and how best to counter it.

The U.S. SST schedule evolved at the October and November 1965 meetings of the PAC seemed to be dictated by a desire to be not more than about two years behind Concorde. The risky one-year overlap of Phase 4 and Phase 3 is one example. In thus reacting, the announced Concorde schedule was accepted as realistic without much examination of its practicality.

Several aspects of the interacting Concorde and U.S. SST programs have been largely overlooked.

First, what counts are (1) the estimated last possible dates that particular airlines having options on the Concorde delivery list must irrevocably risk significant sums, and (2) which of these dates are *before* the time when the U.S. expects to have completed 100 hundred hours of prototype flight *indicating profitable performance* at a price of around $35 million each.

Second, accumulating supersonic flying hours on the prototype aircraft may take much longer than expected, because of accidents, crashes, etc. One economical way to catch-up on the Concorde might be for the U.S. to proceed at a deliberate and prudent pace on design but to construct several more prototype aircraft than planned for Concorde. As the U.S. SST will be *more* of a technological jump it will be attended by more serious physical risks. General Maxwell has long argued privately for more prototype aircraft in the budget. However, because the extra cost might deter some Congressmen, General McKee has not made this plea. (The B-70 warning should not go unheeded.)

Third, having the Concorde available for delivery to airlines will mean little until it has been certified in the U.S. And airlines will have little interest in the U.S. SST until it has also been certified in Britain, France, or possibly the Netherlands. Certification could become very "dirty" and an almost simultaneous exercise in commercial reciprocity. The Concorde will have novel engineering features (e.g. center of gravity control) about which the U.S. can for a while express serious doubts. (Of less importance is the ability of the U.S. to prohibit overland supersonic commercial flight until the U.S. SST is to be placed on such routes.) But much of the commercial advantage to Concorde of being first physically with an SST may well be lost because of circumstances that the USG determines.

In the early spring of 1965 Jeeb Halaby was urging the start of Phase 3, which would probably have been with the Boeing design. Since then Boeing has discovered that the planned location of engines, undercarriage and wing pivots is not feasible, and has been forced into a radical redesign. Also the probable introduction of jumbo subsonics may have drastically reduced the size of market available to supersonics.

It is interesting that the majority view in the U.K. Treasury and Ministry of Aviation is that some way should be evolved of not commiting HMG to more than a token sharing of *production* costs. Even in the French government there are guarded misgivings. Collectively the three national governments concerned are not in control, because each side is being driven by the other, and no one is prepared to take the initiative in breaking out of the dilemma.

APPENDIX 4

International Implications of U.S. Decision to Proceed with or Cancel Supersonic Transport Program

Memorandum to acting administrator, FAA, from Charles O. Cary, assistant administrator for international aviation affairs, 5 February 1969

SOURCE: WASHINGTON NATIONAL RECORDS CENTER, RECORDS OF FAA SUPERSONIC TRANSPORT DEVELOPMENT OFFICE, ACCESSION NUMBER 72A-6174, BOX 4

There are a number of potentially serious problems which could arise internationally as a result of the forthcoming decision to either proceed with or cancel the U.S. supersonic transport program. As the consequences may be quite serious and affect other aspects of our overall international position, I thought it might be useful to summarize the points for your consideration.

If the decision is to continue the SST program, a very careful examination should be made as to the effect which our proposed noise standards could have upon the British-French Concorde. Although the Notice of Proposed Rule Making unequivocally states that the proposed noise standards do not apply to supersonic transports, once a standard has been established and the public in areas surrounding airports become accustomed to that level of noise, it is a matter of some conjecture as to whether a different category of aircraft operating at a substantially higher noise level would be acceptable. It may well be that public protest and political pressure could in fact force the acceptance of then established subsonic noise levels for supersonic operations at airports in high population density areas, such as at Kennedy International Airport.

A second possibility is that a local airport owner, such as the Port of New York Authority, might establish noise restrictions which would bar the Concorde. There is a further possibility that in such an eventuality, a foreign government might misunderstand the FAA's interpretation of Public Law 90-411 with respect to eminent domain, and assume that the Federal Government does have the sole authority to admit or bar Concorde operations. As there has been no court case to test FAA's interpretation of the Act with respect to the eminent domain aspects, we cannot be certain that our own judiciary will uphold the FAA position; an adverse court decision could further complicate the international situation.

If the Concorde were effectively denied access to Kennedy, for whatever reason or by whatever authority, it is almost a foregone conclusion that both the United Kingdom and France would assume that such denial was for the sole purpose of providing the U.S. SST with an opportunity to catch up competitively. This would seem to be particularly credible to a foreigner in view of the schedule delays which the Boeing SST has experienced. In the event that the Concorde could not operate into Kennedy, the reduction in size of its market would be so great that it could not reach the break-even point and the program would in fact sustain a substantial loss.

At varying times, both the Board of Trade and the Ministry of Technology have privately believed that it would be economically desirable to cancel the Concorde program. In one instance, French pressure prevented this, but as the program moves from the prototype to the production stage, and with the attendant requirements for increased capital, the present government in the U.K. cannot afford to back a program of such magnitude if it is likely to sustain further major losses. Profitability of the Concorde program is particularly pertinent in view of the substantial costs involved and the difficult fiscal and monetary situation in the U.K.

Politically, cancellation of the program after the production run has started could cause major embarrassment to the Wilson government, and perhaps even force its fall. The British administration is quite aware of this, and might seek to place the responsibility for market attentuation upon the United States for failing to advise the U.K. or France sufficiently in advance of the possibility of our subsonic noise requirements becoming applicable to supersonic aircraft. They undoubtedly would accuse us of employing the noise regulations to obtain a competitive advantage. The latter point might gain particular public acceptance overseas, because the FAA appears to be both the manager of the SST program and the agency responsible for establishing U.S. noise standards.

The U.K. and France could justifiably point out that the FAA at no time officially advised either government of the character of possible supersonic noise requirements, or even of the possibility of local restrictions banning Concorde operations to Kennedy. Yet, through the Concorde Type Board, the FAUSST meetings, and other sources, the U.S. was presumably aware of Concorde noise levels.

Therefore, if the decision is to continue the program, careful consideration should be given to providing a full official briefing to the appropriate authorities in the U.K. and France as to the potential problems which could arise with respect to noise regulation, including the proposed sideline noise requirements, both Federal and local, so that an Anglo-French decision to proceed with the Concorde production would be based on a full understanding of possible problems within the U.S.

Concurrently, we should discuss with the Department of State the use of airports, by foreign airlines, other than Kennedy, on the eastern seaboard which would be suitable for Concorde operations and which would not bar them because of local noise restrictions. State may have similar reservations on the extension of rights to such airports for foreign SSTs as they have in connection with the congestion problem.

If a decision is made to cancel the SST program, consideration should be given to discussing the possibility of such a decision, in advance of any public announcement or release of information respecting the decision, with the U.K. and the French. It is possible if they knew that such an action was planned by the U.S. Government, that they might wish to take similar action with regard to the production phase of the Concorde. This possibility might be even greater if the French and the British were fully aware of the noise restrictions which the Concorde might encounter and particularly those which might be placed upon its operation into Kennedy, the major traffic gateway to the U.S. In any event, such consultation would serve to disarm them insofar as later public recrimination is concerned if a noise interdiction were placed on the Concorde at Kennedy during some phase of the production program. Fully documented minutes of meetings and correspondence would provide ample evidence that the U.S. had taken every reasonable step to alert the U.K. and France to the problems which might be forthcoming with respect to noise and supersonic flight over land. The fact that the U.S. took such action as soon as it became evident domestically that such problems *might* develop would help to reduce criticism. It should also be made clear that the noise standards would be non-discriminatory in character and would apply to foreign and U.S. aircraft and operators equally.

In the event Kennedy is not available for supersonic transport operations, we should indicate which airports would be available. This will affect not only the U.K. and France, but also the Soviet Union with its Tu-144, and all other countries to whom the Concorde or the Tu-144 might be sold. As many of the countries who may buy foreign SSTs already have bilateral air transport arrangements with the U.S., the above action with respect to airports becomes of some importance.

Prior to a firm decision on cancellation of the U.S. SST being taken, further consideration should be given to possible overall international political effects. The Soviet Union recently approached a second country with what appears to have been a "package" deal in which the sale of the Tu-144 was combined with certain bilateral route advantages which would accrue to the USSR. Aviaexport, the Soviet aircraft marketing arm, has recently been expanded and is making a substantial effort to penetrate new markets, including the offer of exceptionally advantageous financial terms to potential customers. If these are combined with air route negotiations, the U.S. may wish to consider whether the impact of the Soviet SST, or in fact "jumbo" jets or other modern aircraft, can be such as to make them in combination a new air transport route bargaining base. Certainly aviation routes have in the past provided means of economic and political penetration, and may become increasingly important from this standpoint in the future. Since the advent of the jets, U.S. industry both in terms of manufacturing and sales, has expanded in unprecedented fashion overseas. The development of tourism and construction of hotels to accommodate the increased traffic represents a major source of foreign exchange in many countries today.

Regardless of what decision is made—to proceed with the U.S. SST, to cancel it, or to stretch it out—consideration should be given to the various actions suggested above vis-a-vis the U.K. and France.

APPENDIX 5

The Kissinger Letter

Letter from Henry Kissinger, U.S. secretary of state, to William T. Coleman, Jr., secretary of transportation, 6 October 1975

SOURCE: *FAA CERTIFICATION OF THE SST CONCORDE,* HEARINGS BEFORE A SUBCOMMITTEE OF THE HOUSE COMMITTEE ON GOVERNMENT OPERATIONS, 24 JULY, 13 AND 14 NOVEMBER, 9 AND 12 DECEMBER 1975; AND 24 FEBRUARY 1976; 94TH CONGRESS, FIRST AND SECOND SESSIONS

Dear Bill:

I am happy to respond to your request for my views on the foreign policy considerations to be taken into account in your decision regarding the applications by Air France and British Airways to operate the supersonic Concorde aircraft to Kennedy and Dulles Airports.

We have until now addressed ourselves only to the procedural aspects of entry of the Concorde into the United States. In my letter to Chairman McClellan last July 22, I pointed out that the British and French governments had on several occasions expressed to us their concern about possible discriminatory treatment of the Concorde, and that we had assured them at the highest levels that the Concorde would be treated fairly in all aspects of U.S. Government regulation. We were pleased that the Congress agreed to allow the decision with regard to Concorde entry to be taken in accordance with the established administrative procedures and not to take specific legislative action against such entry.

The British and French authorities are fully mindful of the considerations involved in any decision on their applications, in view of the extensive public hearings and Congressional debates on the environmental aspects of the aircraft. In terms of our political relations, we realize that this project, in which both governments have invested very large sums, represents a unique achievement by both Britain and France in a high technology aircraft that commands close attention at the highest levels in both countries, as well as intense public and governmental interest in view of the financial stake and national prestige involved in placing the Concorde into commercial service, and especially into transatlantic service.

Under these circumstances, it is apparent that any Administration decision that would amount to an outright rejection of the applications of the two airlines for a limited service they intend to begin next year would be viewed as a serious blow by two of our closest friends and allies, whose interests coincide with our own in so many areas. The impact would be particularly severe in the case of France in light of the immense disappointment the French felt earlier this year in losing the international competition to the United States in providing a new military aircraft as the replacement for the F-104 fighter aircraft in the hands of certain other NATO countries. We could expect strong public and official resentment against the United States if we were to reach a decision that they would view as not in harmony with the generally excellent relations we now enjoy with both countries on a broad spectrum of important matters. It has been suggested that there would be pressures in one or both countries to respond to such a decision with some form of retaliatory action. Although the immediate practical possibilities in this respect would appear to be limited, protectionist elements would be strengthened, with consequent adverse effects. In any case, in view of our close and mutually advantageous relations with both of these countries, we should take due account of the impact of any decision on their interests.

I hope that in taking the Administration's initial decision with specific regard to the Concorde, you will find it possible to weigh carefully the concerns of these two close allies, together with the environmental and other criteria that you must consider.

Best regards,
Henry A. Kissinger

APPENDIX 6

Extracts from the Secretary's Decision

SOURCE: U.S. DEPARTMENT OF TRANSPORTATION, *THE SECRETARY'S DECISION ON CONCORDE SUPERSONIC TRANSPORT*, WILLIAM T. COLEMAN, JR., SECRETARY OF TRANSPORTATION, 4 FEBRUARY 1976

The Decision

After careful deliberation, I have decided for the reasons set forth below to permit British Airways and Air France to conduct limited scheduled commercial flights into the United States for a trial period not to exceed 16 months under limitations and restrictions set forth below. I am thus directing the Federal Aviation Administrator, subject to any additional requirements he would impose for safety reasons or other concerns within his jurisdiction, to order provisional amendment of the operations specifications of British Airways and Air France to permit those carriers, for a period of no longer than 16 months from the commencement of commercial service, to conduct up to two Concorde flights per day into JFK by each carrier, and one Concorde flight per day into Dulles by each carrier. These amendments may be revoked at any time upon four months' notice, or immediately in the event of an emergency deemed harmful to the health, welfare or safety of the American people. The following additional terms and conditions shall also apply:

1. No flight may be scheduled for landing or take-off in the United States before 7 a.m. local time or after 10 p.m. local time.

2. Except where weather or other temporary emergency conditions dictate otherwise, the flights of British Airways must originate from Heathrow Airport and those of Air France must originate from Charles de Gaulle Airport.

3. Authorization of any commercial flights in addition to those specifically permitted by this action shall constitute a new major federal action within the terms of NEPA and therefore require a new Environmental Impact Statement.

4. In accordance with FAA regulations (14 CFR #91.55), the Concorde may not fly at supersonic speed over the United States or any of its territories.

5. The FAA is authorized to impose such additional noise abatement procedures as are safe, technologically feasible, economically justified, and necessary to minimize the noise impact, including, but not limited to, the thrust cut-back on departure.

I am also directing the FAA, subject to Office of Management and Budget clearance and Congressional authorization, to proceed with a proposed High Altitude Pollution Program (HAPP), to produce the data base necessary for the development of national and international regulation of aircraft operations in the stratosphere.

I herewith order the FAA to set up monitoring systems at JFK and Dulles to measure noise and emission levels and to report the result thereof to the Secretary of Transportation on a monthly basis. These reports will be made public within 10 days of receipt.

I shall also request the President to instruct the Secretary of State to enter into immediate negotiations with France and Great Britain so that an agreement that will establish a monitoring system for measuring ozone levels in the stratosphere can be concluded among the three countries within three months. The data obtained from such monitoring shall be made public at least every six months. I shall also request the Secretary of State to initiate discussions through ICAO and the World Meteorological Organization on the development of international stratospheric standards for the SST. . . .

Concorde's Benefits: International Relations

International aviation as we know it today—the reciprocity of rights and privileges and the widespread exporting and importing of aircraft—is possible only through adherence to a complicated network of treaties and international agreements. Unlike domestic law, treaties and international agreements—because they are not subject to enforcement by any international police power or to the moral suasion of a homogenous culture—are delicate and fragile instruments. Their efficacy is dependent upon the good faith of the parties and upon the recognition of a greater self-interest that is attained only through long-term international cooperation. If provisions of international law are strictly construed or applied in new situations only to further some immediate self-interest, the entire fabric of international law is weakened. Obviously, even where a nation acts according to fair and nondiscriminatory motives, it must take care as well to avoid the appearance of unfairness or discrimination.

The Concorde represents a 13-year commitment of almost $3 billion by the British and French governments, who are among our closest allies and our best customers of United States goods. Prestige, economic vitality, and employment stability are at stake. Service to the United States on the lucrative North Atlantic market was from the first a substantial element in the Concorde program, and denying the aircraft landing rights in this country could well abort the program. The United States must therefore be very careful, in the interests of our relations with England and France and of the continuation of the free and open use of the established international airways, to be wholly fair and nondiscriminatory in making this decision, and to take into account the fact that the decision may in any event be perceived as being unfair and discriminatory.

Although I believe, to the extent one can ever fairly judge one's own actions, that whatever decision I might have made today would have been fairly motivated, a decision totally to deny the Concorde landing rights might easily have been perceived as discriminatory for two reasons. First, the United States would be open to the charge that we treated our own aircraft more favorably than those of foreign countries in regulating aircraft noise. The statutes and historical pattern of aircraft noise regulation, and indeed of most environmental regulation in this country, demonstrate that the promulgation of noise standards has closely followed the development of feasible technology to control noise. FAR 36 was promulgated over a decade after the advent of commercial jet aviation, and 80 percent of the planes in service today still do not satisfy its standard. The regulation was initially written to exempt temporarily aircraft certificated before 1969, which could not comply, and was amended to cover new versions of those aircraft only after the technology became available. The Federal Aviation Act specifically requires the Administrator of the FAA to consider technological feasibility in promulgating regulations. All feasible steps have been taken to control the Concorde noise, and it cannot be modified further to abate the noise levels. Consequently, if we refused to let the Concorde land for noise reasons, the British and the French might well be justified in feeling that the Concorde had been given harsher treatment than we gave our own jets.

Second, the British and French might justifiably feel that the United States was discriminating in its attitude towards stratospheric pollution. There is some risk that even a few Concorde flights may reduce by a slight amount the ozone layer, and that this may cause an increase in the incidence of non-fatal skin cancer. But this is admittedly only speculation. Only recently the United States Consumer Product Safety Commission has denied petitions to initiate rulemaking to ban fluorocarbons, even though the evidence presented would have indicated that the impact of fluorocarbons on the ozone is substantially greater than that of the Concorde. The United States cradles other significant potential sources of stratospheric pollution—military aircraft operations, fertilizers, the space shuttle program—and unless the United States is willing to act against these sources as well, action against the Concorde could well be perceived as discriminatory.

Apart from appearance of discrimination, the British and French might perceive in a negative decision an unfair element of surprise, a defeat of justifiable reliance. No promises have been made to the British or French. However, the United States has never promulgated a noise standard applicable to SSTs. In February 1975 the EPA proposed several alternatives, and expressed a preference for the option that would have exempted the first 16 Concordes manufactured and permitted them to land at federally designated airports with approval of the proprietors under specified restrictions. A total ban at this point might well be perceived by our allies as the imposition of a penalty for which they were not given notice. It is true that we would be applying NEPA, but that Act provides little in the way of definite standards which might have put the British and the French on clear notice of precise limits of the amount of noise pollution the United States was willing to tolerate.

Finally, the British and French might well feel that the United States had taken advantage of the benefits of the relatively free and open international aviation structure while being unwilling to pay the costs. The United States has been the chief beneficiary of the agreements and treaties that permit international use of aircraft based on the airworthiness certificate of the manufacturing country. Almost 95 percent of the commercial and general aviation jet aircraft that have been sold in the free world in the last five or six years have been made in this country. Last year, we exported $2.7 billion in aircraft and aeronautical components—second only to agricultural products in helping to maintain a favorable balance of trade. United States air carriers and aircraft have facilitated commerce throughout the world, opened up new markets for United States products, and created a great many jobs at home. The United States has also been the chief beneficiary of the absence of noise regulations in other nations, for our aircraft—noisy aircraft such as the Boeing 707 and the DC-8—have been welcomed in the great majority of countries in this world, and have been sold to other countries when our air carriers replaced them with newer, quieter jets. A negative decision could well defeat the British and French effort to enlarge their share of the international aeronautical industry. In view of the history of United States dominance of the aviation industry, it would be quite remarkable if such a decision were not considered to be unfair.

SOURCES AND ABBREVIATIONS

Sources used in the U.S. research for this book include the records of the FAA Historian's Office (abbreviated FAA Hist. in the notes); the records of the FAA Office of Supersonic Transport Development (FAA-SST), held in the Washington National Records Center, Suitland, Maryland; the NASA History Office (NASA Hist.); the U.S. National Archives (NA); the John F. Kennedy Library, Boston (JFK); the Lyndon B. Johnson Library, Austin, Texas (LBJ); the National Air and Space Museum (NASM) archives at the Garber Facility, Silver Spring, Maryland; and the records of the Citizen's League against the Sonic Boom, held in the Institute Archives and Special Collections of the Massachusetts Institute of Technology Libraries (MIT) in Cambridge, Massachusetts. The source abbreviations are followed where possible by the relevant collection, box, and file numbers.

Records consulted at the presidential libraries include those of the President's Advisory Committee on Supersonic Transport (LBJ-PAC), Vice-Presidential Files (LBJ-VP), National Security Files (LBJ-NSF), President's Office Files (JFK-POF), and oral history transcripts. The collections consulted in the FAA-SST records have accession numbers 237-70A-905 and 237-72A-6174, here abbreviated to 905 and 6174. Public sources include the *Public Papers of the Presidents of the United States* series; *Federal Reporter, Federal Supplement,* and *United States Reports* volumes; and the *CQ Weekly Reports* and annual *Almanacs* published by Congressional Quarterly Inc. Also consulted were the archives of the Boeing company in Seattle.

British official records held in the Public Record Office, Kew, are indicated by the abbreviation PRO, followed by the group, class, and piece numbers. Also consulted were the archives of British Aerospace (BAe) at Bristol, and the Open University archive collection of recorded interviews (Course D203, Decision-making in Britain).

NOTES

Chapter 1. Quest for Speed

1. Kenneth Owen, *Concorde: New Shape in the Sky* (London: Jane's, 1982).
2. Federal Aviation Agency, *Project Horizon: Report of the Task Force on National Aviation Goals* (Washington: GPO, 1961).
3. Robert J. Serling, *Legend and Legacy: The Story of Boeing and Its People* (New York: St Martin's Press, 1992).
4. T. A. Wilson to Senator William Proxmire, in U.S. Congress, Joint Economic Committee, *The Supersonic Transport: Hearings before the Subcommittee on Priorities and Economy in Government of the Joint Economic Committee*, 92nd Cong., 2nd sess., 27–28 December 1972.
5. Howard Moon, *Soviet SST: The Technopolitics of the Tupolev-144* (New York: Orion Books, 1989).
6. Geoffrey Knight, *Concorde: The Inside Story* (London: Weidenfeld & Nicolson, 1976).
7. Owen, *Concorde.*
8. *The New York Times,* 28 July 1974.
9. Moon, *Soviet SST.*
10. *The Times* (London), 10 August 1984.

Chapter 2. Could We, Should We, Go It Alone?

1. U.K. cabinet, "Aircraft industry," 2 May 1958, memorandum by the chancellor of the exchequer, PRO-CAB 129/92.

2. Cabinet, "The aircraft industry," 18 December 1958, memorandum by the minister of supply, PRO-CAB129/95.

3. Cabinet, 87th conclusions, 23 December 1958, PRO-CAB128/32.

4. Cabinet Committee on Civil Aviation Policy, "The aircraft industry," 27 January 1959, note by the minister of supply, PRO-CAB134/1446.

5. Sir Claude Pelly to firms, 8 May 1959, and replies, PRO-AVIA65/213.

6. Minister of supply to prime minister, note, 2 July 1959, "Supersonic transport," PRO-CAB134/1447.

7. Minister of transport and civil aviation to prime minister, note, 22 July 1959, "Supersonic civil aircraft," PRO-CAB134/1447.

8. Cabinet Committee on Civil Aviation Policy, "Supersonic transport aircraft," 15 September 1959, memorandum by the minister of supply, PRO-CAB134/1446.

9. Cabinet, 52nd conclusions, 18 September 1959, PRO-CAB128/33.

10. Aubrey Jones, letter to author, 20 June 1992.

11. Aubrey Jones, *Britain's Economy: The Roots of Stagnation* (Cambridge: Cambridge University Press, 1985).

12. "Notes of a meeting held in DAC's office on 16 September 1959 between representatives of Hawker Siddeley, Bristols and MoS," PRO-AVIA65/213-4525.

13. "Notes of a meeting held in room 345 on Thursday, 26th November 1959," PRO-AVIA65/213-4725.

14. "Note of a meeting with the French Air Ministry on 10 February 1960 to discuss the possibilities of collaboration on a supersonic transport," PRO-AVIA63/20-E29.

15. "Report of Anglo-French discussions held on the 12th April 1960 (translation of French text)," PRO-AVIA63/20-E64.

16. E. I. R. MacGregor to Sir George Gardner, 29 March 1960, PRO-AVIA63/21-E16.

17. Cabinet, "Supersonic airliner," 12 July 1960, memorandum by the minister of aviation, PRO-CAB129/102.

18. Cabinet, "Supersonic airliner," 19 July 1960, memorandum by the chancellor of the exchequer, PRO-CAB129/102.

19. "Brief for agenda item 2, supersonic transport aircraft," first policy review meeting on Anglo-American cooperation in civil aviation, 7–8 September 1960, PRO-AVIA63/21-E33.

20. "Discussions on Anglo-American cooperation in civil aviation: Note of meeting on 7 September 1960 in room 140, Shell Mex House," PRO-AVIA63/21-E35.

21. "Note of a discussion in CA's office on 20 September 1960," PRO-AVIA63/21-E39.

22. Nicholson, DGSR(A), "The basis of British policy for supersonic transport," 12 October 1960, PRO-AVIA63/21-E46. Morgan, DCA/RD, "Supersonic transport—American cooperation," 12 October 1960, PRO-AVIA63/21-E46.

23. J. A. R. Kay, "Notes on discussion with Mr. Hall Hibbard, senior vice-president, Lockheed Aircraft Corp. on 8th September 1959," in Hawker Siddeley Aviation, *Feasibility Study on Supersonic Transports: Report APG 1000/2305*, 1960, addendum B, appendix 12, BAe.

24. Hibbard to Kay, 8 March 1960, in Hawker Siddeley Aviation, *Feasibility Study,* addendum B, appendix 12.

25. S. D. Davies, "Notes on discussion with Mr. George S. Schairer, Boeing Airplane Co. on 18th and 21st February 1960," in Hawker Siddeley Aviation, *Feasibility Study,* addendum A, appendix 12.

26. R. Verdon Smith to the director of civil aircraft, Ministry of Aviation, 23 May 1960, PRO-AVIA65/1508-1488 and 1215.

27. Hawker Siddeley Aviation, *Feasibility Study,* appendix 12.

Chapter 3. Seriously Seeking a Partner: The Quest Continues

1. U.S. House, Committee on Science and Astronautics, *Supersonic Air Transports: Hearings before the Special Investigating Subcommittee of the Committee on Science and Astronautics,* 86th Cong., 2nd sess., May 1960.

2. House Committee on Science and Astronautics, *Supersonic Air Transports: Report of the Special Investigating Subcommittee,* 86th Cong., 2nd sess., June 1960, H. Rept. 2041.

3. Federal Aviation Agency, Department of Defense, and National Aeronautics and Space Administration, "A national program for a commercial supersonic transport aircraft," October 1960, FAA Hist.

4. Federal Aviation Agency, "Commercial supersonic transport aircraft report," December 1960, FAA Hist.

5. Thorneycroft to Quesada, 27 October 1960, PRO-AVIA63/21-E58.

6. Quesada to Thorneycroft, 9 November 1960, PRO-AVIA63/21-E63.

7. Russell to Satre, 11 January 1961, PRO-AVIA63/20-E74.

8. Satre to Russell, 27 January 1961, PRO-AVIA63/20-E74.

9. Russell to N. V. Meeres, 23 January 1961, PRO-AVIA63/21-E72.

10. J. G. Ashcroft, note for files, 18 January 1961, PRO-AVIA63/20-E72.

11. N. E. Halaby, memo for the record, 22 February 1961, FAA Hist.

12. Thorneycroft to Halaby, 7 March 1961, PRO-AVIA63/21-E77.

13. Paul T. Preuss, memorandum for Mr. Halaby, 16 March 1961, "Thorneycroft correspondence," FAA-SST 6174/14.

14. "Notes for Minister's visit to Paris, 1 June 1961: Possible Anglo/French collaboration on a supersonic transport project," PRO-AVIA63/20-E80.

15. British Aircraft Corporation, "Supersonic transport aircraft: International collaboration," 6 July 1961, PRO-BT242/184.

16. U.K. Ministry of Aviation, "Supersonic transport aircraft: Review of position near the end of the design study period and recommendations for further action (draft)," 13 July 1961, PRO-AVIA63/20-E101.

17. U.K. cabinet, "The future of the aircraft industry," 6 October 1961, memorandum by the minister of aviation, PRO-CAB129/106.

18. Foreign service dispatch, American embassy Paris to Department of State, Washing-

ton, 9 October 1961, "Civil aviation: Supersonic transport: Buron-Thorneycroft meeting and other recent developments," FAA Hist.

19. Cabinet, "The aircraft industry," 11 October 1961, memorandum by the chancellor of the exchequer, PRO-CAB129/107.

20. Georges Hereil, "European cooperation on research, development and production in the fields of aviation and astronautics," Fourth Dr. Albert Plesman Memorial Lecture, Technological University, Delft, 22 September 1961.

21. Hereil, Open University interview, 1976.

22. "MoA/FAA meeting, Washington, 6–8 November 1961. Advance brief on item 2: Status of supersonic transport program," FAA Hist.

23. FAA, "Discussions on Anglo-American cooperation in civil aviation," 6–8 November 1961, FAA Hist.

24. Wright to Rochte, 31 January 1962, and Wright to Halaby, 27 April 1962, FAA-SST 6174/14.

25. Rochte to Wright, 21 March 1962, FAA-SST 6174/13.

26. Kotz to Frank E. Loy, memo, 31 July 1962, "Consortium research, development and production of the supersonic transport," FAA-SST 6174/14.

27. Loy to Shank and Maloy, memo, 6 August 1962, "Supersonic transport," FAA-SST 6174/14.

28. Maloy to Shank and Loy, memo, 10 August 1962, "International cooperation on supersonic transport," FAA-SST 6174/14.

29. Beall to Allen, memo, 15 March 1962, "French supersonic commercial transport," Boeing archives.

30. Beall to Halaby, 16 April 1962, FAA-SST 6174/12.

31. Crudge to Beall, transcription of disks, 1 June 1962, Boeing archives.

32. U.K. cabinet, 38th conclusions, 29 May 1962, PRO-CAB128/36.

33. Cabinet Committee on Civil Scientific Research and Development, minutes of second meeting, 26 June 1962, "Supersonic airliner," PRO-CAB134/1585.

34. Cabinet Committee on Civil Scientific Research and Development, 26 June 1962, "Case for British participation in the development of a supersonic airliner," note by minister of aviation, PRO-CAB134/1585.

35. Cabinet Committee on Civil Scientific Research and Development, minutes of third meeting, 13 July 1962, "The supersonic airliner," PRO-CAB134/1585.

36. Cabinet Committee on Civil Scientific Research and Development, minutes of fourth meeting, 27 September 1962, "Supersonic airliner," PRO-CAB134/1585.

37. Cabinet, "The supersonic airliner," 3 November 1962, memorandum by the first secretary of state, PRO-CAB129/111.

38. Cabinet, 66th conclusions, 6 November 1962, PRO-CAB128/36.

39. Cabinet, 70th conclusions, 20 November 1962, PRO-CAB128/36.

40. "Agreement between the Government of the United Kingdom of Great Britain and Northern Ireland and the Government of the French Republic regarding the develop-

ment and production of a civil supersonic transport aircraft," 29 November 1962, PRO-FO93/33/475.

Chapter 4. The Race Begins

1. Halaby, memorandum for the president, 15 November 1962, "Race to the supersonic transport," JFK-POF (Departments and agencies) /78.
2. Halaby, report to the vice president, May 1963, "Supersonic transport," LBJ-VP (1963 subj.) /192.
3. Gordon and Heller, memorandum for the vice president, 23 May 1963, JFK (Theodore Sorensen papers) /41.
4. Halaby, memorandum for the president, 3 June 1963, "The commercial supersonic transport—the next steps," FAA Hist.
5. "Remarks of the President at graduation ceremonies, United States Air Force Academy, Colorado Springs, Colorado," White House press release, 5 June 1963, JFK-POF/44.
6. Halaby to Shank, memo, 31 January 1963, "Intensification of supersonic transport program," FAA-SST 6174/12.
7. Najeeb E. Halaby, *Crosswinds: An Airman's Memoir* (Garden City, N.Y.: Doubleday, 1978).
8. Allen to Gilpatric, 30 March 1962, Boeing archives.
9. Allen to President Kennedy, draft, 31 March 1962, Boeing archives.
10. Supersonic Transport Advisory Group, report to the chairman, Supersonic Transport Steering Group, 11 December 1962, "Supersonic transport program planning," JFK-POF (Departments and agencies) /78.
11. FAA, "Supersonic transport," 19 June 1963, LBJ-VP (1963 subj.) /192.
12. Halaby, "The development of the supersonic transport," AIAA Los Angeles, 19 June 1963, JFK (FAA papers) NK-32 film roll 15.
13. U.S. Senate, Committee on Commerce, *United States Commercial Supersonic Aircraft Development Program: Hearings before the Aviation Subcommittee of the Committee on Commerce,* 88th Cong., 1st sess., 16 October 1963.
14. Eugene R. Black and Stanley de J. Osborne, report to President Johnson on the supersonic transport, 19 December 1963, LBJ-PAC/69.
15. Halaby, "Report by the Administrator on the visit of Sir George Edwards," 14 December 1962, JFK-POF (Departments and agencies) /78.
16. Chester C. Spurgeon to Halaby, memo, 13 June 1963, "Report of discussions between Mr. Alan Greenwood, Mr. Charles Gardner and myself regarding BAC-Sud position on United States SST development," FAA Hist.
17. Joseph A. Califano, Jr., memorandum for the record, 15 May 1964, "Supersonic transport program; conversation with the French Ambassador, General Puget, President of Sud-Aviation, Paul Simonet, Secretary of Sud-Aviation, and David Downey, Vice-President (American representative) of Sud-Aviation," LBJ-PAC/46.

18. Bain to Halaby, memo, 12 June 1964, "Memorandum for the record dated 15 May 1964 by Joseph A. Califano, Jr.," FAA Hist.

19. Bain, memorandum for Mr. Halaby, 22 June 1965, "Summary information—Paris air show," FAA-SST 6174/95.

20. Briddon to Maxwell, route slip and attached report, 23 March 1967, FAA Hist.

21. Halaby, "FAA Concord evaluation by Mr. N. E. Halaby, Administrator," 1 October 1964, LBJ-PAC/24.

22. *The Economic Situation: A Statement by Her Majesty's Government,* 26 October 1964, HMSO.

23. U.K. Foreign Office, "Record of conversation between the Right Honourable Patrick Gordon Walker, Foreign Secretary, and Mr. Rusk at the State Department on Monday, October 26 [1964] at 10 a.m," PRO-PREM13/117.

24. U.K. Foreign Office, "Meeting between the Foreign Secretary and the U.S. Secretary to the Treasury, Mr. Dillon, at the U.S. Treasury on Monday, October 26 [1964]," PRO-PREM13/117.

25. Cabinet Committee on Economic Development, "Future of the Concord project," 13 November 1964, memorandum by the minister of aviation, ED(64)14, PRO-CAB134/1736.

26. Foreign Office to Paris, 1 December 1964, "Concorde," Foreign Office telegram 3320, PRO-PREM13/117.

27. "Foreign Office note on explanatory remarks made by the French Ambassador," 18 December 1964, PRO-CAB130/212.

28. Lord Jenkins of Hillhead, letter to author, 7 July 1992.

29. Maloy to Halaby, memo, 27 November 1964, "Evaluation of Concorde project," FAA Hist.

30. American embassy Paris to SecState, telegram, 22 December 1964, "Concorde supersonic transport," LBJ-NSF (subj. SST) /45.

31. Halaby, memorandum for the president, 4 December 1964, "U.S./U.K. aviation problems," LBJ-PAC/46.

32. Halaby, memorandum for Mr. Bundy, 26 January 1965, "British/French plans for SST (Concorde)," LBJ-NSF (subj. SST) /45.

33. Ministry of Aviation (Air A.2), "Note of a meeting held in London on 16th February 1965 between the U.K. Minister of Aviation, Mr. Roy Jenkins, M.P., the French Minister of Transport, M. Marc Jacquet, and the U.S. Federal Aviation Agency Administrator the Hon. Najeeb Halaby, for a general discussion of supersonic transport problems," 22 November 1965, LBJ-PAC/13.

34. Roy Jenkins, *A Life at the Centre* (London: Macmillan, 1991).

35. Plowden Committee, *Report of the Committee of Inquiry into the Aircraft Industry,* Cmnd. 2853 (London: HMSO, 1965).

36. Black and Osborne to McNamara, 16 November 1964, LBJ-PAC/24.

37. Halaby, "FAA Concord evaluation," 1 October 1964, FAA-SST 6174/11.

Chapter 5. Mr. McNamara and His Systems Men

1. McNamara, letter to author, December 1994.
2. Enke, "The SST venture—issues and questions," SST 1965 task force internal paper 1, 12 April 1965 (revised), LBJ-PAC/100.
3. Edwards, "Some aspects of SST development," SST task force internal paper 9, 29 April 1965, LBJ-PAC/100.
4. "Draft proceedings of the President's Advisory Committee on Supersonic Transport, 5 May 1965," LBJ-PAC/76.
5. U.S. Treasury, "Comments on the 'list of issues' for the 21 May meeting," 20 May 1965, LBJ-PAC/28.
6. "Overall strategic issues affecting the SST program," Department of Defense paper for 21 May 1965 meeting, LBJ-PAC/28.
7. Halaby, memorandum for the president, 1 July 1965, FAA-SST 6174/95.
8. Enke to Meadows, 11 October 1965, LBJ-PAC/46.
9. Henderson to Enke, 12 October 1965, LBJ-PAC/74.
10. Alain Enthoven, memorandum for the secretary of defense, 15 September 1965, "Visit to OSD of P. D. Henderson, Economic Advisor, U.K. Ministry of Aviation," LBJ-PAC/74.
11. Enke, "Summary of findings to date 5/17/65," 18 May 1965, LBJ-PAC/28.
12. Enke, memorandum for Honorable Charles J. Hitch, Califano, Enthoven, 23 June 1965, "Discussions in Britain on SSTs," LBJ-PAC/45.
13. Enke, "On the urgent need to limit wasteful supersonic transport competition through agreements with the U.K. and/or France," 4 November 1965, attachment to letter, Enke to Charles Schultz, 4 November 1965; and Enke to Walt W. Rostow, 20 December 1965, LBJ-PAC/11.
14. Enke, memorandum for Mr. McNamara, 18 January 1966, "Some French and British officials want a 'deal' on the Concorde," LBJ-PAC/11.
15. Enke, "Continued interest of French and British officials in an agreement with the U.S. to rationalize SST competition," 24 January 1966, LBJ-PAC/13.
16. John M. Steadman, memorandum for record, 1 February 1966, LBJ-PAC/11.
17. Halaby, *Crosswinds*.
18. Memorandum for the president, 14 May 1964, "First interim report of the President's Advisory Committee on Supersonic Transport," LBJ-PAC/76.
19. Lockheed California Company, "Answers to questions asked by Department of Defense and Federal Aviation Agency representatives during the meeting in Burbank on 16 April 1965," 18 April 1965, addendum to program planning study (report SST-874), LBJ-PAC/27.
20. Joe C. Jones, memorandum for record, 22 April 1965, "Discussion of alternative SST programs with Boeing Airplane Company on 15 April 1965," LBJ-PAC/27.
21. FAA, "United States supersonic transport program questions and answers," July 1965, SST 65-11, FAA Hist.

22. "Agreements reached at informal 9 March meeting of several members of the PAC-SST," enclosed with letter, McNamara to General W. F. McKee, 12 March 1966, LBJ-PAC/33.

23. "Draft proceedings of the President's Advisory Committee on Supersonic Transport, 6 May 1966," LBJ-PAC/77.

24. Osborne, "Notes on PAC/SST problems," 27 June 1966, LBJ-PAC/12.

25. McCone to McNamara, 27 May 1966, LBJ-PAC/11.

26. "1. The effect of a longer interval between the Concorde and the U.S. supersonic transport," FAA paper for 9 July 1966 meeting, LBJ-PAC/34.

27. Enke, "Comments on the FAA paper on the PAC assignment of the effect of a longer interval between the Concorde and the SST," for 9 July 1966 meeting, LBJ-PAC/34.

28. Dr. Stephen Enke, Dr. Edward H. Rastatter, and Dr. John A. Walgreen, "Competition of Concorde with U.S. SST introduced 1974 or 1975," 5 May 1966, LBJ-PAC/34.

29. "2. Concorde impact on SST schedules," FAA paper for 9 July 1966 meeting, LBJ-PAC/34.

30. Enke, "Concorde impact on SST schedules," for 9 July meeting, LBJ-PAC/34.

31. Draft proceedings, 9 July 1966, LBJ-PAC/77.

32. Draft proceedings, 7 December 1966, LBJ-PAC/77.

33. Department of Commerce, "Potential effects of the U.S. supersonic transport program on balance of payments, domestic employment, and defense readiness," with 2 May 1963 Martin letter, LBJ-VP (1963 subj.) /192.

34. Clarence D. Martin, Jr., to the vice president, 2 May 1963, LBJ-VP (1963 subj.) /192.

35. Gordon and Heller, memorandum for the vice president, 23 May 1963, "Comments on the FAA report and recommendations on a U.S. supersonic transport development program," JFK (Theodore Sorensen papers) /41.

36. Draft proceedings, 10 December 1966, LBJ-PAC/77.

37. Fourth interim report, 22 December 1966, LBJ-PAC/78.

Chapter 6. The Intelligencers' Tale

1. Najeeb E. Halaby, memorandum for the vice president, 30 January 1963, "The supersonic transport program," FAA Hist.

2. Heller, memorandum for the vice president, 12 March 1963, "Supersonic transport," LBJ-VP (1963 subj.) /192.

3. Hornig, memorandum for Mr. Kermit Gordon, 2 March 1964, "The Black-Osborne report," LBJ-Hornig/1.

4. Gordon M. Bain to Halaby, memo, 1 April 1964, "Intelligence estimate of Concorde," FAA-SST 6174/96.

5. McCone to Califano, note, 21 May 1964, LBJ-PAC/46.

6. Pursley, memorandum to Mr. Califano, 28 May 1964, "Supersonic transport," LBJ-PAC/46.

7. T. C. Muse, memorandum for Mr. Califano, 11 September 1964, "NASA Concorde report," LBJ-PAC/46.

8. Califano, memorandum for Secretary McNamara, 6 November 1964, "Supersonic Transport Advisory Committee," LBJ-PAC/24.

9. "Draft proceedings of the President's Advisory Committee on Supersonic Transport, 21 May 1965," LBJ-PAC/77.

10. FAA Office of Supersonic Transport Development, "Concorde intelligence summary," 29 October 1965, LBJ-PAC/11.

11. CIA Directorate of Intelligence, "The supersonic transport race: The European side," special report, weekly review, 17 March 1967, LBJ-PAC/11.

12. Concorde questions, unsigned, undated (1969), NASM-Vierling/9.

13. "Notes on telephone call between Mr. Luppi, State Department, and General Maxwell, FAA," 9 December 1966, LBJ-PAC/11.

14. E. Drexel Godfrey, Jr., to Office of Supersonic Transport Development, FAA, memo, 9 December 1966, "FAA request for political evaluation of the Concorde as related to British entry in the EEC," LBJ-PAC/11.

15. Maloy, untitled note (reply to questions), undated (December 1966), LBJ-PAC/11.

16. "Supersonic transport development, daily highlights," 28 December 1965, FAA-SST 6174/95.

17. FAA, "Summary status report to the President's Advisory Committee on Supersonic Transport: U.S. supersonic transport program, and foreign programs," 30 June 1966, LBJ-PAC/12.

18. Summary status report, 31 August 1966, LBJ-PAC/12.

19. Enke, comment on CIA report, for 6 October 1966 meeting, LBJ-PAC/12.

20. Charles O. Cary to director, Office of Supersonic Transport Development, memo, 21 March 1968, "Foreign SST intelligence," FAA-SST 905/2.

21. American embassy Paris to Department of State, airgram, 25 April 1968, "Concorde aircraft—pacing items," FAA-SST 6174/1.

22. "Minutes of meeting, Supersonic Transport Steering Group, 26 February 1962," FAA Hist.

23. Warnick to the administrator, memo, 30 June 1964, "SST Sooner boomer," FAA-SST/11.

24. Maloy to administrator, memo, 13 July 1964, "Sonic boom tests—observations by foreign air attaches," FAA-SST 6174/11.

25. ACEP document 179, 24 May 1965, "Use of United States-origin materials, equipment supplies and technical data in the design, engineering and construction of the British-French supersonic aircraft Concorde," LBJ-PAC/46.

26. "Talking paper for DOD representative on the Advisory Committee on Export Policy Structure, rough draft," 28 May 1965, LBJ-PAC/46.

27. B. J. Vierling to assistant administrator for international aviation affairs, memo, 6 February 1967, "Policy determination on export of technology," FAA-SST 6174/93.

28. FAA, "Dissemination of information concerning development of U.S. supersonic aircraft," for 9 July 1966 meeting, LBJ-PAC/12.

29. Vierling, memo to the record, 19 December 1966, "Meeting with State Department Officials," FAA-SST 6174/93.

30. Frutkin to Frank E. Loy, 17 February 1967, NASA Hist.

31. Vierling to assistant administrator for international aviation affairs, 7 March 1967, "Possible Concorde wind tunnel testing program in U.S," FAA-SST 6174/93.

32. American embassy London to SecState, telegram, 29 May 1967, "Civair: Cooperation on Concorde," LBJ-PAC/11.

33. Maxwell, memorandum for General McKee, 1 November 1967, "Concorde information," FAA-SST 6174/95.

34. British Aircraft Corporation–Sud, "World's first SST unveiled," attachment to news release, 11 December 1967, BAe.

35. European Aerospace Corporation–BAC (U.S.A.), "U.S. companies working on Concorde," news release, September 1973, BAe.

36. Julian Amery, Open University interview, 1976.

37. Knight, *Concorde*.

38. Jock Bruce-Gardyne and Nigel Lawson, *The Power Game* (London: Macmillan, 1976).

39. Denis Healey, *The Time of My Life* (London: Michael Joseph, 1989).

40. McNamara, telephone interview with author, 4 May 1994.

41. Lord Jenkins of Hillhead, letters to author, 4 August and 12 October 1994.

42. Foreign Office telegram 3387, Foreign Office to Paris, 11 December 1964, "Concorde," PRO-PREM13/117.

43. Maxwell, memorandum for record, 10 March 1966, "Meeting of President's Advisory Committee for Supersonic Transport members," FAA-SST 6174/96.

44. Lord Callaghan of Cardiff, letter to author, 18 March 1993.

Chapter 7. The Nixon Years

1. FAA, "Issues paper—SST program," December 1968, NA-RG398/70.

2. Agger to the under secretary, memo, 6 January 1969, "SST issues paper," NA-RG398/70.

3. Thomas, memorandum for under secretary of transportation, 9 January 1969, NA-RG398/70.

4. Robson to the secretary, memo, 29 January 1969, SST, NA-RG398/70.

5. Cary to acting administrator, memo, 5 February 1969, "International implications of U.S. decision to proceed with or cancel supersonic transport program," FAA-SST 6174/4.

6. D. D. Thomas to George A. Spater, Harding L. Lawrence, Robert F. Six, Charles H. Dolson, Floyd D. Hall, Donald W. Nyrop, N. E. Halaby, Charles C. Tillinghast, Jr., and George E. Keck, telegraphic message, 19 February 1969, FAA-SST 6174/4.

7. Beggs to Shaffer, 25 February 1969, FAA-SST 6174/4.

8. Beggs to the secretary, memo, 6 March 1969, "New British 'feeler' on SST-Concorde," FAA-SST 6174/4.

9. Halaby to Thomas, 1 March 1969, FAA-SST 6174/4.

10. DuBridge to Beggs, 20 March 1969, FAA-SST 6174/4.

11. *Final Report of the Ad Hoc Supersonic Transport Review Committee of the Office of Science and Technology*, 30 March 1969, BAe.

12. "Panel report to SST ad hoc review committee: Balance of payments and international relations," in SST reports submitted to Congress by the Department of Transportation, October 1969, FAA-SST 6174/95.

13. U. Alexis Johnson to Beggs, 26 March 1969, FAA Hist.

14. Nixon, "Remarks announcing decision to continue development of the supersonic transport," *Public Papers of the Presidents of the United States: Richard Nixon,* 23 September 1969.

15. FAA, "Summary of current economic studies of the United States supersonic transport," September 1969, FAA Hist.

16. Edwards to Magruder, two letters, 17 September 1970, FAA-SST 6174/90.

17. Department of Transportation news release, 2 October 1970, "Remarks prepared for delivery by William M. Magruder, Director, Office of SST Development, Department of Transportation, to the New York Society of Security Analysts, New York City, 2 October 1970," BAe.

18. Department of Transportation news release, 27 October 1970, "Remarks prepared for delivery by William M. Magruder, Director, Supersonic Transport Development, Department of Transportation, to the International Committee/AIA, Washington, D.C., 27 October 1970," BAe.

19. Boeing leaflet, May 1970, "$22 billion at stake: a reassessment of U.S. balance of payments and the supersonic transport," FAA Hist.

20. G. Worrall to E. H. Burgess, memo, 18 January 1971, "Preliminary notes on BAC / Aérospatiale / Boeing 'environment' meeting 13th and 14th January 1971"; and Aérospatiale Direction Technique Avions, Paris, 14 January 1971, "Environment meeting Boeing / BAC / Aérospatiale, 13th and 14th January 1971," BAe.

21. "BAC, Concorde and the environment: Proceedings at a press conference held in Millbank Tower, SW1, on Wednesday, 10th February 1971," BAe.

22. Department of Transportation, "SST question and answer index, February 1971. Section 8—competition," FAA Hist.

23. Richard J. Kent, Jr., *Safe, Separated, and Soaring: A History of Federal Civil Aviation Policy, 1961–72* (Washington: U.S. Department of Transportation, 1980).

24. Sir George Edwards, "Speech to American Chamber of Commerce at the Savoy Hotel, London, 15 December 1971," BAe.

25. Richard J. Barber to the secretary, memo, 14 April 1970, "Briefing: Meeting with Ambassador-designate Arthur K. Watson, Jr," FAA Hist.

26. Department of Transportation, "Summary of discussions between the Secretary and the U.K. Minister of Technology, 17 April 1970," FAA Hist.

27. Department of Transportation, "Memorandum of conversation," 22 July 1970, FAA-SST 6174/90.

28. "'Ban the Concorde' summary opinion," attachment to letter, Magruder to Senator Henry M. Jackson, 19 August 1970, FAA-SST 6174/90.

29. Civil Aeronautics Board, "Ban the Concorde" questions and answers, 28 July 1970, attachment to letter, Magruder to Jackson, 19 August 1970, FAA-SST 6174/90.

30. Department of Commerce, "Prohibition of Concorde," 31 July 1970, attachment to letter, Magruder to Jackson, 19 August 1970, FAA-SST 6174/90.

31. Department of State, "Introduction of the Concorde into U.S. service," attachment to letter, Bert W. Rein to Magruder, 20 July 1970, FAA-SST 6174/90.

32. John R. Petty to Magruder, memo, 27 July 1970, FAA-SST 6174/90.

33. Flanigan, "Memorandum for Cabinet: Problems affecting the use of the Concorde in the United States, 27 November 1972," in U.S. House, *Review of the Secretary of Transportation's Decision on the SST Concorde: Joint Hearing before Certain Subcommittees of the Committee on Government Operations and the Committee on International Relations,* 94th Cong., 2nd sess., 26 May 1976 [hereafter cited as *Review of the Secretary's Decision*], appendix.

34. Volpe, memorandum for cabinet, 8 December 1972, in *Review of the Secretary's Decision,* appendix.

35. "Minutes of review group discussion of problems connected with certification of the Concorde for use in the United States," 11 December 1972, in *Review of the Secretary's Decision,* appendix.

36. Nixon to Heath, 19 January 1973, in *Review of the Secretary's Decision,* appendix.

37. Barnum, "eyes only" note on Nixon letters, 25 January 1973, in *Review of the Secretary's Decision,* appendix.

38. Robert H. Binder to assistant secretary for policy and international affairs, memorandum, "Summary of status of Concorde problem," 26 January 1973, in *Review of the Secretary's Decision,* appendix.

39. "Letters revealed: Nixon promise on Concorde," *CQ Weekly Report,* 20 December 1975.

Chapter 8. Environmental Impact

1. L. J. Schefer, "First cut proposal for Concorde publicity in North America," 1 September 1972, BAe.

2. G. Perol to Charles Cary, 14 February 1975, and F. S. Tanner to Cary, 19 February 1975, in U.S. Department of Transportation, FAA, *Concorde Supersonic Transport Aircraft: Draft Environmental Impact Statement,* March 1975 (Washington: GPO) [hereafter cited as *Draft Environmental Statement*], appendix A.

3. *Draft Environmental Statement.*

4. Andy Logan, "Around City Hall: Three If by Air," *New Yorker,* 4 April 1977.

5. Migdon R. Segal, *The Concorde SST Controversy,* 14 August 1975, Congressional Research Service, HE 9901 Gen., 75-177SP.
6. William C. Clarke to director, flight standards service, FAA, 5 May 1975, attachment to U.S. Department of Transportation, FAA, *Concorde: Final Environmental Impact Statement,* 30 September 1975 (Washington: GPO).
7. P. M. Innes to Charles R. Foster, "Concorde: Written response to draft EIS," 2 May 1975, attachment to *Concorde: Final Environmental Impact Statement,* 30 September 1975.
8. Department of Transportation, "Public Hearing: Amendment of operations specifications to permit Concorde flights to John F. Kennedy International Airport and Dulles International Airport," attachment to letter, William T. Coleman, Jr., to "Those interested in the Concorde," 13 November 1975, FAA Hist.
9. "The Concorde: Written submission to Secretary Coleman," submitted by the governments of France and the United Kingdom, 2 January 1976, BAe.
10. Department of Transportation, "Public hearing on applications of Air France and British Airways to operate Concorde aircraft in limited commercial service to New York and Washington," transcript, 5 January 1976.
11. Ruckelshaus, letter to author, 11 April 1994.

Chapter 9. Decision and Dissension

1. U.S. Department of Transportation, *The Secretary's Decision on Concorde Supersonic Transport,* 4 February 1976 (Washington: GPO).
2. U.S. House, Committee on Government Operations, *FAA Certification of the SST Concorde: Hearings before a Subcommittee of the Committee on Government Operations,* 94th Cong., 1st and 2nd sess., 24 July, 13 and 14 November, 9 and 12 December 1975; and 24 February 1976 [hereafter referred to as *FAA Certification*]. *Review of the Secretary's Decision.*
3. Kissinger to Coleman, 6 October 1975, in *FAA Certification.*
4. Jerome A. Ambro, "The Concorde," *Congressional Record,* extension of remarks, E3141, 12 June 1975.
5. Coleman, interview with author, 7 June 1993.
6. Brian Calvert, *Flying Concorde* (London: Fontana, 1981).
7. Coleman, interview with Edmund Preston, 14 July 1986, FAA Hist.
8. "Letter agreement regarding program for U.S. authorizations for Concorde supersonic commercial transport service," DGA International Inc. and SNIAS, 7 and 17 February 1975, U.S. Justice Department records.
9. *Attorney General of the United States of America* v *DGA International Inc.*, U.S. District Court for the District of Columbia, civil action 75-2040, December 1975.
10. Final judgment, U.S. District Court for the District of Columbia, civil actions 75-2040, 2041, 2042, December 1975.

11. "Amendment Number 1 to 'Letter agreement regarding program for U.S. authorization for Concorde supersonic commercial transport service,'" DGA International Inc. and SNIAS, 19 January 1976, Justice Department records.

12. DGA International, "Supplemental statements pursuant to Section 2 of the Foreign Agents Registration Act of 1938," 28 April 1976 to 28 April 1979, Justice Department records.

13. "Rider to Form OBD-64, Question 12, Aérospatiale," in DGA supplemental statement for period to 28 October 1977, Justice Department records.

14. "Statement to form DJ-307," in Edelman International Corporation amendment to registration statement, 24 December 1976, Justice Department records.

15. "Extension of letter agreement regarding U.S. public relations program," SNIAS and International Public Relations Co. Ltd., 15 September 1975, Justice Department records.

16. Ramsbotham, interview with author, 12 October 1992.

17. Coleman, interview with author, 7 June 1993.

18. *Review of the Secretary's Decision.*

19. Booth, interview with author, 3 February 1993.

20. Brown and Rowlands, interview with author, 27 May 1993.

21. Preslar, interview with author, 27 April 1994.

22. Shurcliff to Philip Boffey, 7 May 1971, MIT MC12 Box 3/115.

23. Shurcliff to Wiggs, 13 August 1970, MIT MC12 Box 7/283.

24. Shurcliff to CLASB members, card, 8 April 1971, MIT MC12 Box 8/340.

25. Shurcliff to Proxmire, 2 April 1971, MIT MC12 Box 3/114.

26. *CLASB Newsletter* 39A (22 June 1971), MIT MC12 Box 8/317.

27. New Jersey Legislature, *Public Hearing before the Senate Transportation and Communications Committee on Use of Kennedy International Airport by the SST Concorde,* 15 March 1976.

28. New Jersey Legislature, Senate Transportation and Communications Committee, *Report on the Landing of the Concorde,* April 1976.

29. Philip B. Raflo, "Concorde landing rights at Dulles International Airport: A case study in political influence, or, 'The second battle of Concorde,'" 20 April 1977, B.A. thesis, Princeton University.

30. U.S. Court of Appeals for the District of Columbia Circuit, 1976, Dockets 76-1105, -1213, -1259, -1260, -1321.

31. *United States Reports, vol. 429,* 15 November 1976, Case 76-231.

32. U.S. District Court for the District of Columbia Circuit, 1976–79, Docket 76-0139.

33. President Carter to Prime Minister Callaghan and President Giscard d'Estaing, 15 February 1977, attachments to memorandum for the secretary of transportation from Stuart E. Eizenstat, 15 February 1977, FAA Hist.

34. American embassy Paris to SecState, telegram, 23 February 1977, "Civair: Barre remarks on Concorde," FAA Hist.

35. American embassy Paris to SecState, telegram, 24 February 1977, "Civair: Press invites write-in campaign in support of Concorde," FAA Hist.

Chapter 10. The Battle for New York

1. Clarke, letter to author, 12 December 1994.
2. Port Authority of New York and New Jersey, "Kennedy International Airport—Concorde operations," Report of Board Meeting, 11 March 1976.
3. Goodell to P. J. Farley, telegram, 7 March 1977, attached to Port Authority of New York and New Jersey news release, 8 March 1977.
4. Port Authority of New York and New Jersey, news release, 7 March 1977.
5. Goodell to William J. Ronan, telegram, 7 March 1977, attached to Port Authority of New York and New Jersey news release, 9 March 1977.
6. U.S. District Court, Southern District of New York, No. 76 Civ. 1276, 11 May 1977, *431 Federal Supplement,* 1216–1226.
7. U.S. Court of Appeals, Second Circuit, No. 1403, docket 77-7237, 14 June 1977, *558 Federal Reporter 2d,* 75–86.
8. U.S. Court of Appeals, Second Circuit, docket 77-7237, 25 May 1977, "Brief for the United States, Amicus Curiae."
9. U.S. District Court, Southern District of New York, No. 76 Civ. 1276 (MP), 17 August 1977, *437 Federal Supplement,* 804–820.
10. H. Perrier and R. McKinlay to Charles Foster, 7 April 1977, FAA Hist.
11. Foster to British Aircraft Corporation, 14 April 1977, FAA Hist.
12. Port Authority of New York and New Jersey, news release, 17 August 1977.
13. U.S. Court of Appeals, Second Circuit, No. 287, docket 77-7438, 29 September 1977, *564 Federal Reporter 2d,* 1002–1018.
14. *United States Reports, vol. 434,* 17 October 1977, Order no. A-327.
15. Port Authority of New York and New Jersey, news release, 17 October 1977.
16. Davidson, interview with author, 20 October 1944.
17. Calvert, *Flying Concorde.*
18. Binning, interview with author, 11 August 1994.
19. Gordon-Cumming, interview with author, 27 July 1994.
20. Booth, interview with author, 3 February 1993.
21. Schefer, interview with author, 3 June 1993.
22. Clarke, letter to author, 12 December 1994.

Chapter 11. Through the Political Sound Barrier

1. "Giscard Speaks Out," *Newsweek,* 25 July 1977.
2. U.S. Senate, Committee on Commerce, *Oversight Hearings on the SST,* 20 February 1976. *FAA Certification.*
3. Roy W. Haney, memorandum for file, 5 May 1961, "Summary report, FAA/ARB discussions on supersonic transport safety criteria, 10–14 April 1961," FAA Hist.
4. "Digest of the minutes of the first supersonic transport meeting of the Sud–BAC committee of directors, Paris, 7 December 1962," PRO-BT242/4.

5. Rochte, memorandum for the record, 10 January 1963, "Meeting of FAA/MOA regarding possible collaboration on the supersonic transport in various environmental areas," FAA/SST 6174/13.

6. "FAA holds conference with British and French on certification standards for the SST," FAA news release T63-20, 17 April 1963, FAA Hist.

7. "Report of final plenary: Meeting between United Kingdom Ministry of Aviation and Federal Aviation Agency, 3–5 March 1964," FAA Hist.

8. "Position paper for U.S. delegation to British-French-American meeting on supersonic transport standards to be held in Paris, June 1–9, 1964," FAA Hist.

9. P. C. Spiess, "Summary of French-Anglo-U.S. meeting on supersonic transports (FAUSST), June 1–9, 1964," FAA Hist.

10. N. E. Halaby, "FAA Concorde evaluation," 1 October 1964, attachment H, regulatory activity, FAA/SST 6174/11.

11. British Aircraft Corporation/Sud-Aviation to Federal Aviation Agency, "Application for type certificate" for Concorde, 15 July 1965, FAA Hist.

12. McKee to Thomas C. Mann, 22 September 1965, FAA Hist.

13. Frank E. Loy to Cary, 26 October 1965, FAA Hist.

14. Maloy to J. Delacroix and R. E. Hardingham, 16 February 1966, FAA Hist.

15. Project engineer, Concorde, to chief, aircraft certification staff, FAA, memorandum, 19 December 1967, "Notes on France/U.K./U.S.A. Concorde administrative meeting—Brussels, 18 December 1967," FAA/SST 6174/91.

16. H. C. Black to Maloy, 29 December 1967, FAA/SST 6174/91.

17. Maloy to deputy administrator, memorandum, 5 July 1968, "Status of Concorde certification," FAA/SST 6174/1.

18. Maloy to deputy administrator, memorandum, 28 January 1969, "Concorde status report," FAA/SST 6174/3.

19. R. D. Forrest, "Chronology of events: SST airworthiness standards development 1974–1969," NASA Ames Research Center.

20. S. Sloan Colt to Halaby, 31 January 1964, LBJ-PAC/69, 70, 74.

21. Loy to Donald G. Agger, 15 March 1968, FAA/SST 905/2.

22. Agger to Loy, 10 April 1968, FAA/SST 905/2.

23. U.S. Department of Transportation, "Secretary Adams announces proposed Concorde noise rule," news release DOT 101-77, 23 September 1977.

24. Department of Transportation, "DOT issues final SST noise rules," news release DOT 96-78, 27 June 1978. Department of Transportation, FAA, "Civil supersonic airplanes: Proposed noise and sonic boom requirements," *Federal Register,* 13 October 1977.

25. Department of Transportation, FAA, *Final Environmental Impact Statement: Noise Regulation and Type Certification Alternatives for Civil Supersonic Aircraft,* June 1978 (Washington: GPO).

26. U.S. House, Committee on Government Operations, *Aircraft Noise and the Concorde,* seventeenth report, 10 February 1978, H. Rept. 95-879.

27. Comptroller General, *The Concorde: Results of a Supersonic Aircraft's Entry into the United*

States: Report to the Subcommittee on Environment, Energy, and Natural Resources of the House Government Operations Committee, General Accounting Office, 15 September 1977.

Chapter 12. A Second Generation?

1. U.S. Department of Transportation, "Suggested policy for United States advanced high speed transport," 26 July 1971, FAA-SST 6174/90.

2. F. Edward McLean, *Supersonic Cruise Technology,* 1985, NASA SP-472.

3. U.S. Congress, Joint Economic Committee, *Federal Transportation Policy: The SST Again,* report of the Subcommittee on Priorities and Economy in Government, 16 March 1973 (Washington: GPO).

4. Fletcher to George P. Shultz, 9 March 1973, NASA Hist.

5. Fletcher to Roth, 25 February 1975, NASA Hist.

6. "Effect of SST market on U.S.—GNP, 20 October 1976," NASA chart HQ RA77-261(1), NASA Hist.

7. *Proceedings of the SCAR Conference Held at Langley Research Center, Hampton, Virginia, 9–12 November 1976,* NASA CP-001.

8. U.S. House, Committee on Science and Technology, *The Future of Aviation,* report prepared by the Subcommittee on Aviation and Transportation R&D, October 1976, Committee Print.

9. *CQ Weekly Report,* 19 March, 26 March, 28 May, and 30 July 1977.

10. U.S. Congress, Office of Technology Assessment, *Impact of Advanced Air Transport Technology: Part 1, Advanced High-speed Aircraft,* April 1980 (Washington: GPO).

11. NASA, "Three contracts awarded for supersonic flight studies," news release 80-51, 22 April 1980.

12. Pennell to Halaby, 5 January 1965, FAA Hist.

13. FAA, *U.S. Supersonic Transport "Grey Book,"* February 1971, FAA Hist.

14. Gilbert Cormery, "Tomorrow . . . Concorde's successor?" *Revue Aérospatiale,* February 1986.

15. British Aircraft Corporation, "Advanced supersonic transport for the 1990s," May 1976, report SST/MGW/17553, BAe.

16. P. LeComte, C. Leyman, and Richard D. FitzSimmons, "Supersonic transportation prospects," December 1978, BAe.

17. C. Robert Nysmith to director of Office of Legislative Affairs, memo, 5 June 1981, "Utilization of Concorde in NASA Supersonic Cruise Research (SCR) program," NASA Hist.

18. William T. Hamilton to Dr. A. M. Lovelace, 4 March 1981, "Comments on use of the Concorde to expand the technology base for an advanced supersonic transport or other large supersonic aircraft," NASA Hist.

19. *National Aeronautical R&D Goals: Technology for America's Future,* Executive Office of the President, Office of Science and Technology Policy, March 1985.

20. James P. Loomis, ed., *High Speed Commercial Flight: The Coming Era* (Columbus, Ohio: Battelle Press, 1987).

21. *National Aeronautical R&D Goals: Agenda for Achievement,* Executive Office of the President, Office of Science and Technology Policy, February 1987.

22. U.S. Senate, *Commercial High Speed Aircraft: Opportunities and Issues,* report prepared for Committee on Commerce, Science, and Transportation, March 1989, Committee Print.

23. James P. Loomis, ed., *High Speed Commercial Flight: From Inquiry to Action* (Columbus, Ohio: Battelle Press, 1989).

24. *Proceedings of the European Symposium on Future Supersonic/Hypersonic Transportation Systems, Strasbourg, 6–8 November 1989* (Toulouse: Cepadues-Editions, 1990).

25. T. Barrie Bryant, "Super Concorde," letter published in *Aerospace,* April 1990.

26. British Aerospace, "Second generation supersonic airliner: A joint British Aerospace and Aérospatiale study," news release BAe 61/90, 9 May 1990.

27. "BAe/Aérospatiale Alliance: 'Super Mach' for 2005," *Revue Aérospatiale,* June 1990.

28. British Aerospace, "International group explores civil supersonic transport," news release BAe 69/90, 23 May 1990.

29. British Aerospace, "Supersonic transport international studies show progress," news release BAe 63/91, 17 June 1991.

30. Kenneth Owen, "Tupolev Joins SST Study Group," *Aerospace America,* November 1991.

31. U.S. National Research Council, Aeronautics and Space Engineering Board, *Aeronautical Technologies for the Twenty-first Century* (Washington: National Academy Press, 1992).

Chapter 13. Once More, with Hindsight

1. Boeing Commercial Airplanes, "High-speed civil transport study," NASA contractor report 4233, 1989. Douglas Aircraft Company, "Study of high-speed civil transports," NASA contractor report 4235, 1989.

2. NASA Office of Aeronautics and Space Technology, *High-speed Research Program: Briefing Book,* November 1989.

3. Williams, interview with author, 26 April 1994.

4. NASA Office of Aeronautics, "High Speed Research Program," *NASA Facts,* April 1993.

5. Jay R. Swink and Richard T. Goins, "High speed research system study: Advanced flight deck configuration effects," NASA contractor report 189650, June 1992.

6. NASA, "High-speed engine cycles tapped for further research," news release 94-41, 14 March 1994.

7. Daniel S. Goldin, "It's time to go supersonic," *Air and Space Smithsonian,* June-July 1993.

8. U.S. House, Committee on Science, Space, and Technology, *Enhancing U.S. Competi-*

tiveness (NASA High Speed and Subsonic Research Programs): Hearing, Subcommittee on Technology, Environment, and Aviation of the Committee on Science, Space, and Technology, 103rd Cong., 2nd sess., 10 February 1994.

9. British Aerospace, "Aérospatiale, British Aerospace and Deutsche Aerospace agreement on supersonic research," news release BAe 29/94, 7 April 1994.

10. M. Pacull and P. K. Green, "European second-generation supersonic transport," paper presented at the Seventh European Aerospace Conference: The Second-generation Supersonic Transport, Toulouse, 25–27 October 1994.

11. Henderson, interview with author, 22 September 1993.

12. MacKinnon, interview with author, 22 September 1993.

13. Henderson interview, 22 September 1993.

14. British Aerospace, "Very Large Commercial Transport," news release BAe 64/95, 10 July 1995.

15. Kenneth Owen, "Engine Makers Pursue Supersonic Goals," *Aerospace America,* September 1991.

16. Richard Wiggs and John Connell, letters to *Flight International,* 4 May and 29 June 1994.

17. Davies, interview with author, 21 April 1994.

18. R. E. G. Davies, "SST Market Limitations: A Simple Matter of Arithmetic," in *From Airships to Airbus: The History of Civil and Commercial Aviation,* vol. 1, ed. William M. Leary (Washington: Smithsonian Institution Press, 1995).

19. Davies, letter to author, 20 October 1994.

20. Davies, letter to author, 3 November 1994.

21. "Conversations with Louis J. Williams," *Aerospace America,* February 1995.

22. B. L. Bunin, I. G. Gray, E. Khaski, M. W. Olszewski, and D. Schmitt, "SCT: A Case for Global Cooperation," Seventh European Aerospace Conference, Toulouse, 25–27 October 1994.

23. "The Future SST: Implementation," *Revue Aérospatiale,* December 1994–January 1995.

Chapter 14. Lessons and Prospects

1. Owen, *Concorde.*

2. McNamara, letter to author, December 1994.

3. Julian Amery, Open University interview, 1976.

4. Loomis, *Inquiry to Action.*

5. Nick A. Komons, "A history of the civil supersonic transport development program," unpublished manuscript, FAA Hist.

6. Halaby, interview with author, June 9, 1993.

7. Halaby, Open University interview, 1976.

8. Bruce-Gardyne and Lawson, *The Power Game.* Haviland, interview with author, 3 August 1992, and letter to author, 5 July 1994.

9. Edwards, letter to author, 16 June 1992.

10. Lighthill, letter to author, 29 June 1992.

11. Jones, letter to author, 15 January 1995.

12. William C. Clarke, letter to author, 15 January 1995.

13. Lowe, interview with author, 7 December 1994.

14. British Airways, "Concorde set to fly for another 20 years," news release, 21 January 1996.

15. International Air Transport Association, *Annual Report* (Geneva: IATA, 1994).

16. Halaby, interview with author, 9 June 1993.

17. Bunin et al., "SCT."

18. Mel Horwitch, *Clipped Wings: The American SST Conflict* (Cambridge, Mass.: MIT Press, 1982).

19. James R. Hansen, "What Went Wrong? Some New Insights into the Cancellation of the American SST Program," in *From Airships to Airbus.*

20. *Washington Post,* 3 June 1993.

21. *Independent on Sunday* (London), 2 September 1990.

22. Robert M. McKinlay, "Concorde: First or Last?" Royal Academy of Engineering paper, London, 14 October 1992.

23. Louis J. Williams, "Is a second-generation supersonic airliner possible?" *Financial Times* Conference: Commercial Aviation and Aerospace—Towards the Year 2000, Paris, 6–7 June 1989.

INDEX

225